NEATH ABBEY
ABBEY
AND THE
INDUSTRIAL REVOLUTION

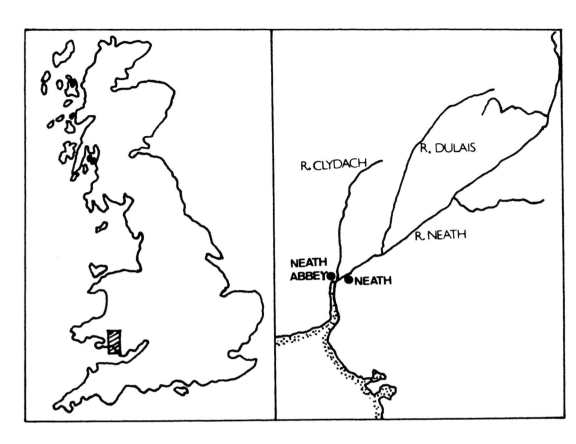

The position of Neath Abbey in South Wales.

NEATH ABBEY

AND THE
INDUSTRIAL REVOLUTION

Laurence Ince

TEMPUS

First published 2001

PUBLISHED IN THE UNITED KINGDOM BY:

Tempus Publishing Ltd
The Mill, Brimscombe Port
Stroud, Gloucestershire GL5 2QG
www.tempus-publishing.com

PUBLISHED IN THE UNITED STATES OF AMERICA BY:

Arcadia Publishing Inc.
A division of Tempus Publishing Inc.
2 Cumberland Street
Charleston, SC 29401
(Tel: 1-888-313-2665)
www.arcadiapublishing.com

Tempus books are available in France, Germany and Belgium
from the following addresses:

Tempus Publishing Group	Tempus Publishing Group
21 Avenue de la République	Gustav-Adolf-Straße 3
37300 Joué-lès-Tours	99084 Erfurt
FRANCE	GERMANY

© Laurence Ince, 2001

British Library Cataloguing in Publication Data.
A catalogue record for this book is available from the British Library.

ISBN 0 7524 2145 X

Typesetting and origination by Tempus Publishing.
PRINTED AND BOUND IN GREAT BRITAIN.

Contents

Preface

It is now over fourteen years since my book *The Neath Abbey Iron Company* made its first appearance. As soon as it was published I still felt that there was more to discover about the industrial history of the Neath Abbey area. To this end, I continued searching for further documents concerning the Neath Abbey Iron Company. More information was discovered and important photographic archives of the Waring and Price families were located. However, the event that prompted me to take on a major project on the industrial history of the area occurred at a Newcomen Society meeting in Birmingham. It was here that I heard of the recent discovery of another collection of engineering drawings from the Neath Abbey Iron Company. These records had been deposited at the West Glamorgan Record Office. I found this information difficult to come to terms with, especially as the new deposit was certainly equal to the first large cache of drawings.

This event galvanised me into action and I started to examine the plans with a view to rewriting my work on the Neath Abbey Ironworks. However, I soon realised that to expand my earlier work would be a straightforward task but this would be a disservice to the overall industrial heritage of the area. My work took on a broader aspect with research undertaken in the histories of the early iron, coal and copper industries. I soon discovered that important documents had survived which meant that I could piece together the stories of these industries in the Neath Abbey area. One topic, however, produced an abundant amount of preserved material, namely, the Main Colliery Company. Therefore, most of the following chapters are my reconstruction of the progress of the industrial undertakings in the Clydach valley. However, I have used a different technique for the Main Colliery Company chapter and have allowed the documents to tell the whole story with a few comments from my own pen.

It is possible this work would never have been completed had it not been for the constant encouragement I received from the staff of the West Glamorgan Record Office, Swansea. I must thank Miss S.G. Beckley, County Archivist and her staff for efforts beyond the call of duty in aiding my research. Thanks must also be communicated to Mr and Mrs P. Havard for their efforts to allow me to examine material in the archives of the Neath Antiquarian Society. I am also indebted to Peter King who informed me of the early history of the Bryncoch Furnace and to Jeremy Hodgkinson who was able to communicate to me the career of Thomas Pryce as a gunfounder.

The photographs in this volume, I believe, are as important as the text. In this spirit I must thank the Talbot family of London and Dorothea Ellison for allowing me to copy and use their Waring and Price photographs in this work.

I am also indebted to Neath Museum for copying and their permission to use the Main Colliery Company photographs.

I must also thank the principals of Tempus Publishing for helping me to bring this project to fruition.

So the efforts of many have come together to help tell the fascinating story of one of the pioneering areas of the Industrial Revolution. I sincerely hope that the readers of this volume can join with me in praising the Neath Abbey area as one of the cradles of the Industrial Revolution.

Laurence Ince, Solihull, 2001

Acknowledgements

Permission to reproduce photographs is gratefully acknowledged to Ros Wakeman, Kent, p 44.
The Taylor family and West Glamorgan Record Office, Swansea, pp 47, 52, 53, 57, 58, 61, 65, 67.
Professor Marilyn Palmer, University of Leicester, p 48.
The Welsh Industrial and Maritime Museum, p 50 and cover.
Kingston upon Hull Museums and Art Galleries, p 64.
Real Photographs Company, p 66, Neath Museum, pp 69, 107, 111, 115, 118, 121, 124, 125, 126, 128, 133.
The Talbot family of London, pp 73, 74, 76, 77, 79, 80, 84, 85.
Dorothea Ellison, pp 81, 83.

1

Rivers, Geology and Estates

The valley of the River Clydach and its adjoining lands were blessed with many features which attracted industrialists from an early date. The river rises at Cilybebyll near Pontardawe and is a fairly swift-flowing stream for its six and a half mile length. Close to its confluence with the River Neath at Neath Abbey, where it would be expected that the stream would be of a more docile character, faulting has endowed it with a surge of power. The fault at Cwm Felin has produced a waterfall which provided an ideal water power site for the early industrialist. The Cwm Felin site was close to the navigable junction of the Rivers Clydach and Neath which allowed the import of raw materials and the export of coal and various finished products. Coal seams abounded along the valley and readily provided raw materials for industrial development. It is no wonder that from the late seventeenth century the valley of the Clydach attracted development. This early industrial activity must surely earn the area the description of being one of the cradles of the Industrial Revolution.

The valley of the River Clydach must owe this accolade to the geology of the area. The structure of the Vale of Neath is dominated by a series of faults known as the Neath Disturbance.[1] This is expressed along the Clydach valley by faulting which has produced a trough-like structure, known as the Dyffryn Trough, and is dominated by the Dyffryn, Cwm Felin and Rhyddings faults. Within this structure rocks of the Upper Coal Series have dropped down and have been preserved in the rift-like valley along which the River Clydach developed. Several workable coal seams occur in this series of rocks and further outcrops can be found along the valley.

Even in the medieval and Tudor periods there was industrial activity in the area, aided by a gift of land to the monks of Savigny. The benefactor was Sir Richard de Granville who had helped establish Norman power in the region. In 1130, faced with the prospect of dying without an heir, he granted his lands between the Rivers Neath and Tawe to the Savignac monks. Within twenty years the Savignac monks had merged with the powerful Cistercian order. The monks not only farmed their lands, but also actively encouraged others to undertake economic activity on their estates. Coal mines existed around the abbey and metal mining may have taken place on land held by the monks of Neath Abbey at Exford in Somerset. In 1536-1538 Leland visited Neath and noticed considerable activity in digging for coal and in shipping. The coal mines he saw were probably in the Neath Abbey area. At the time of the dissolution of the monastery the bailiff was collecting twenty shillings 'for the rent of a coal pit late in the hands of Leyson Thomas late Abbot therein and now in tenure of the aforesaid Richard Crumwell.'

After the dissolution of the monasteries Sir Richard Cromwell purchased the abbey and its lands. His main home lay in Huntingdonshire and he soon sold off his Neath Abbey property to local Glamorgan gentry. Much of the Neath Abbey land was acquired by Sir John Herbert (1550-1617), Second Secretary of state to Elizabeth I and James I. From Sir John Herbert, the abbey and lands passed to Sir William Dodington, husband of Herbert's daughter and heiress, Mary. Later, the estate descended to Edward Dodington who left the lands to his nephew Philip Hoby. He took up residence at Neath Abbey and became High Sheriff of Glamorgan in 1669. The Hoby family increased their holding in this area by purchasing the adjoining Court Rhydir Estate. Philip Hoby died in 1678 and was survived by his widow and three daughters. The mother died in 1699 and the Neath Abbey Estate was inherited by the daughters as co-heiresses.[2]

The three daughters were married, Elizabeth Hoby to Henry Compton, Ann to William Stanley and Katherine to Griffith Rice of Dynevor, Carmarthenshire. The Compton and Stanley families hailed from Hampshire, so it was soon decided that the Neath Abbey Estate would be divided between the three families. The Stanley family took the Graig and Longford lands of the Court Rhydir Estate and the remaining lands were divided between the Rice family, later the Lords Dynevor, and the Comptons.

It has often been stated that the Comptons took a large share of the mineral rights while the Dynevor family held title to the land. The Dynevors did hold a considerable portion of the land but there was also a joint estate held by the Dynevors and Comptons. Mineral rights were shared by the two families who administered the estate as Lords of the Abbey with a joint agent for the Neath Abbey Estate.

Other estates also had a part to play in the industrial development of the area. The Rhyddings, Tennant and Drymma Estates all made a contribution to the story. However, one other land holding was also to play a crucial part in the later industrial development of the Clydach valley; the Dyffryn Estate situated to the north of the Neath Abbey Estate. The Dyffryn Estate was owned by the Williams family with its important coal bearing land being centred on the village of Bryncoch.

The owners of the Neath Abbey Estate leased out land for various industrial under-takings. However, like many other great landowners during the eighteenth century, they were prepared to indulge in coal mining themselves. This activity by the landowner was mirrored on the other side of the Neath valley on the Vernon Estate.[3] As long as the coal could be won fairly easily, without a great deal of equipment and management, then landowners were prepared to exploit their own coal resources. Certainly coal mining was an important activity in the Neath Abbey area during the 1690s. Edward Lhuyd recorded in about 1697, that an important coal mining industry existed around Neath, 'but ye most considerable are near the Abbey of Neath where many workmen are employed.' [4]

During the eighteenth century the high quality of Neath Abbey culm or thro coal was commented upon. In 1772 it was noted that, 'There was a vein of coal at Neath Abbey which by order of the Revenue authorities, was allowed to be shipped promis-cuously as it came from the pit's mouth'.

By 1767 remarks were being made concerning Neath coal being shipped to Cornwall for the use of smelting houses and fire or steam engines. The importance of the coal export trade can be gauged from the following document:

Amount of the Number of Coasters who Loaded Coals at Neath
Yearly from 30 June 1748 [5]

Date Ending	No of Vessels	Chaldrons	Tons	Av. Tons per Ship
30/6 1749	501	9,959	12,448	28.84
30/6 1750	574	11,260	14,075	24.52
30/6 1751	601	12,077	15,096	25.12
30/6 1752	658	13,502	16,877	25.65
30/6 1753	616	12,657	15,821	25.68
30/6 1754	602	11,636	14,545	24.16
30/6 1755	595	11,165	13,956	23.45

Most of the exported coal was sold to Somerset, Devon and Cornwall with the occasional cargo going to Ireland, the Channel Islands and France. These six areas proved to be important markets for Neath Abbey coal until the collapse of the industry in the 1920s.

The demand for Neath Abbey coal prompted the Lords of the Abbey to sink their coal workings deeper in an attempt to increase production. This caused problems for the owners as, in the late 1750s, an explosion occurred at Wern Fraith Colliery at Neath Abbey.[6] No less than seventeen workers were killed and this grim figure gives an idea of the scale of production at a single pit. Increased working depths also prompted the Lords of the Abbey to construct a steam engine to drain the Wern Fraith Colliery. In 1766 Thomas Williams of Court Herbert, the agent for the Lords of the Abbey's collieries, took delivery of a 54in x 10ft steam cylinder weighing 70cwt. This and other unspecified parts were made by the Coalbrookdale Ironworks in Shropshire and cost £289.[7] These parts would have been component parts for a Newcomen engine to drain the pit of water.

The Lords of the Abbey continued to operate their coal mines until 1791. Many of the landed gentry found that their coal mining operations expanded to a point where they could not afford the time to manage the pits or to keep up with technical developments. Therefore, on 29 January 1791, the Lords of the Abbey leased their three collieries to Richard Parsons.[8] He was born at Clydach in the Swansea valley and had become involved in the working of the Ynyscedwyn furnace. Whilst there he married the daughter of David Tanner who owned the ironworks. Parsons had operated forges at various sites in west Wales and also had experience of the potential of the Clydach valley, having owned collieries at Cilybebyll. The Lords of the Abbey leased the Wern Fraith Vein Colliery to Parsons and it was at this colliery that the steam engine was built. The lease values it at £638 8s 4d and next to this steam engine was machinery driven by a waterwheel valued at £108 10s. There were two further waterwheels at this colliery which were valued at £67 1s 4d and £51 13s 6d respectively. Parsons also took over the Abbey Colliery and Ynisscinen Colliery. The annual rent for the Wern Fraith Colliery was £600, comprised of 6s per wey for 2,000 weys. The Abbey Colliery was let out at £88 per year made up of 8s per wey for the first 2,000 weys. The wey was a measure that had increased its weight during the eighteenth century. In the coal industry this was due to the colliery owners of a district putting extra coal into the measure to attract more business. At the start of the nineteenth century the wey in the Neath area was equivalent to five tons. This steadily rose to reach nine tons and by the 1790s the wey was equivalent to 216 Winchester bushels or ten tons.

Parsons had gained control of three lucrative collieries but the lease bound him to mine at least 40,000 tons of coal yearly from two of the mines. For a coal mine in the eighteenth century this was a large output. It was now important for Parsons to find new customers to enable the Neath Abbey collieries to produce the yearly 40,000 tons of coal or more so that he could maximise his profits. Parsons decided that attracting industrial customers to the Clydach valley could create a larger market for Neath Abbey Coal. This strategy was to have important results with regards to the development of the metalliferous industries of Neath Abbey.

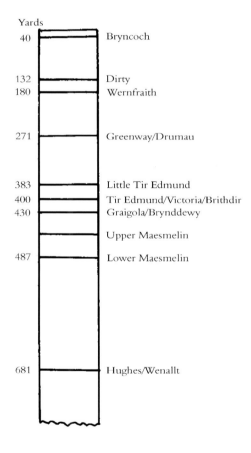

The principal coal seams of the Neath Abbey area.

2

The Copper Industry

The copper smelting industry has been associated with the Neath valley since Tudor times. In order to promote the industry, Elizabeth I granted charters in 1568 for two companies to exploit the mineral resources of her realm. They were the Company of Mineral and Battery Works, which concerned itself with the making of brass and the drawing of iron wire, and the Society of Mines Royal which mined, smelted and refined copper. The Society of Mines Royal mined copper ore in the Lake District and Cornwall and set up a smelting house at Aberdulais near Neath in 1584.[9] Smelting at Aberdulais was sporadic and soon after 1598 the site was abandoned. The Queen's attempts at cultivating a copper industry were not successful and by the 1680s the British copper industry was virtually non-existent.

However, patents were soon taken out for the use of reverberatory furnaces to make lead and copper. This type of furnace allowed the use of coal as a fuel to smelt copper ore. This revived the industry and together with the Acts of 1689 and 1692 which freed lead, copper and tin mines from all claims by the crown gave the impetus for growth. Copper and brass wares had previously been imported from Holland and Germany but British merchants could see the imminent growth of the copper and brass industry in supplying ordnance, coinage and slave and plantation goods. Several copper works were built in Britain during the 1690s and one of these pioneering works was placed at Neath Abbey. The lease for the founding of this concern survives and is dated 10 September 1694. It consisted of:

> *A lease for 42 years from Elizabeth Hoby of the Parish of Cadoxton, co Glamorgan, widow, Henry Compton of Bisterne, co Southampton, esq., and Elizabeth his wife, Griffith Rice of Newtown, co Carmarthen, esq. and Katherin his wife, and William Stanley of Poulton, co Southampton, esq. and Anne his wife, to Thomas Scawen of London, merchant, Thomas Leeke of Chelsea, co Middlesex, gent. Thomas Neale Of London, esq., and Benjamin Gyles of London, mercer, of a parcel of land whereon an iron smelting furnace formerley stood, a messuage and lands in the Tenures of David William, Elizabeth Howell ,and, Friswith Lewis, $\frac{1}{2}$ acre of waste land adjoining, Having the river Clydach on the east, the highway Leading from Neath Abbey to Courtride on the west, Lands and houses in the tenures of Evan John, David Griffith, and Hopkin Jeffery, on the south, and a Little brook running from the said highway to the River Cledach, and a little garden in the tenure of Rees Llewelin on the north; also the right of making wears on the east bank of the River Clydach and to Import and land on the north side of the Abbey coal Bank all commodities requisite for the use of the copper mill. Yearly rent, £14 for the first 21 years of The said term, and thereafter, £19 17s 6d payable to the said Elizabeth Hoby for her life, and thereafter, to the said Henry Compton and Elizabeth his wife, Griffith Rice and Katherin his wife, and William Stanley and Anne his wife; suit at the Abbey Mill, and 2s in lieu of suit at the court of the manor of Cadoxton by Neath.[10]*

Thomas Neale (d.1699), Master of the Mint and a partner in the first Neath Abbey copper works.

First a copper battery mill was constructed to produce copper plate with water powered hammers. However, by the end of 1694 copper ores were being imported by the company demonstrating that smelting furnaces had also been built at Neath Abbey. The partners in Benjamin Gyles & Company were London merchants, although the landowner, Madam Hoby, seems to have taken a share in the company. The copper mill and other works would have been situated around the Cwm Felin waterfall area.

This partnership contained an important speculator who had a thorough knowledge of the growing market for copper, Thomas Neale MP, later Master of the Royal Mint in 1686. He was one of the great projectors of his time, who was said to have made and lost two fortunes.[11] Neale had been appointed by Charles II as groom porter for life in 1678. Charles also conferred on him the reversion for life of the mastership of the mint on a vacancy. In 1681 he was awarded a patent authority to construct a waterworks at Shadwell and he formed a Governor and Company of the Waterworks and Water-houses there.

Neale worked hard to carry out the work planned by the company. He also developed the Seven Dials area near Leicester Square in London and founded the penny post in the American colonies. In 1693, when Neale had been Master of the Mint for seven years, he ran a private lottery of 50,000 ten-shilling tickets with prizes up to £3,000 with a commission of £2,500 for the manager. The following year saw him promote and manage the first state sweepstake, the Million Pound Lottery, after obtaining a special act to exempt him from the disqualification of MPs from the post. Neale was prolific in setting up joint stock companies which included ventures to work lead mines, develop steel and wire screens, to raise valuables from sunken ships and promote his invention of Brown Paper. He died in late 1699.

The copper works at Neath Abbey seems to have worked only intermittently during its early life. Copper ore was purchased for the works in the period 1694 to 1696, John Champion being the manager. In 1700 ten hundredweights of copper plate were shipped to London and regular shipments from Neath Abbey to Bristol are recorded from 1702 to 1710. The yearly totals of these shipments varied from $5\frac{1}{2}$ to 44 tons and, at its peak, the production of Neath Abbey copper matched the output of other large works.[12] During this period of copper production there appear to have been a change in the ownership of the works. From 1706 it was Thomas Collins who paid the rent on the property. He then took two new partners into the concern, namely Dr John Lane and Lane's father-in-law, John Pollard.

Lane was baptised at Banbury, Oxfordshire in 1678.[13] He entered Exeter College, Oxford in 1694 and studied medicine at Leyden from 1702. Lane established a medical practice in Bristol where he appears to have earned a high reputation in his profession. Like many professional men he invested widely in industrial undertakings. Along with Pollard he had invested in shares in Cornish mines before they both took third shares in the Neath Abbey Copper Works. Lane had a troublesome business career and the Neath Abbey partnership was dissolved around 1716, with Lane moving on to establish another copper works at Landore in the Swansea valley. During this period not only copper but also lead was being smelted at Neath Abbey but in 1716, the works was making no profit and was described as being in a state of disorder.

The next phase in the history of the copper industry at Neath Abbey began in 1720 when the Welsh Copper Company took over the abandoned copper works. The complete title of this concern was the Governor and Company of the Copper Mines in the Principality of Wales, founded in 1694, the time of the government's freeing up of the metaliferous mining and smelting industries. However, the drowning of their lead mine at Talorgoth in 1715 nearly destroyed the company. The Welsh Copper Company was also debilitated by the death of the Governor, John Cooper, in the same year. After these events the company took no action until 14 June 1720 when a newly elected court tried to augment the stock to get the company mines in order and enter the smelting trade.[14] This was not an entirely successful manoeuvre as the South Sea Bubble had affected speculation, although enough money was subscribed to take over the Neath Abbey works, with Thomas Collins acting as manager. The leading members of the company involved in the resuscitation were the Duke of Richmond, the Earl of Clarendon, Sir R. Knipe, Sir Fisher Tench and Mr Ward.[15] Although smelting operations were soon under way, the company was still trying to entice more capital into the venture in 1722.

The progress of the Neath Abbey Copper Works was severely affected by the death of Thomas Collins in 1724 and the rent for the land became eighteen months overdue. The affairs of the Welsh Copper Company then spiralled into confusion with writs being issued between partners.[16] In 1730 Caleb Wynd received a shipment of lead, copper ores and Cornish clay from Hayle in the name of the company. However, two years later part of the works was solely leased to Caleb Wynd of Neath. On 1 November 1732 he took over 'the ruined buildings called the Lower Copper house and the waste ground around it at or near the Abbey bridge – late in the occupation of the Welsh Copper Company for smelting ores.' On gaining the lease he set up a new works on the site buying tools and equipment from the Melyncryddan Copper Works in 1733 and 1744 for use in the smelting works. Some of the equipment he purchased suggests that he was also operating a rolling and slitting mill on this site.[17]

The Welsh Copper Company continued to occupy the Upper Copper Works for smelting copper and lead ores. The manager of this works was Edmund Moore, who in 1731 took out a lease of Neath Abbey and the lands around it and began to use them as a dump for the slag from smelting. Edmund Moore, acting for the Welsh Copper Company, continued to receive shipments of ore from Cornwall until 1751 but the small and intermittent character of the copper ore deliveries suggests the company was concentrating on lead smelting. Smelting seems to have come to an end soon after this date.[18]

It is possible that another copper works operated in the area during the 1720s. There has been a long tradition that the copper used in producing 'Wood's Halfpence' was produced at Neath Abbey. The rent roll of the Neath Abbey Estate 1720 – 1725 does record a Mr Wood & Partners paying rent for an unspecified building adjoining Neath Abbey. The rental of £3 a half year could represent a small smelting works set up to fulfil coinage contracts.[19] Wood was born in Wolverhampton in 1671 and was a projector of schemes equal to Thomas Neale.[20] His schemes included a Company of Ironmasters that would have been the first £1,000,000 corporation. Although his main interest was in the iron industry, he did have a connection with the copper industry. By a patent of 12 July 1722 he produced copper coins for the American colonies at the American Mint near Seven Dials, London. In the same year Wood obtained a patent to coin halfpence and farthings for Ireland at the Bristol Mint. However, the Irish populace, stirred by Drapier's Letters written by Dean Swift, refused to accept the coinage.

It has often been advanced that the Mines Royal Society had an unbroken relationship with the Neath valley from the reign of Elizabeth I to the mid-nineteenth century. However, by 1600 the Society of Mines Royal had closed down its undertakings and the monopolistic powers of this company and the Company of Mineral and Battery Works had begun to waste away. The two companies were later amalgamated and meetings were held in the first decade of the eighteenth century to revive the joint company but little came of this.

It was in 1757 that a company was formed that adopted the Mines Royal name and in that year land was leased close to Neath Abbey for building a copper works. The company was probably made up of a mixture of London merchants and Cornish smelters. There had been some smelting of copper ores taking place in Cornwall but as the scale of the industry increased so did the advantages of the coalfields for smelting. It was economic sense for the smelting industry to be situated on the coalfield of south-west Wales for each ton of ore smelted took upwards of three tons of coal. Furthermore the ships bringing copper ore from Cornwall to Neath Abbey could return with cargoes of coal for the steam engines on the mines. Sampson Swaine, a well known Cornish smelter, seems to have been involved in the setting up of this company and it was Robert Place, his son-in-law, who was sent to Neath Abbey to manage the works.

The Mines Royal Company seems to have operated successfully, as shown by the company taking an additional lease of land from the Lords of the Abbey in order to expand the works in 1771.[21] The building of the Mines Royal Copper Works at Neath Abbey was part of a general expansion of the industry in south Wales with many works being built, particularly in the Swansea valley. However, soon after the taking of the additional Mines Royal lease in 1771, the industry was thrown into a period of turmoil. Already there had been problems between the three factions operating in the industry, namely the Cornish miners, the Associated Smelters of South Wales and the Birmingham merchants whose trade represented a large share of the market. The mutual distrust of these factions was exacerbated when a large mass of copper ore was discovered in 1768 on Parys Mountain on Anglesey. Although this ore was of a poorer quality than Cornish ore it occurred at about six feet below the ground and so could be easily quarried rather than mined. [22]

The Parys Company and other copper concerns came to be controlled by Thomas Williams of Llanidan. He realised that the Associated Smelters had been paying low prices for Cornish ores and so decided to smelt his own ores and wrest control of the copper market from the Swansea ring. To combat this the Associated Smelters forced down the price of Cornish ore with the result of all these actions being a recession for the Cornish mining industry. To try to rectify these problems, the half million pounds Cornish Metal Company was set up in 1785 with offices in Truro.[23]

The main initiator of this move was Matthew Boulton, a Birmingham tradesman who used large amounts of brass and copper in making various metal goods. Boulton was convinced that the Cornish miners were suffering unjustly at the hands of the Welsh smelters. The company's policy was 'to maintain and keep the price of copper ore at a proper standard' and it was committed to buying at a fixed price the output of ore from the mines involved for an eleven year period. For a time all went well but stocks of ores and metal rose in the face of the market domination of Williams and the opposition of the Welsh smelters. The new company failed to dominate the industry and many Cornish mines were forced to close. One of the main difficulties was that Williams could still make a profit when selling his ore at £50 a ton against which the Cornish mines needed a figure of £80 a ton to survive. This intractable problem caused the Cornish Metal Company to be liquidated with the shareholders being fortunate in regaining their capital.

As has already been stated, Williams not only controlled the mining of ore in Anglesey but also entered the smelting side of the business. He was involved in the Parys Mine Company, the Mona Mine Company and the Stanley Company, as well as holding copper mills in his own name. The Middle Bank Copper Works in the Swansea valley was taken over in the 1780s by the Stanley Company, who had also held the Penclawdd Copper Works. Around 1782 the Parys Mine Company took over the Upper Bank Copper Work and there was a need for still more rolling mills to make copper plate, plus the product was in great demand due to the introduction of copper sheathing for ships. Indeed, the demand for mill capacity for the copper industry was such that the Williams' organisations leased the copper rolling mills at Cwm Felin, Neath Abbey during the period 1786-1790.[24] These mills were held by the Parys Mine Company and Williams & Co. and were probably producing plate from the copper produced by the Williams' works in the Swansea valley.

The Mines Royal Copper Works at Neath Abbey also entered the copper sheathing market in about 1780. It could well have been that the Williams' organisations occupied the Cwm Felin rolling mills from the early 1780s for the Mines Royal Company was forced to roll their copper into plate at other sites. Initially the company chose Rogerstone in Monmouthshire, conveniently situated on the coast near the Bristol market.[25] However, this site was soon abandoned and rolling mills were constructed in Middlesex.

These mills had the advantage of being close to the great naval dockyards of south-east England. The most important of these mill sites was at Harefield. At that time one of the managing partners was Robert George Spedding, a Harefield landowner and merchant of Dowgate Wharf, London.

Some details of the Mines Royal Company's smelting operations in the 1790s have survived.[26] In 1795 copper was being produced for the East India Company and by contract for the Rose Copper Company of Birmingham. The Rose Copper Company was a Birmingham co-operative venture inspired by Matthew Boulton. Obviously Boulton's disappointment at the lack of success of the Cornish Metal Company had not dulled his appetite for copper industry schemes.

In 1796 production at the Mines Royal Copper Works was severely disrupted when a stack fell, bringing down a roof and some arches. However, the roof of Mackworth's Gnoll Copper and Lead works was purchased and erected and production resumed. For the week ending 23 May 1796, twenty tons of copper were made and for the week ending 10 October 1796, seventeen tons of copper were made by thirty-eight furnaces. This amount of copper was made using 136 tons of ore and 315 tons of coal as the fuel. So successful was copper production at this time that the Mines Royal Company was considering taking the lease of the Gnoll Copper Works. This development came to nothing for Lady Mackworth objected on the grounds that the copper smoke would damage her Gnoll House.

The company did experience some production problems which were mainly related to the supply of coal from Richard Parson's collieries. As with many of the industrial under-takings on the Neath Abbey Estate, the Mines Royal Company were locked into using coal from the estate by the terms of their lease. A lease of 1 June 1798 bound the company to receive, for a term of forty years, coal from the Neath Abbey Estate after the expiration of the Parson's lease.[27] The company agreed to take:

> *from Level Coal Works – 600 weys of coal containing 216 Winchester bushels at the price of 39s per wey and from Cwm Velin Coal Works – 200 weys to contain 216 bushels to be delivered without being picked for coaking or any other purpose and in the case of the failure of these coal works to be supplied from some other vein of good binding quality at the price of 45s per wey.*

The yearly output of copper from the Mines Royal works in 1797 was 650 tons.[28] This would have required about 1,204 weys of coal for fuel. The sensible course at this time would have been to obtain the extra coal over the 800 weys from the collieries on the Neath Abbey Estate. The supply of coal above that was stipulated in Neath Abbey leases caused a problem that was to surface later in the nineteenth century.

The Mines Royal Copper Company continued to smelt at Neath Abbey during the nineteenth century but the works remained a fairly small establishment while other larger neighbouring works in the Swansea valley continued to grow. At the Mines Royal site in 1842, the company employed ninety-three people compared with 450 at the Morfa Copper Works in Swansea. Another indication of the scale of operations can be gauged from the following sales of copper ores to the Mines Royal Company at Cornwall and Swansea.[29]

		ore purchased in tons	copper purchased in tons	% of total ore for sale
Cornwall,	1855	10,099	595.85	5.2
Swansea,	1855	2,614	337.60	5.9
Cornwall,	1856	10,060	601.25	4.9
Swansea,	1856	2,259	290.80	5.3
Cornwall,	1857	9,003	524.85	4.7
Swansea,	1857	2,039	261.55	5.4
Cornwall,	1858	8,969	524.25	4.9
Swansea,	1858	1,879	239.00	5.0
Cornwall,	1859	6,863	379.75	3.8
Swansea,	1859	2,658	326.70	6.1
Cornwall,	1860	6,753	348.10	3.7
Swansea,	1860	2,278	311.50	—
Cornwall,	1861	3,776	197.70	2.1
Swansea,	1861	1,434	207.65	3.8

These figures certainly show declining purchases of copper from the Cornish ticketings. During the period 1858 to 1862 the average price of a ton of fine copper fell from £108 1s to £100 6s and a small firm like the Mines Royal Company would have had great difficulty in withstanding the competition from the larger Swansea firms who had access to better transport facilities. When the lease of the works terminated in 1862 the Mines Royal Company withdrew from the industry and sold their works. The Neath Abbey site was then occupied by the Neath Copper Company who purchased ore in Cornwall and Swansea in 1862 and 1863. After this date this firm disappears from the records. It seems that the Swansea firm of Williams, Foster & Company smelted at the Mines Royal site during the period 1875-1881 but after this the buildings were abandoned.

During the 1790s the Mines Royal Copper Works provided Richard Parsons with an assured market for a large amount of Neath Abbey coal. However, Parsons had to mine and sell 40,000 tons of coal each year. Parsons therefore set out to attract further industrial concerns to the Neath Abbey area. In 1792 he leased the land around the Cwm Felin waterfall which contained the then redundant copper rolling mills and he also started negotiations with the Lords of the Abbey for leasing land around the Abbey Wharf and saltmarsh near the confluence of the Rivers Clydach and Neath.[30]

Parsons main aim in 1792 was to attract another copper works to the Neath Abbey area. As luck would have it an established copper company was looking to move one of its smelting establishments from near Liverpool. This was the Macclesfield Copper Company or, as it is often known, as Roe & Company. Charles Roe, the originator of the company, was born in Castleton, Derbyshire on 7 May 1715.[31] He was the son of the Reverend Thomas Roe MA, the vicar of Castleton. In 1742 Charles Roe was admitted as a freeman of Macclesfield and was described as a gentleman. He built a silk mill in Macclesfield but withdrew from the trade to enter the copper industry. Roe & Company leased land at Macclesfield in 1758 for smelting after taking a mining lease at Coniston in the Lake District. In 1763 a site near the Macclesfield-Congleton turnpike was acquired and houses and mills were built for the rolling of brass and copper. This establishment became known as the Havannah, named after a recent successful British siege. At Bosley, six miles from Macclesfield, the company erected a mill for the rolling and hammering of copper and then later built a calamine house at Bonsall in Derbyshire.

The Macclesfield area could not have been the most convenient situation for importing ore; therefore Roe and Company leased land on the banks of the River Mersey and built a copper smelting works on the site in 1767.[32] However, because of complaints about pollution the works was moved to Harrington in 1770 on land acquired from Lord Sefton. The Macclesfield Copper Company had been involved in the early development of the Parys Mine but after a dispute had withdrawn from the enterprise.

Charles Roe died in 1781 but this had little effect on the company as there were enough experienced partners to continue operations in the copper trade. Of the partners it was Edward Hawkins who not only had great mercantile experience, but also good practical knowledge of copper making technology. Hawkins was a merchant from Congleton who had taken out a patent for the 'art or method of making shaven or bright latten by rolling, battering, hammering and shaving sheet brass' in 1778 and also set up the first bank in Macclesfield in 1787.

On 16 August 1785, none other than James Watt visited Roe & Company and was impressed by what he saw. He recorded that:

> *I was at Messrs Roe and Co.'s Brass Works; their consumption of water is amazing. They have 5 wheels; the one belonging to the wire mill requires constant water and may be replaced by a 20 horse rotative engine. Mr Hawkins (one of the partners) was exceeding kind. After we had seen the mills he took me to dine at Congleton at Mr Hodgson's, his brother-in-law, who is also a partner, and is just returned from Scotland, where the Company have just taken a lease of lead and copper mines of Islay; he says the latter are very promising and I have heard so formerly.[33]*

Additional smelting capacity was added on 22 September 1785 when the company leased land from Thomas Pennant in Flintshire. On this land Roe and Hawkins built the River Bank Works which were, 'employed for the double purpose of calcining calamine for the brass works at Cheadle and Macclesfield and for melting lead ore'. The Macclesfield Copper Company's mining interests also expanded by leasing mines near Llanberis in North Wales.

Further expansion occurred in 1787 when Edward Hawkins, William Roe and partners found great difficulty in purchasing enough ore for their smelters. To solve this problem they entered into an agreement with others to buy the Cronebane Mines in County Wicklow along with other mines in Ireland. This subsidiary concern became known as the Associated Irish Mine Company and £40,000 was spent on developing these mines. Soon these mines were yielding about 1,000 tons of ore each year which was sent to Liverpool for smelting.

The removal of the Macclesfield Copper Company's smelting works from Liverpool to Neath Abbey was initiated by the partners' dissatisfaction with the price and quality of coals they were receiving for their smelter in Lancashire. A contemporary observer stated that the company was thinking of moving the works, 'on account of the scarcity and dearness of coal at Liverpool.' Between 2 June and 22 September 1791, Roe & Company advertised in Gore's *Liverpool Advertiser* inviting tenders for contracts to supply their Liverpool smelter with coal for one or two years commencing 1 May 1792. The company's committee book records that the closing date for tenders was 24 December 1791 and that this information should also be sent to Sir Herbert Mackworth.

Here we can see the start of the process that brought Roe & Company to Neath Abbey. Mackworth knew Lancashire well for he had invested heavily in a plate glass factory in the county, and while on business in the area would have seen the advertisements. It could be that Mackworth wanted to sell some of his coal or offer a deal in which the Macclesfield Copper Company took over one of his redundant copper works in Neath. Mackworth, however, died on 25 October 1791 though Richard Parsons seems to have known of his plans and stepped in to offer his commercial services.

The Committee Book of the Macclesfield Copper Company for the years 1774-1833 survives and records the move of the company's Harrington smelting works to Neath Abbey.[34] In the early 1790s the meetings of the company were held alternately in Liverpool and Macclesfield on the third Thursday in November, February and May. However, important decisions had to be made and this routine was soon changed with Liverpool being dropped as a venue for the meetings. The main partners in the concern at this time were Abraham Mills, who was chairman of the company, Thomas Smythe, Edward Hawkins, William Roe, Robert Hodgson, John Johnson and Charles Caldwell.

In August 1792 it was decided that all the company's copper ore would be smelted in South Wales; the contracted work to be completed by Fenton & Company in the Swansea valley. It was also resolved to build a copper works near the River Neath for smelting and 'Mr Parsons of Cadoxton' was requested to attend a meeting of the Committee bringing with him such deeds as would enable the partners to judge the eligibility of erecting works on his premises.

Parsons was walking a tightrope as he still had not yet signed a lease for the Neath Abbey land. Despite this, in November 1792, Mills was instructed by the partners to journey to Cornwall and then visit Neath to inspect the site for the new copper works. The furnaces in the north range of the buildings at the Harrington copper Works and the calciners were taken down and shipped to Neath by order of the committee dated 8 March 1793. Parsons was finally able to complete the signing of the lease of the Neath Abbey lands on 30 May 1793, several weeks after the decision had been made to move the works. The lease was then transferred to Edward Hawkins and Abraham Mills representing Roe & Company on 22 June 1793. The land carried a yearly rent of £40 and the lease ran for sixty-one years. The company signed a further lease with Parsons sometime after August 1794. The leases achieved what Parsons had hoped for; another major user of coal had been enticed into the area and was locked into using Neath Abbey coal by the terms of the lease.

A reading of the Committee Book of the Macclesfield Copper Company shows that Parsons had to make an incredible bargain to attract the company to Neath Abbey. Instead of offering coal at a set charge per wey or per ton, Parsons contracted to supply enough coal to smelt each ton of ore at a set price of 8s. On 14 April 1794 Roe and Johnson were instructed to offer the buildings of the Harrington Copper Works to Lord Sefton for £2,500 and also to offer him the slag bank at the works for £1,000. In the following August it was decided to send all the fire bricks and wrought iron at Harrington to Neath Abbey and to sell off the remaining cast iron. At this time William Roe and Thomas Weaver were confirmed as joint directors of the Neath Abbey works with Weaver visiting the works every quarter day and Roe visiting annually on 5 July and one other quarter day. The Macclesfield

Copper Company's premises were valued in August 1794 in the following way:

Macclesfield Works	£8,013 12s 2d
Havannah Works	£9,239 10s 1d
Bosley Works	£14,936 6s 6d
Harrington Works	£2,500
Slag bank at Liverpool	£1,000
Holywell Works (one share)	£1,053 15s 8$\frac{1}{2}$d
Neath Smelting Works	£2,961 5s 9d.

The value of the Neath Abbey works seems to reflect the slow progress in its completion. On 24 August 1795 it was decided to build a house for the copper works' agent at Neath Abbey and also to send the horse engine, rollers and other bricks from the Liverpool works. As well as the slow progress of the Neath Abbey works other problems began to surface in 1796, particularly with Parson's coal contract. It was decided that Parsons would deliver coal for the Neath Abbey works consisting of $\frac{6}{7}$ from the New Level Coal unpicked, $\frac{1}{7}$ of the Skewan binding coal plus one wey at 36s of the Cwm Valyn Coal per week for the refineries. This was accepted as long as the price of 8s per ton of ore smelted was not exceeded. In 1797 both Roe & Company and the Mines Royal Copper Company complained about the quality of the coal supplied by Parsons. He countered this by claiming that the workmen at the copper works were stealing some of the coal supplied. This seems to have been a frequent claim by Parsons and in August 1796 Roe & Company had ordered that a weighing machine should be constructed at the copper works at the end of the railway leading to the coal bins.

The unfinished nature of the works can be gauged from the fact that in 1797 it produced 320 tons of copper, less than half of the Mines Royal output. The problem with Parsons' coal contract led to a reorganisation of the terms in 1797. The price of coal per ton of ore smelted had by then risen to 8s 3d and on 12 May 1797 it was agreed that the figure rise to 9s 4d per ton of ore smelted. This was still a good enough bargain for Roe & Company to try to get Parsons to supply coal at that price for exporting to Ireland for calcining copper ore. During 1798 efforts were made to complete the Neath Abbey works including putting the roof on the agent's house and the Neath Abbey works of the Macclesfield Copper Company seem to have finally been completed in 1799 when preparations were made to make their own firebricks at the site.

However, these were troubled times for the partnership. The Coniston mine had been an unproductive investment for Roe & Co. Between 1758 and 1867 a total of 904 tons of ore was raised at this mine. After this period the mine produced little until 1792 when money, effort and time were expended again on this venture but by August 1794 the company decided to give up the Coniston mine. In 1795 Abraham Mills wrote: '...the Coniston Mine has for some years been so unproductive that it has been determined to discontinue the working...'

Problems also existed with the supply of copper ore from Ireland. The ore was subject to an import duty against which Roe & Company appealed to the Board of Customs on 15 February 1794 couched in the following terms:

Our House is Roe & Company…extensively concerned in smelting & manufacturing copper ore & are likewise concerned in Copper Mines in various parts of this kingdom & also in the kingdom of Ireland, our smelting works were situated within a short distance of the Town of Liverpool, & by…indulgence we were permitted to land our ores…but the high price of labour & coals at that Port, has obliged us to remove our Works to the Port of Neath…and in the month of January of the present year, we imported from Wicklow in Ireland to the Port of Neath, per our Brig, the Irish Minor, a Cargo of Copper Ore which is subject to an heavy duty on importation…For several years past we have been almost the only importers of Irish Copper Ore and of course the only British subjects on whom the duty falls.[35]

There were yet more problems with the Irish copper ore to come when a rebellion in Ireland disrupted the trade during 1798.

In 1799 Edward Hawkins was made director of the copper trade at a salary of £250 per annum, the company decided to withdraw completely from the brass trade although Mr Weaver continued as superintendent of the Neath Abbey works at a yearly salary of £60. Conditions worsened in the trade during 1800 with Mr Morgan, the works' agent, being denied a rise in salary as the company deemed his move into the works' house the equivalent to an increase in wages. The problems affecting the partnership's operations came to a head in 1800 and it was decided to close down all the firm's activities in the brass and copper trade.

In 1801 Edward Hawkins offered to buy the Neath Abbey works from the partnership. The Macclesfield Copper Company's Committee Book records that on 6 July 1801,

That the Neath Works having been offered to Mr Hawkins and he has accepted them, he is now become the purchaser of them as they stand and in our books and also the workmen's tools for the sum of £7,000 payable half in six months and the remainder in nine months from the time of his taking possession of them – such time of Entry to be at Mr Hawkins' option not later than 25th day of December next…

The ores and the furnace bottoms were later valued independently and sold to Hawkins who took over the lease of the works and the coal contract with Parsons. There is no doubt that Hawkins then operated the works alone as a later Victorian lease marks a row of homes in Neath Abbey called Hawkins Cottages on the accompanying map. Hawkins appears to have made his home in the Vale of Neath for he was still living in the area when he was involved in a later law case concerning the land around the works.[36]

Hawkins was an experienced and well-known businessman and it appears that the copper works at Neath Abbey traded successfully under his ownership. However, the Neath Abbey works came to the notice of the Cheadle Brass Wire Company and this Staffordshire firm made an enquiry in August 1803 'that Mr Hawkins be applied to know if he will dispose of a part of Neath Copper Works and part of his lease of a colliery which supplies the same.'[37]

The Cheadle Brass Wire Company was started up by the Patten family who built a copper smelting works in Warrington.[38] In 1734 Thomas Patten built a brass works and a brass wire mill to make use of his copper from Warrington. The Cheadle area was chosen because of the combination of coal supplies, waterpower and a location relatively close to the important brass market of Birmingham. Patten's industrial empire grew larger with copper and brass mills being built in North Wales and in 1771 he built the Stanley Copper Works for smelting on the outskirts of St Helens, Lancashire. However, despite this growth, Patten's empire was not large enough to resist pressure from Thomas Williams and he eventually sold his interests in the Greenfield Valley and the Stanley Copper Works to Williams and consolidated his holdings around Cheadle and Alton.

The company did still operate a copper smelting works at Penclawdd near Swansea but problems existed with the lease of this site. In 1809 the Cheadle Company was discussing building or buying a copper works if the Penclawdd lease could not be renewed. Attempts were made to find an alternative smelting site in South Wales. On 11 December it was reported that 'Mr Hawkins, having offered to dispose of his copper works to the company, resolved that Mr Plumbe be requested to wait upon him on his return to Swansea in order to know his term and report the same to the principal partners for their future consideration.' The directors of the company at this meeting were Thomas Wilson, John Watkins, Ralph Fisher, William Ingleby, Jos. [sic] Ingleby and John Plumbe, at that time superintendent of the company's business in South Wales with a salary of £200 per year.[39] The purchase of the Neath Abbey works went ahead during what came to be the company's golden age. In 1795 the company's stock was valued at nearly £60,000 but within just ten years this had grown to over £100,000.

In September 1813 John Plumbe was asked to call on the neighbouring Crown Copper Works at Neath Abbey to 'try to make an arrangement with them for a regular supply of spelter and, in the event of his failing, that he be further requested to look out for a foreman accustomed to the making of spelter preparatory to the company entering (upon a small scale) upon the trade themselves.' This emphasis on the need for a supply of or for production of spelter was because it had replaced calamine in the manufacture of brass.

This was not the only technical development at the Neath Abbey works as in September 1818 the directors of the company asked that:

> ...the sum of £256 11s together with the interest due from Mr W.E. Sheffield to the company be allowed to him as the account balance in consideration of his having gone down to Neath Abbey Copper Works to teach his new method of smelting having in the sale of his patent to Mr Vivian reserved to the company the right of working and enjoying every advantage from it.

Although the Neath Abbey works smelted successfully for several years the Cheadle Brass Wire Company was badly affected by the economic depression that followed the Napoleonic Wars. In 1821 all company salaries and wages were cut and William Keates was, 'presented with £30 for his good conduct in winding up the Neath copper concern.' [40]

In 1821 the works were closed and the buildings remained abandoned for a few years until leased by the Neath Abbey Iron Company for boiler making and ship building.

The copper industry expanded at Neath Abbey after 1800, with a works operated by the Crown Copper Company of Birmingham on land leased from the Lords of the Abbey in 1806. The main partners in this concern were Pritchit, Ledsam & Jukes.[41] The Crown Copper Company was one of three Birmingham co-operatives formed to serve the interests of the city's merchants who operated in the copper and brass trade. By 1842 the Crown Copper Works was employing 143 people which indicates that the concern was half as big again as the neighbouring Mines Royal Copper Works.

However, Williams & Foster of Swansea had absorbed the Crown Copper Works into their organisation by 1850. The works at the time had thirty-five copper furnaces and nine furnaces for making zinc spelter. Ore was also processed in six calciners.

Williams & Foster gave up the Crown Copper Works on the expiration of the lease in 1866. It was then leased for a short period to E.A. Moore, who was involved in the Dynevor Coal Company, and John Thomas, the mineral agent for the Neath Abbey Estate. The works was again operated under the title of the Crown Copper Company and during 1866 the concern bought 880 tons of ore and just over 44 tons of copper from Cornwall. [42] In the same year the company was also active at the Swansea ticketings and purchased 89 tons of ore and just under 9 tons of copper. During 1867 the Crown Copper Company purchased 675 tons of ore in Cornwall and just less than 26 tons of copper.[43] However, renewed smelting at this site did not prove successful and the company abandoned its operations during this year.

The buildings did not stay redundant for long as the thirty-three acres of land belonging to the works were leased to James Humby on 20 November 1867.[44] Humby's address was Wellington Buildings, Liverpool and he agreed to pay a yearly rent of £495. Humby then floated the Laxey Neath Smelting Company Ltd and started to turn the Crown Works into a spelter works. Humby had a rather long history of founding companies that attracted capital but which soon went into liquidation. He was involved with the Great Western Iron Ore, Smelting & Coal Company who were concerned with iron making at Seend in Wiltshire.[45] This company's operations ended in chaos in the bankruptcy court where it was revealed that Humby, who was one of the company's original promoters and the manager of the North Wiltshire Banking Company, had bought land at Seend for £500 and sold it to the company for £2,500. In 1871 Humby was involved in launching the Welsh Ironworks Company, formed to take over the Hirwaun Ironworks, but this failed in its objective.

Humby's Neath venture also failed and went into liquidation and subsequently, in January 1871, the works were advertised for sale.[46] The works were described in the following terms:

> *The works are admirably situated, including an extensive quay on the river frontage, where vessels can load and discharge cargoes. The canal also passes through the works on the other side, whilst the railways are close at hand, giving facilities of communication to all parts of the kingdom. There is also a tramway into the works for the supply of coal and advantageous terms with coal mines adjacent are included in the lease. The works contain twenty four furnaces (some not yet completed but requiring a small expenditure to finish); six calciners, with three floors each; very large retort house, two stories high; pug mill; excellent retort machine; horizontal engine, 15in x 3ft, all complete and almost new; pipe or condenser house, with three large kilns, blacksmith's and joiner's shops; suitable offices and every requisite for turning out 10 tons of spelter per day.*

Later these works were occupied by the British & Foreign Construction Company Ltd., (1902-1903), the British Silver Zinc Company Ltd, (1903-1906), and the Neath Spelter Company Ltd, (1919-1924) and during this last occupation the site was known as the Emu Works.[47] Later the works were converted to produce patent fuel, bringing to a close the metaliferous smelting history of the Neath Abbey area that had been in existence from the late seventeenth century to the early twentieth century.

3

The Eighteenth Century
Iron Industry

The lease of 1694 for the land of the Neath Abbey Estate to be used as a copper mill states that the site was previously host to 'an iron melting furnace',[48] and further interest was shown during the eighteenth century for using land along the River Clydach for the iron trade. This may well seem surprising for the coal measures along the valley contained no iron stone – ore for smelting would have to be brought from the Swansea or Upper Neath valleys or imported by sea to Neath Abbey. However, the Clydach valley did have the advantages of plentiful water-power sites, abundant coal and the ease of export and import through the tidal rivers at Neath Abbey and these factors appear to have outweighed the one serious disadvantage.

The early eighteenth century was a time of great progress for the British iron industry. Abraham Darby at Coalbrookdale in Shropshire had been the first to use coked coal in iron smelting sometime after 1709; up to this time the predominant fuel was charcoal. Although Abraham Darby's use of coal as a fuel was a major breakthrough there were still problems associated with this new method of iron making. The coke iron made at Coalbrookdale was not suitable for refining into wrought iron at a forge but this did not worry the Darby family as the iron produced using this method was highly suitable for the products that were to be made at Coalbrookdale. Abraham Darby wanted to make pots and other vessels using cast iron and the coke iron made at Coalbrookdale produced an excellent foundry iron for casting such utensils. However, the unsuitability of this iron for refining in a forge meant that the adoption of coke smelting was a slow process.

One of the first, if not the first, coke fired furnaces used outside the initial sites in Coalbrookdale, was at Bryncoch in the Clydach valley. A furnace using coal as a fuel was built at Primrose Bank on land leased in June 1727.[49] The partners involved in this historic venture were James Griffiths of Swansea, merchant Joseph Hiscox of London, Augustine Rock, a drugget maker from Bristol, ironmonger William Donne, distiller Edward Garlick, glass maker Stephen Collier and drugget maker Isaac Mills. The land was leased from Llewellin Williams of Duffryn and included the 'liberty to build one or more blast furnaces for making or working or casting pig iron or other iron castings'. The lease also allowed the taking of water from the Clydach and to 'dig coal and culm…sufficient to supply a blast furnace and one air furnace that might be erected on land demised and for supplying workmen and servants employed by tenants'.

This Quaker partnership had some experience in smelting metals in South Wales for James Griffiths was also involved in the Cambrian Copper Works in Swansea. The connection of coke smelting with this partnership can be easily followed for Abraham

Darby was himself a Quaker and at one time involved in Bristol with other Quakers in a company making cast brass pots. Many of the Bryncoch partners were also involved in setting up the Welch Iron Foundry Company in Bristol which was founded to make pots and other cast iron goods. The Bristol group that held the Bryncoch furnace later evolved into Reynolds, Getley & Company who were important ironmasters and merchants in the mid-eighteenth century.

Abraham Darby had experimented with various coals for iron making and in 1713-1714 three cargoes of coal were brought up the River Severn from Neath to Coalbrookdale.[50] It is quite probable that the Bristol Quakers already knew that the coal along the Clydach valley was suitable for iron smelting before taking out the lease in 1727. Later visitors to the area often mentioned the low sulphur content of Neath Abbey coal.

The Bryncoch furnace appears to have been operated successfully by the Bristol company until 1757. The furnace was then sold by the partnership consisting of Edward Garlick, James Hillhouse, Richard Reynolds, gunsmith Samuel Page, ironfounder Richard Palmer and the ironmonger James Getley. The furnace was sold to Thomas Pryce of Cwrtrhydir (Longford Court), a local man who had entered the iron trade through being related to the Popkin family.[51] Pryce's father had married Mary Popkin and Thomas was their second son. The Popkin family had extensive interests in the iron industry. They operated the Ynyscedwyn Ironworks in the Swansea valley and in 1739 Thomas Popkin took out a lease for the Llandyfan Forge in the Upper Lougher valley, Carmarthenshire.[52] There are also scattered references to the Popkin family holding a forge in the Neath Abbey area in the early eighteenth century. Thomas Pryce seems to have taken over the family's interests in the iron trade for he was also involved at the Ynyscedwyn furnace and in 1752 he took over the lease of Llandyfan Forge. The acquisition of the Bryncoch furnace was sound as it occurred during the Seven Years War, a time of increased demand for iron products.

Clearly Pryce took over the furnace for a particular reason. This is revealed by John Vaughan, the owner of the land the Llandyfan Forge stood on, in a letter dated May 1758 that states '[Thomas Pryce] has made a Contract with the Government to cast cannon & shot & deliver the same of [several thousand] pounds value'.[53]

Despite the favourable international situation, an attempt to enter the ordnance trade at that time was not without risk. The expertise in casting cannon was mainly to be found in the Weald district of south-east England. New firms who tried to break into the trade often had great difficulty in producing cannon to the correct specifications and quality. The main problem facing the supplier was the stringent proof tests carried out by the government before the cannon were accepted. The first test was in the visual examination of the exterior of the piece for obvious gross casting failures and for surface flaws that exceeded accepted standards. The bore was then examined by probes and mirrors for flaws or 'spongy areas' and the piece was also gauged for calibre and the accuracy of the bore about the horizontal axis. Secondly, if the cannon survived these examinations, it was subjected to firing tests using graduated powder charges, well above the maximum. These firings were often carried out with double, triple or more shot.

At the beginning of 1758 Pryce had proposed to the Surveyor General of the Ordnance that he should cast 200 tons of iron ordnance and 300 tons of round shot.[54] Pryce was asked by the Government in February 1758 to deliver seventy-two 9-pounder cannons of 7ft, seventy

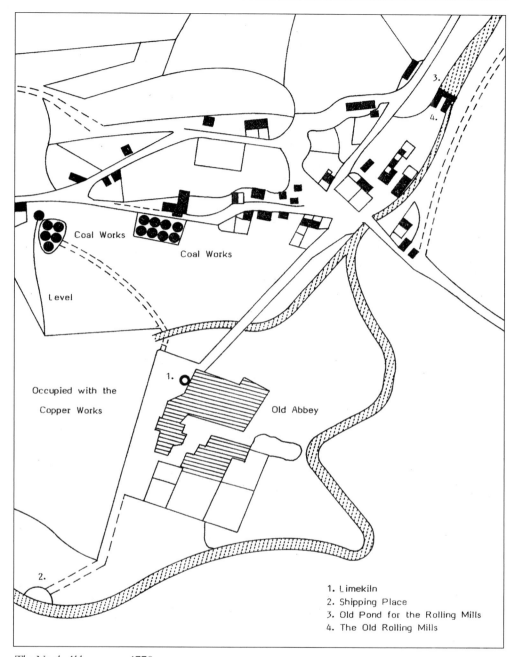

Coal Works

Coal Works

Level

Occupied with the

Copper Works

Old Abbey

1.

2.

3.

4.

1. Limekiln
2. Shipping Place
3. Old Pond for the Rolling Mills
4. The Old Rolling Mills

The Neath Abbey area, c.1770.

6-pounder cannons of 6ft, fifty 4-pounder cannons of $5\frac{1}{2}$ft and ninety 3-pounder cannons of 4 $\frac{1}{2}$ft together with 4,000 32-pounder round-shot, 6,000 18-pounder round-shot, 5,000 12-pounder round-shot, 15,000 9-pounder round-shot and 4,000 6-pounder round-shot.[55] By October 1758, despite being forced to decline an order to cast shells, matters were proceeding well with ships leaving Neath Abbey for London carrying Pryce's ammunition and guns.[56]

As with many concerns that tried to enter the cannon trade with the Government, disaster awaited Pryce's cannon at the proving tests. On 26 and 28 February 1759 nine of Pryce's 4-pounder cannon and five 3-pounders were tested. Of the 4-pounders, only three passed the first series of tests. Of these three, only two passed the second tests to be received into Government service. Not one of the 3-pounders got through both tests.[57]

On 30 April and 3 May 1759 sixteen of Pryce's 9-pounders were tested. Fifteen failed the first tests and one survived to be accepted into service.[58] Three more 9-pounder cannon were tested on 4 and 5 July and they all failed.[59] This prompted Pryce to write to the Surveyor General of Ordnance in August 1759 asking to be released from the cannon contract due to his lack of success.[60] As an alternative he offered to cast no less than 1,200 tons of shot in the next sixteen months. It is highly likely that this would have been all of the 900 tons output yearly from the Bryncoch furnace but it was agreed that Pryce should become a major supplier of cast iron shot to the Government.

However, even supplying shot during wartime appears to have been a trade laced with difficulties. In June 1760 Pryce wrote to the Board of Ordnance asking for extra time in delivering 200 tons of shot because of the difficulty in procuring vessels and in waiting for a convoy.[61] He was forced to write again in October 1761 to explain delays in the previous year because of troubles with convoys and winds which meant that ships that set off in November did not arrive until February.[62] Problems with customs officers meant that Pryce was forced yet again to write to the Board of Ordnance to explain further delays. It seems that Pryce's offer to cast 1,200 tons of shot in sixteen months was not taken up by the Board, although between February 1758 and September 1764 he did cast just over 1,230 tons of shot for which he received £13,609. Records have not survived to indicate what happened to the furnace's output after the end of hostilities.

The next development at Bryncoch was the transfer of the furnace on 25 March 1772 to Coles, Lewis & Company who also operated other ironworks in the Vale of Neath. Philip Williams of Duffryn granted a thirty-five year lease on the Bryncoch property with the company paying a yearly charge of £20 for the first five years and £25 thereafter. The lease also included a colliery at Warndee with a charge of 4s per wey of fifty-four bags with each bag containing three Winchester bushels. There seems to have been little activity at the furnace after this date for in the 1790s, when detailed statistics were compiled of furnaces both in and out of blast, there is no mention of Bryncoch.

Probably the most important event in the industrial history of the Neath Abbey area occurred in the late eighteenth century, the building of the Neath Abbey Ironworks.[63] With the foundation of this concern we can again see the guiding hand of Richard Parsons.[64] On the 29 May 1792 Parsons leased land from the Lords of the Abbey in the Cwm Felin area of the Clydach valley for an annual rent of £60 plus £6 per acre.[65] Having become possessed of this land Parsons then leased it within a few months to a Cornish partnership that wished to build an ironworks at Neath Abbey. This partnership took over:

...all that Mill and Foundry with all the other Erections...in a certain Vale or Dingle called Cwm Velin in the parish of Cadoxtone...theretofore made use of as Mills for battering copper and then lately for the purpose of rolling Iron Plates and making Cast Iron goods then in the occupation of the said Richard Parsons...

The partners of the Neath Abbey Iron Company were the same people who had set up the Perran Wharf Foundry, Cornwall in 1791. The partnership consisted of George Croker Fox, Robert Were Fox, Thomas Were Fox, Mary Fox, George Fox, Thomas Fox, Edward Fox, Peter Price, Samuel Tregelles, copper-smelter Thomas Wilson of Truro, 'Doctor of Physic' John Gould of Truro and ironmaster William Wood of Swansea. The partners were mainly related and were Quakers.

To fully understand the reasons behind the formation of these two widely separated ventures it will be necessary to investigate the fortunes of the Fox family in Cornwall in the eighteenth century.

George Croker Fox moved from Fowey to Falmouth in 1762 and brought with him the family bank of G. Fox & Co.[66] The move was probably due to his interests in the local pilchard fishery. In the same year he established a ships' agency and merchanting business under the title of G.C. Fox & Co. This company must have soon become involved in the lucrative shipping of copper ore to the smelters in South Wales and the return cargoes of Welsh coal for the pumping engines then at work on the Cornish mines. In the late 1790s the Fox family became involved in the development of the harbour at Portreath and leased the port under the title of Foxes & Portreath Company. They were to develop it into one of the largest copper exporting ports in Cornwall.

Members of the Fox family were soon taking a more active part in Cornish mining as individuals and as adventurers under the style of Fox, Philips & Fox. At a later date they were involved in copper ore purchasing and smelting as Fox, Williams & Company.

They were active in Cornish copper mining during the period of turmoil associated with the mining of copper ore on the Parys Mountain, Anglesey. In an effort to compete with the Parys ore the Cornish miners attempted to reduce their mining costs. One option was to reduce the charges for pumping the mines by adopting the more efficient Boulton & Watt steam engine with its separate condenser.

In 1776 a Cornish deputation visited Boulton & Watt. The members were taken to the colliery at nearby Tipton where Boulton & Watt's first engine was at work. The partners offered to erect an engine in Cornwall at their own expense and an order was received for a 52in engine for Ting Tang Mine. A second engine with a 30in cylinder was ordered by Chacewater Mine and in September 1777 was the first engine to be put to work. The engines certainly proved their worth and Cornwall became the largest market for Boulton & Watt engines. However, as time passed the annual dues to be paid on the engines became a source of dispute between Boulton & Watt and the mine adventurers. This led to the Birmingham partners taking shares in the mines as part payment and thus became involved in the mining and smelting of copper.

It must have been as fellow adventurers that the Fox family became acquainted with Boulton & Watt. This acquaintance developed into a firm and valuable friendship. The parts of the first Boulton & Watt engine for Cornwall were shipped through Falmouth and the Fox family were adventurers in many mines that acquired Boulton & Watt engines such as Polgooth (Edward Fox and Fox, Phillips & Fox), North Downs (Fox, Phillips & Fox) and Hewas. As disputes between adventurers and Boulton & Watt grew it was often the Fox family that interceded and placated both sides.[67] The Fox family also kept Boulton & Watt in touch concerning activity in the county and on such matters as the availability of shares.[68] Attempts were made to circumvent Watt's patent in Cornwall by such engineers as Trevithick, Edward Bull and the Hornblower family and information concerning their activities was readily sent from Falmouth, a typical example is a letter written in 1782 by George Fox to Boulton & Watt:

> *Doubtless thy agent in Cornwall will inform thee that some of the Hornblowers are returned and report great feats of their engines. Yesterday they were at friend Tremayne's and today I apprehend are at Truro. I have not seen Capt. Paul but hear he is almost a convert to their plans and indeed the County pretty generally seems to be prejudiced in their favour and I regret thy absence from Cornwall at this juncture. I know not the particulars of the proposals that Hornblowers are making to the adventurers, but thought it right to give these hints and with much respect am,*
> *Thy assured friend*
> *Geo[rge] Fox.*[69]

George Croker Fox, George Fox, Robert and Thomas Were Fox again wrote to the Birmingham partners in 1797 giving valuable information to them on engine building in Cornwall. They informed Boulton & Watt about rumours that were circulating in the county to the effect that:

> *Edw[ard] Bull is a partner with R. Trevithick in one or more steam engines that he is about to erect by your permission, we have had some conversation with R.T. on the subject who seems to be much hurt by a report which he aparts is invidious and totally void of foundation – this we are disposed to believe and at his request take freedom of intimating this much to you.*[70]

The Fox family held a powerful position in Cornish mining during the 1790s and had given valuable assistance to Boulton & Watt for many years. The Birmingham partners were aware of the debt that they owed to the Fox family and in 1792 they informed Edward Fox that:

> *…and we beg that you would believe us when we say in sincerity and truth that there is no set of adventurers in the county to whom we consider ourselves so much indebted on the score of good offices as to your family and connections…'*[71]

The Fox family's industrial interests were further expanded by establishing the Perran Foundry to supply castings and machinery parts for the Cornish mines.[72] This was the second foundry in Cornwall after John Harvey set up his own foundry at Hayle in 1779. The Fox partnership had some advantage in this venture for being Quakers they could purchase pig iron from the Quaker family of Coalbrookdale at more reasonable prices than Harvey.[73] In 1792 the site for the Neath Abbey Ironworks was leased by the partnership, giving them their own means of producing pig iron.

The Quaker partnership certainly possessed enough industrial and mercantile experience to make this venture into iron making a success. The partnership consisted of George Croker Fox, Robert Were Fox and Thomas Were Fox, who were the sons of George Croker Fox who set up in business in Falmouth in 1762, and their cousins Edward, Thomas, George and Mary Fox. Edward and Thomas Fox were also engaged in serge making at Wellington in the county of Somerset. Thomas Fox had also set up a banking department as Fox, Fowler & Company.[74] Dr Gould was the Falmouth Foxes doctor and was probably rewarded for his services with an invitation to join the partnership[75] while Samuel Tregelles was a merchant of Falmouth whose sister had married Robert Were Fox. Thomas Wilson though had a widespread knowledge of Cornish industry.[76] He was at Chacewater when the Wheal Busy engine was ordered, an agent for the Fenton Copper Company and Watt stayed at his house on his first visit to Cornwall. Wilson was appointed Boulton & Watt's agent for Cornwall but would appear to have been severely over-extended in his activities. In 1785 he had several shares in ships, the accounts of the copper works to oversee, several mine accounts to supervise plus partnerships in several farms. Furthermore, he was involved in the candle trade, held partnerships in several pairs of mules and was later a partner in the Cheadle Brass Wire Company. To crown it all there was the Boulton & Watt business in Cornwall to manage. For his services to Boulton & Watt, Wilson was paid a commission of $2\frac{1}{2}\%$ on the premiums collected in Cornwall. For the period 1781-1800 he received the sum of £3,485 or a little over £174 per annum.

Another partner with a widespread knowledge of industry was Peter Price who had been apprenticed in the iron trade and had practical experience of building furnaces and making steam engines.

The new works at Neath Abbey took some time to complete. The site possessed the advantages of proximity to a tidal river and the resource of water power at the waterfall site. The Quakers were not to neglect the natural resource of falling water but they were determined to have their furnaces blown by a steam engine.

The Quakers had not leased any land for coal mining so it was prudent for them to have their furnaces blown by an efficient steam engine. In June 1792 the Foxes wrote to Boulton & Watt concerning an engine:

> We request you will be pleased to furnish us with a note of the premium you will expect for an engine to be erected in Wales for working some blast furnaces. We propose to erect two and have sufficient blast for three; indeed of such power as there will be no doubt of our making 100 to 110 tons p[er] week. What would be the size of the single and that of the double? With the cost of each complete or as near as you can calculate – for the larger coal fit for coaking [sic] we shall most likely pay upwards of 3/- per ton, but coals for the engine ought to be reckoned at a much less rate.[77]

The Birmingham partnership replied in September informing the partners that the engine required would be the most powerful blowing engine ever erected and that:

> We cannot help recommending a double engine for this particular purpose in preference to a single one as the blast becomes more uniform and requires less of what is commonly called Regulating Belly. Such an engine when blowing the 3 furnaces will consume about 5 bushels of good coal an hour whereas the common engines we have seen applied to blowing, burn 4 times that quantity in proportion to the work done.

> As to the Blowing Cylinder and Regulating Belly, we will undertake to be your engineers
> in them and make such drawings for the founders, the smiths etc. as may be necessary without
> charging for the same and perhaps our knowledge and experience in that part of the machinery
> may be found of some importance.'[78]

There was some disagreement between the Quaker partners and Boulton & Watt over the premium payment but in September 1792 the blowing engines for Neath Abbey were ordered:

> As it is your opinion that an engine worked by a double 40in cylinder will be fully equal to
> the blowing of three large furnaces to make the greatest quantity of iron that you can produce.
> We desire that you will get us such an engine made and send it to Neath in Glamorganshire
> together with a proper person to superintend the erection of it. We also desire that you will
> furnish us as soon as you can with those drawings which are necessary for setting out the
> ground for the engine house boilers etc., and the distances you would wish the two furnaces to
> be from each other and to instruct us in any other matter which will forward the business so
> as to ensure the speedy completion of the engine which we wish to have at work in six months
> from this time. You'll of course take care of the engine be made of the best material and
> completed in the best manner in your own power for we need not inform you that if the same
> should get out of repair it will be attended with a heavy loss to the concern. We further
> recommend that you have the whole completed at the cheapest rate you can.[79]

The erecting of the engine was delayed and the Neath Abbey partners wrote on 30 May 1793 the following letter to Boulton & Watt:

> The concerned at the Ironworks at Neath are much disappointed that the engine for the
> business is not yet erected, nor the materials on the spot, we entreat the favour of your advising
> us how this delay arises and when you think it will be ready for work, one furnace has been
> completed near 2 month and the second we expect will be finished in 3 or 4 weeks, so that the
> disappointment is great to us.[80]

However, the furnaces were soon being blown by a double engine acting with a cylinder cast in Coalbrookdale of 40in diameter and 8ft in length. The engine was able to:

> ...work a blowing cylinder of 70 inches diameter and eight feet long in the stroke, both
> upwards and downwards where the piston of the said blowing cylinder is not charged with a
> resistance greater than [$2\frac{1}{2}$ lbs] on every square inch of the said piston.[81]

The Neath Abbey Iron Company paid an annual premium of £120 for the use of the engine. Although the cylinders were cast at the Coalbrookdale Ironworks the remaining parts were made at the Perran Wharf Foundry. The engine was erected by William Murdock, James Watt's main engineering assistant. After the completion of the engine Murdock visited the Neath Abbey Ironworks on several occasions to check that the engine was working in a satisfactory way. At this time Murdock was experimenting with extracting gas from coal for lighting. He seems to have successfully used coal gas in this way in experiments at the Neath Abbey Ironworks. Later, Thomas Wilson was asked to substantiate these events and several of the Neath Abbey partners were able to confirm that:

> *...I do hereby swear that betwixt the month of November 1795 and February the 7th 1796 the said W[illiam] Murdock did exhibit to me in the Counting House of the Neath Abbey Iron Works in the County of Glamorgan an apparatus for extracting gasses from the substances above mentioned, and that the said apparatus consisted of an iron retort with an iron tube of from three to four feet in length through which the gas from the coal then used in the retort issued, and at the end thereof was set fire to and gave a strong and beautiful light, which continued burning a considerable time.*[82]

The construction of the ironworks would have needed large initial outlay. The two furnace Madeley Wood Ironworks in Shropshire were valued at £15,000 in 1803 and it is quite possible that a capital of £20,000 was needed to complete the Neath Abbey concern, purchase new plant and attract new workers to the area. This money would have been sourced quite easily from the Foxes own industrial concerns and from the two banks the partners operated.

The supply of ironstone for the furnaces was also sourced relatively easily as the Quakers had leased land for ironstone mining as early as 1792. The area mined was on the Aberpergwm Estate at the head of the Vale of Neath where they could:

> *...work, extract and raise as many tons annually of the said ironstone or iron ore as they may...think fit...exceeding the seven thousand five hundred tons hereafter covenanted to be by them paid for...[sic]*[83]

The mining of ore in that area was made feasible by the recent opening of the Neath Canal which allowed easy transportation of materials from Aberpergwm to Neath Abbey. Soon, the Neath Abbey furnaces were able to produce between 60 tons and 80 tons of iron each week when working at full capacity.

When Joshua Gilpin visited the works in 1796 he not only saw local iron ore being used but also ore from Lancashire making up the furnace charge. Gilpin described the works in the following terms:

> *They are of the most modern and capital construction. Furnaces about 60 feet high dotted the yard and produced 80 tons of iron per week. A steam engine built by Boulton and Watt provided power. Before use the coal was coked by setting it on fire in long beds and later covering it with earth or by burning it in ovens, which were then closed. This process exhausted the caluminous parts in the coal. The furnaces were built of common blue 'slaty' fire or grit stone and lined with two lengths of local fire brick. The iron ore was brought from Pontyvan 13 miles away by canal.*[84]

The pig iron made at Neath Abbey was sent to Perran Wharf for casting into machine parts and also sold on the open market. In 1796 the company was sending prices and terms for the supply of iron to Belfast and London and also casting grate backs and kitchen ranges.[85] During the period 1797-1800 the Neath Abbey Iron Company sold 23.8 tons of iron to the Knight family for conversion into wrought iron at their Stour forges. This iron was sold to the Knights at a charge of between £5 18s to £7 a ton.[86]

The first ironmaster at Neath Abbey was William Wood but he seems to have left the partnership in its early stages. The name of John Williams of Scorrier then appears as a partner on minute papers for the company dated 14 November 1797.[87] The Williams family had made a fortune through Cornish mining and were co-partners with the Foxes in many ventures. At a later date John Williams' holding was increased when he purchased Thomas Wilson's share after the latter's bankruptcy.[88]

In 1794 Edward Fox offered his share to Boulton & Watt who turned down the offer.[89] Although they declined a share in the Neath Abbey Ironworks, they did show a healthy interest in the progress of this venture. One of the Birmingham partnership's employees visited the works in October 1796 and recorded that the works was paying 4s per ton for coal, 12s per ton for ironstone, 4s per ton for limestone and 21s per ton for Lancashire ore delivered on the furnace bank. He also noted that each furnace was 62ft high and each produced on average 33 tons of iron.[90]

These costs had altered by the end of the century for the Birmingham partners received a detailed statement of expenses at Neath Abbey during the period 30 June 1799 to 1 July 1800.[91] Coals still cost four shillings per ton and 17,000 tons had been used during the year which means approximately 5.6 ton of coal made 1 ton of iron. Welsh ironstone cost 14s per ton and 3.25 tons of this, together with 3cwt of Lancashire ore at 20s per ton, were used to make 1 ton of iron.

During the same year 3,025 tons of iron had been made at Neath Abbey with 430 tons being refined. Wages at the furnace cost a little over six shillings per ton. None of the iron was puddled and the company never made an attempt at producing their own wrought iron throughout its history.

James Watt, Jnr. who visited Neath Abbey in 1800 and recorded in detail what he saw, may well have collected the statement from which this information is gleaned.[92] He noted that the works were supplied under contract from two of Parsons' collieries, one a mile away and the other a half mile away to the north-west. The company was paying 4s 6d per ton for coal, this price had been increased to encourage Parsons to supply good coal.

Limestone used at the works came from Mumbles and Plymouth.

Watt, Jnr. reckoned that it took $4\frac{1}{2}$ tons of coal to make 1 ton of pig iron at Neath Abbey but the previous higher figure probably included the coal used to fire the boilers for the blowing engine and calcining the iron ore.

The produce of the furnaces was chiefly pig iron with approximately one tenth of the total sold to London. Neath Abbey also used its pig iron to make cylinders, pipes, wheels and grate bars. Any scrap from the castings was melted in a finery and sold ready for puddling. It was estimated that 22cwt of scrap produced 20cwt of refined metal. One important development that Watt, Jnr noted was that a boring mill was being erected at the site by the Downing family of Bell Broughton, Worcestershire. It was to have a 34ft overshot waterwheel which was 4ft wide. The wheel was to power three rods, one for working barrels and two for cylinders. The waterwheel could also be used to power a forge hammer.

This latter development was important demonstrates that the company had decided to seriously enter the engineering trade and build steam engines. It was a decision that would bring both fame and fortune to the Neath Abbey Ironworks.

4

The Neath Abbey Iron Company 1800-1890

In 1803 Neath Abbey was visited by a Swedish tourist who noted:

Not far from here lay, on the left-hand side of the road, an ironworks belonging to Mr. Fox & Company of Cornwall. We had letters from Mr Lockwood to a Mr Gould who lived here, and we were allowed quickly to go through the workshops; these consisted of a blast furnace, a founding furnace, and a large hearth, which was presumably used for the production of so-called 'fine metal' for a wrought-iron works erected for the purpose, or perhaps also for sale. All these hearths received their blast from a large cylinder blower which was driven by a steam engine, and which had a regulator with a movable cover of 9 feet diameter. There was nothing special about the blast furnace, the shaft of which was 63 feet high, and which produced 15-16 tons of pig iron per week, except that the shaft was dug out and built into the side of a hill which encroached into the works. The ironstone was by comparison with that of Merthyr Tydfil poor, but it was said that production could be pushed higher, if they did not primarily consider the quality of the iron. The coal had, after it had been converted to coke, almost the appearance of carbonised oak wood, and was said to be more free from sulphur than usual. Ironstone and coal were brought down from the hills above by railway. Besides the workshops mentioned a turning shop had also been established, where by means of a steam engine with the strength of three horses, rollers and various machine parts were turned.[93]

Within the next few years the making of machine and steam engine parts had graduated to the building of complete engines. The first engines built by the works in the period 1804-1806 included several of the Trevithick high-pressure type.[94] In 1806 the partners of the ironworks took out a lease to exploit the minerals on the Dyffryn Estate and over the next few years they built beam engines to aid their coal mining activities there. Three years later the works were building beam engines for sale to customers including John Williams of Scorrier.[95]

Many of the engines built at Neath Abbey were destined for duty on the Cornish mines and it appears that several Cornish engineers found employment in the workshops of the Neath Abbey Ironworks. The Cornish engineer, John Taylor, is a perfect example of this movement. He designed many of the company's early steam products and his family served the works until the 1870s.

The range of Neath Abbey steam products was increased after 1817 when the paddle steamer *Britannia* called at Neath Abbey. This ship had been used on the Holyhead to Howth mail service but was travelling to Bristol when she came to the Neath Abbey Ironworks for alterations to her 20hp engines.[96] The sight of these marine steam engines must have filled the Neath Abbey engineers with enthusiasm and from 1817 until the early 1820s preparations were made to commence the building of marine steam engines.

By 1817 the partnership that controlled the Neath Abbey Ironworks had become unwieldy. Many of the original partners had died and their shares were in the hands of inheritors or executors. It was decided to address this problem by selling the works. On 6 December 1817 the Neath Abbey Ironworks was advertised for sale and described as:

> *All those valuable Ironworks, Collieries and C. & C. consisting of two blast furnaces, ready to work at a short notice; a very extensive foundry, well furnished with all the necessary implements and capable of making the largest castings; a powerful boring mill worked by water, with complete apparatus for boring and turning all kinds of castings; also an excellent site for a rolling mill, for iron, copper or other purpose, with an unemployed fall of water of about twenty five feet; commodious buildings now employed making steam engines on the most approved plan, being furnished with an excellent steam engine, turning lathes and all the necessary apparatus; extensive smithery,[sic] with most complete blowing apparatus, and all kinds of tools and implements; – and all in complete repair, situated about a quarter of a mile from the navigable River Neath, with rail roads to a Wharf on the said river, as well as to the Neath Canal. The collieries consist of several valuable veins of coal adopted for the supply of iron, coal and other works and for general sales to Ireland, Cornwall, Devonshire & C. with four steam engines now at work; rail roads leading towards the navigable River Neath; waggons and every requisite for carrying on a most extensive trade.[97]*

Although advertised widely the ironworks was taken over by a new partnership between Fox and Price. The sale of the works was probably associated with the slump in the iron trade which followed the end of the Napoleonic Wars. However, the lease of 1818 clearly shows how unwieldy the partnership had become:

The Neath Abbey blast furnaces, c.1970.

This Indenture made the thirty first day of March in the year of our Lord one thousand eight hundred and eighteen between Thomas Fox of Wellington in the county of Somerset, Merchant, George Fox of Perranwharf in the county of Cornwall, Merchant and Robert Phillips Fox of the same place Merchant (which said T. Fox, G. Fox and R.P. Fox are the executors…of George Fox late of Perranwharf…deceased) the aforesaid Thomas Fox, Edward Coode of St. Austell…Gentleman and the aforesaid George Fox (which said T. Fox, E. Coode and G. Fox are the executors of Edward Fox late of the parish of Egloshayle…deceased) Dorothy Fox of Kingsbridge…Devon, Widow, William Matravers of Westbury…Wilts, merchant, Samuel Tregelles of the Parish of Budock…Esquire, Peter Price of Neath Abbey…Merchant, Elizabeth Fox of Falmouth…Widow Executrix…of Robert Were Fox late of the same place Esquire deceased, Catherine Fox of Falmouth…widow, George Croker Fox of Falmouth, aforesaid Esquire and Catherine Peyton Fox of Falmouth…Spinster (which said Cath. Fox, G.C. Fox and Cath P. Fox are Executrixes and Executor…of George Croker Fox of Falmouth…deceased) Thomas Were Fox of Falmouth…John Williams of Scorrier House in the county of Cornwall aforesaid Esquire (carrying on business as Iron Founders at Neath Abbey aforesaid under the Name Style and Firm of Foxes and Neath Abbey Iron Company) of the one part and Joseph Tregelles Price of Neath Abbey aforesaid Merchant, Henry Habberley Price of the same place Merchant, Alfred Fox of Falmouth…Merchant and Thomas Were Fox the Younger of the Borough of Plymouth…Merchant of the other part.[98]

The area of land leased extended from a point 20yds above the waterfall on the Clydach, down to the bridge on the main road. It included all the buildings in the dingle – the mill, foundry, nine dwelling houses and two parcels of flat land extending from the said bridge to the river, in holding which it was forbidden to do any injury to the old abbey.

No.2 blast furnace and the charging bank.

The rear of the engine manufactory showing the supports of a trough that took water to a waterwheel in the building.

One of the first actions of the new partnership was to change the name of the concern from Foxes & Neath Abbey Iron Company to the Neath Abbey Iron Company and the new company experienced a period of great expansion during the 1820s. At this time Joseph Tregelles Price was the managing partner at Neath Abbey and the engineering career of his brother, Henry Habberley Price, undoubtedly helped the firm attract orders.

Joseph T. Price's years as managing partner coincided with the boom years of the Welsh iron industry. To a large extent, the development of the Neath Abbey Ironworks reflects the increased fortunes of the local iron industry. It seems that in the late 1820s Neath Abbey pulled out of the Cornish market to concentrate on local outlets for their products. Although only a few engines were supplied to Cornwall after this date the partners still extracted some profit from this sector by selling pig iron to the Cornish engineering works. The 1820s also saw the beginnings of marine steam engine manufacture.

To deal with the increased capacity this expansion into new markets necessitated, the machine shops were enlarged during the period 1821-1823 and, indeed, in 1824 the company leased the buildings of the old Cheadle Copper Works and converted them for building marine engines and boilers. Expansion continued when in 1825 a forge and rolling mill were constructed alongside the waterfall on the River Clydach.

In 1829 the works began to construct railway locomotives and thus, under the direction of Joseph T. Price, every type of steam engine was built at Neath Abbey and output increased helped by the concurrent growth in the iron and coal industries.

Neath Abbey was certainly a major supplier of machinery to ironworks and collieries in the region. In the period 1840-1849 the works constructed approximately 128 stationary steam engines and over two thirds of these products were supplied to the coal, iron and tinplate industries of South Wales. The majority of these engines were of the beam type for blowing, rolling, winding or pumping. Such was the popularity that virtually every ironworks in South Wales was supplied with Neath Abbey engines and therefore helped to further the industrialisation of the entire country.

The works' reputation as suppliers of these products clearly spread outside the country with fifteen engines being exported to Europe during the period 1840-1849.

By 1850 the company had added the construction of iron ships to its already impressive repertoire. An indication of the scope of the work undertaken at Neath Abbey at this time is provided by the inventory for May 1847 which lists the following items under construction at the works:

> *Castings for Briton Ferry Iron Co., castings for C.H. Leigh Esq., sawing machine for Taibach, Swansea Dock Gates, locomotive engine for sale, two 45in blowing engines for France, 36in engine for Amman Iron Co., 30in engine for White Bros., water wheel for boring mill, 40in engine for Briton Ferry, 12in engine for Gadlys, 12in engine for sale.*[99]

The increasing output of engineering products called for yet more expansion but at Neath Abbey this was becoming difficult because of the constraints of the valley site. A decision was therefore made to expand the activities of the partners at the head of the Vale of Neath. In 1845 two furnaces were constructed at Abernant in close proximity to the company's iron ore mines and anthracite colliery and a third furnace was added in 1851.[100] A separate company was formed to operate these furnaces and was called the Abernant Iron Company.

The engine manufactory, early 1970s. The main part of this building was later destroyed by fire.

The main entrance to the forge and rolling mill of the Neath Abbey Ironworks. This building was completed in 1825.

It is probable that smelting ceased at Neath Abbey and was concentrated at Abernant from 1845 onwards although the furnaces at Neath Abbey were listed as being in blast in 1849 and the company was listed as Iron Masters in 1852. Smelting at Abernant meant that the company could save money on the costly transportation of ironstone down the Neath canals to Neath Abbey.

All of the expansion of the Neath Abbey Iron Company noted above was financed from within the Fox and Price families. Indeed, many members of the Fox family appear to have entered into the company as partners bringing new capital from their numerous business interests. The financial strength of the Fox family was further increased by society marriages into the notable banking families of Lloyd and Backhouse.

The continued progress of the Neath Abbey Iron Company undoubtedly suffered a serious setback upon the death of Joseph T. Price in 1854. Price had been the managing partner since 1818 and had transformed the company into one of the most versatile and respected engineering concerns in Britain. His death occurred during a period of great upheaval in the partnership. In 1852 the experienced businessman Alfred Fox retired to concentrate his resources on the development of the harbour at Falmouth and a new partnership had then been constituted consisting of Theodore Fox, Joseph T. Price, his nephews

Henry H. Price and Edwin Price and Robert Barclay Fox, the son of Robert Were Fox. Then in the period 1854-1856 three partners died in relatively quick succession, Joseph T. Price in 1854, Robert Barclay Fox in 1855 and Edwin Price in 1856. This left the partnership as Theodore Fox, Henry Price and Jane Gurney Fox, the widow of Robert Barclay Fox.[101]

The 1850s saw a slight decline in the production of stationary steam engines at Neath Abbey with around 102 engines being constructed. However, this was balanced by the good performance of other sectors. During this time the works completed five locomotives and ten iron ships. A large dry dock was constructed at the Cheadle Works in 1854; at this time Neath Abbey was building iron sailing ships of over 1,000 tons.[102]

The works reputation was still attracting engineering apprentices from a wide area.[103] In the 1850s Benjamin Baker was apprenticed at the works after being educated at Cheltenham Grammar School. As the designer of the Forth Railway Bridge he later became one of the most famous engineers of his day.

One of Baker's fellow apprentices was Henry Taylor, a member of a family who had served the works for several generations. He first worked in the pattern shop in 1858 and then moved to the fitting shop in 1862. The following two years saw him working on the screw cutting lathe and then in the erecting shop. In 1865 he was travelling with Tom Taylor, erecting steam engines at several localities. His wages illustrate a method of payment which helped to produce a disciplined work force. In the first year as an apprentice he was paid 3s a week plus 1s per week for good conduct. This rose to 4s 6d for the second year, 6s in the third year, 7s 6d for the fourth year and 9s for the fifth, all with the 1s extra for good conduct.[104]

The serious decline of the works began in the early 1860s when the Quaker partners ceased their smelting activities at Abernant. It appears that for a while the furnaces were leased to the neighbouring Aberdare Iron Company and one of the furnaces was in blast in 1861. However, the closure of the Abernant Iron Company meant that the Neath Abbey Ironworks had to buy in all the pig iron for their products. This meant in turn that the company was now involved in the expense of buying large amounts of pig iron for the beam of a large engine which could weigh over 30 tons. The closure of the Abernant Ironworks was an illustration of how unsuccessful the anthracite iron industry was in West Wales.[105] The bituminous ironworks were also in decline. The valley ironworks were suffering from exhaustion of their own ore and growing competitive disadvantages against the newer, more favourably placed coastal ironmaking districts. Newer sources of rich ore were now being exploited in areas such as Cleveland where, compared to the Welsh valleys, profits were higher and costs lower. Importing richer ores could not solve the new problem as it proved to be too expensive because of the position of the Welsh ironworks on the northern rim of the coalfield.

The developments in the Cleveland district attracted many of the Welsh managers and in 1863 Theodore Fox, who had managed the activities of the partnership at Abernant, left the company and moved to Middlesbrough.[106] The general decline exhibited itself at Neath Abbey in a reduction of orders for equipment from the Welsh works. The Neath Abbey Iron Company produced about 103 stationary steam engines in the 1860s but the majority of these were only small horizontal or vertical engines and only eighteen small engines were supplied to Welsh ironworks.

The output at Neath Abbey was seriously hampered by a combination of outside factors. There was a drop in orders for iron ships, only three small vessels being built in the 1860s, and to compound this, the works found itself in direct competition with the Cornish foundries for the first time.

The great decline of the Cornish copper industry had forced Cornish engineering companies to find new markets and the closure of many Cornish mines had resulted in a flood of second-hand engines coming onto the market, many of which found homes in South Wales. In 1870 Harvey & Company of Hayle had no less than eighteen second-hand engines for 'immediate delivery'. Harvey & Company had been supplying engines to South Wales since the 1830s but at that time Neath Abbey was working at full capacity. The 1860s saw too many engineering works chasing too few orders. The Cornish incursion into the South Wales market is well illustrated by Harveys of Hayle delivery of an 80in engine to the Gellygaer Coal Company in 1869. In the following year Harveys produced a 45in engine for the New Lodge Colliery, Pembrey, in 1872 a 90in engine was delivered to the Ebbw Vale Company and in 1873 an 85in engine was supplied to the Newport Abercarne Black Vein Steam Coal Company.[107] Perran Foundry was also building very large engines for South Wales at this time. In 1865 they built a 72in beam blowing engine for the Ebbw Vale Steel and Iron Company and in 1872-1873 a 100in engine was completed for the Harris Navigation Colliery, Quakers Yard. [108]

A concentration on the production of locomotives during the 1860s could well have postponed the closure of the works. The locomotives built at Neath Abbey had a fine reputation and they specialised in industrial locomotives for varying gauges. In 1862 the works exhibited an 0-4-0 tank locomotive built to a gauge of 2ft 8in at the International Exhibition in London.[109] However, the decision to concentrate their efforts was never made and the

The water powered forge and rolling mill beside the River Clydach.

Ty Mawr, the ironmasters' house.

works continued to build a wide range of engineering products in ever more competitive markets. In 1871 the Neath Abbey Iron Company was listed as makers of marine, locomotive and land engines, iron ship builders, boiler makers and general founders.[110]

It was inevitable that the early builders of stationary steam engines were the ones with the necessary engineering skills to pioneer the building of marine engines and locomotives. Thus the Soho Foundry in Birmingham and Harvey & Company of Hayle built marine steam engines and the Round Foundry of Leeds went on to build railway locomotives. In the second half of the nineteenth century many firms grew rapidly by specialising in one product. Their economy of scale meant that the products of the versatile works like Neath Abbey were not economical.

The Quaker partners closed down the Neath Abbey Ironworks in 1874 during a period described in *The Engineer* as one of great depression in iron, tinplate and coal.[111] The evidence suggests that since 1870 the works had built around forty-four stationary engines, one steam barge and four locomotives. However, the works were reopened by a partnership of local men consisting of Edward Davies, Henry Jones and John Howell. [112] Henry Jones took on the role of managing partner. Little information is available concerning the activities of the new partnership but the Neath Abbey engineering drawings show that again the company tried to construct the complete range of products. A paddle tug was completed in 1876 but the company did not possess the requisite knowledge or skills to build the side lever engine for the ship and one was purchased second-hand, having been built in 1863 by W. Scott of North Shields.[113] No major shipbuilding took place after this date.

Some stationary engines were completed by the works, one of the last examples being built in 1882. This product was a fitting reminder of the works in its heyday for it was a

70in x 12ft rotative beam pumping engine built for Henry Crawshay's Shakemantle Pit in the Forest of Dean.

In 1884 the company was listed only as engineers. The new partnership had taken out a fifty-three year lease on the Neath Abbey Ironworks on 3 July 1876 at an annual rent of £600 but the lease was surrendered on 3 July 1885. [114]

However, industrial activity continued at Neath Abbey for the buildings were briefly used as a tinplate works.[115] In fact the 1876 lease had specifically given permission for the works to be adapted for the manufacture of tinplate. The Neath Abbey Iron Company was also listed in a directory for 1890 but no later listings have come to light. The final years must have seen the works survive on repair work and appears to have sunk into obscurity for its closure is not mentioned in engineering journals or local newspapers.

Neath Abbey's closure was accompanied by many of early engineering works suffering a similar fate. The Copperhouse Foundry of Hayle closed in 1869, Perran Foundry closed in 1879 and Harvey & Company of Hayle managed to survive until 1903, although on a much reduced scale.

The closure of the Neath Abbey Ironworks was part of a pattern to be repeated through a period of twenty years dubbed the Great Depression, although recent researches have questioned the existence of this period of depression in a unified sense. However, it is a fact that at some time during the last quarter of the nineteenth century Britain and several countries overseas went through unusually worrying economic experiences.

Henry Jones, one of the last partners of the Neath Abbey Iron Company.

At this time major facets of the British economy were suffering from competition from foreign countries that had caught up on the early start experienced by Britain's major industries. Certainly this seems to have been compounded by lethargy present in British industry during this period that stifled innovation. The latter years of the Neath Abbey Iron Company provide the perfect example of a company experiencing difficulties due to this particular problem.

It is clear that the 1840s were the most successful years of the company, although the experiences of the 1850s show there was still much vitality in the concern with the introduction of the newer type of compact horizontal and inverted vertical engines and with several large ships under construction. However, it was the period 1860-1874 which saw a failure in the rational management of the company. During this period the company produced no new designs of stationary steam engine. The Neath Abbey Iron Company had sent a tank locomotive to the International Exhibition of 1862 where the first of Allen's high speed stationary engines was displayed and this had heralded the future developments of steam power.[116]

While it is true to say that the traditional markets exploited by the company were declining there was still a demand for colliery engines and compact engines for the tinplate industry. The failure to keep up with technical developments can be seen in the production of marine steam engines at the works. There appears to have been little interest in building compound marine engines although this design had been commonplace from the late 1850s with the shipbuilders of the Clyde.[117]

One successful product of the company during the years of decline was their tank locomotives. The works was one of the pioneering steam engineering works and had manufactured many types of steam product but in the second half of the nineteenth century most firms started to specialise in one product. The Neath Abbey Iron Company with its low output of locomotives could not hope to compete even with a relatively small locomotive building firm like Andrew Barclay, Sons & Co. of Kilmarnock who built eighteen locomotives in 1876 alone.[118] Neath Abbey's output of locomotives between the years 1870-74 had been four.

Perhaps a switch to producing locomotives only could have averted the closure of the works. This would have entailed a tremendous capital outlay for, like many of the early engineering works at this time, Neath Abbey was operating under the burden of ageing buildings and obsolete equipment. These management mistakes were later repeated by the partnership of 1875 who made the same questionable decision to continue with the complete range of engines, locomotives and ships.

However, the engineering tradition founded by the Neath Abbey Iron Company did continue despite the closure of the works. Henry Taylor, who had left the works in 1877, founded his own engineering business and five years later were joined by Messrs Eaton, Struvé and Henry H. Price. The company later became Taylor & Sons and this concern is still active in engineering. In 1889 David James, D.W. Prosser and Richard Owen founded the Dynevor Engineering Company in Neath. The partners had been trained at Neath Abbey and again this company is still in existence.

5

The Products of the
Neath Abbey Iron Company

A detailed examination of the products of the Neath Abbey Iron Company has been allowed by the preservation of the engineering drawings of the firm. These give a valuable insight into the development of steam power after the Boulton & Watt era. The documents are of three main types. The first are pen and ink drawings of engine parts; the second consists of more elaborate colour washed drawings of component parts and the third type contains elevations of complete engines. The elevations of engines sometimes lack details of valve gear and so give an uncluttered view of the engine. The elevations are elaborately finished and this seems to indicate that these drawings would be the ones shown to prospective customers to indicate the types of engine produced at the works.

The Neath Abbey Iron Company was founded at a time when great advances were being made in steam power. Thomas Newcomen (1666-1729) designed the first practical steam engines and his first engine appears to have been erected on a colliery near Dudley Castle, Staffordshire in 1712.[119] The engine had a vertical cylinder which was open at the top and was supplied with steam from a boiler underneath. The piston, which was packed with leather and sealed with a layer of water on top, was hung by a chain from the arch head of a rocking beam. From the other end of the beam hung the pump rods. The running cycle of this engine comprised the following events: admission of steam into the cylinder and the drawing up of the piston by the weight of the pump rods and any air or water in the cylinder was blown out through water-sealed non-return valves. Then the steam valve was closed and the steam in the cylinder was condensed by a jet of cold water. The imbalance of atmospheric pressure above the piston and partial vacuum below drove the piston down so raising the pump rods: the working stroke. The operation of the engine was controlled by a plug rod triggering the valves. The valves controlled the intake of steam, the injection of the condensing water and the removal of the condensate and the air introduced into the cylinder. The simple atmospheric Newcomen engine was readily adopted in coal mining areas for pumping and also in the metal mining areas such as Cornwall and Devon.

A great advance in steam engineering took place in 1769 when James Watt took out his patent for the separate condenser. Watt had perceived that the Newcomen engine was inefficient because for each stroke the cylinder had to be alternately heated and cooled. This inefficiency was reduced by condensing the steam in a separate vessel, connected by a valve to the steam cylinder. The cylinder could now be jacketed to keep it hot, while the condenser could be kept cool. Watt applied his condenser to a beam engine with a pump operating off the beam to clear water from the condenser. In the period 1780-1795 other

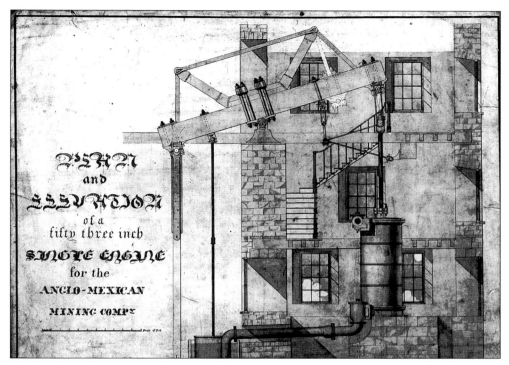

One of a series of beam engines built at Neath Abbey in the early 1820s for the Anglo-Mexican Mining Company.

important improvements were pioneered by Watt: the sun and planet gearing to obtain rotary power; double action, with the famous parallel motion mechanism, and the centrifugal governor for automatic speed control.

After initial business difficulty, Watt became a partner with the Birmingham manufacturer, Matthew Boulton, and they successfully produced over 500 engines before the patent lapsed in 1800. The more efficient Boulton & Watt engines were adopted in areas where it was expedient to save on the large quantities of coal burned by Newcomen engines. Cornwall was a particularly lucrative market for the partnership's engines as they helped save on the great cost of importing Welsh coal.

The Neath Abbey Iron Company had experience of Boulton & Watt engineering when the partners erected a double acting 40in blowing engine in 1793. Further experience was gained when the Neath Abbey Iron Company purchased Boulton & Watt's first winding engine second-hand. This engine had been erected at Wheal Maid, Cornwall in 1784 and was disposed of on the closure of the mine. [120] It had sun and planet gearing, but no eccentric or reversing gear. The engine was removed to a colliery in the Vale of Neath to be sold back to Cornwall in 1797.

In 1800 Watt's patent, which had to some extent hampered the development of the steam engine, lapsed. Until this time Boulton & Watt had a virtual monopoly of the erection of efficient steam engines. Developments came quickly after 1800 and the two main themes were the adoption of high-pressure steam and the building of a compact beamless engine.

The Cornish engineer Richard Trevithick considered both of these problems. He had built a high-pressure beam winding engine in 1800 at Cook's Kitchen Mine in Cornwall and in 1802, with Andrew Vivian, took out a patent for 'methods for improving the construction of steam engines' and 'the application thereof of driving carriages and for other purposes'.[121] Trevithick's ideas were applied in his various designs of high-pressure stationary engines. These were non-condensing and could have the cylinder vertically or horizontally sunk into the boiler which was either spherical or cylindrical. Trevithick was experimenting with steam pressure of 145psi at Coalbrookdale in 1802 but 50-60psi was the usual pressure used in his early engines.[122]

Trevithick entered into partnership with Samuel Homfray of the Penydarren Ironworks, Merthyr Tydfil and together they promoted his engines.[123] In 1804 a Trevithick engine was mounted on wheels and succeeded in hauling 10 tons of iron down a tramway from Penydarren to Abercynon. The partners allowed other interested parties to construct stationary steam engines on Trevithick's plan on paying a premium of twelve guineas a horse power up to 6hp, nine guineas from 6-7hp and seven guineas a horse power above 9hp.

Several firms began to build stationary steam engines on Trevithick's plan and these included the Neath Abbey Iron Company. There is evidence that Neath Abbey was building Trevithick engines in the period 1804-1806 and these were the first stationary steam engines manufactured at the works. The company appeared to be on good terms with Trevithick even though Trevithick had quarrelled with the Fox family at an earlier date when he attempted to cheat George Croker Fox over the sale of shares in Dolcoath Mine.[124]

The Neath Abbey engineers made a drawing of a typical Trevithick stationary engine at Penydarren and this drawing, which is preserved in the Neath Abbey Collection, shows

The remains of another Neath Abbey combined pumping and winding engine built in 1849 for one of John Calvert's collieries in the Rhondda. This engine is preserved in the grounds of the University of Glamorgan, Treforest.

an engine with a cylindrical boiler 8ft long and 4ft in diameter, with a horizontal 9in x 4in cylinder.[125] Neath Abbey's first Trevithick engine was probably erected at the Swansea Pottery in 1806.[126] Another of these engines was supplied in that year to Wheal Crenver and Abraham, Cornwall and was described by Captain G. Eustace who moved the engine in 1820.[127] Eustace recollected the following:

> *About 1820 I removed one of Captain Trevithick's early high-pressure whim engines from Crenver and Wheal Abraham and put it as a pumping engine in Wheal Kitty, where it continued to work for about fifteen years. The boiler was of cast iron in two lengths bolted together, about 6 feet in diameter and 10 feet long. At one end a piece was bolted, into which the cylinder was fixed so that it had steam and water around it. There was an internal wrought-iron tube that turned back again to the fire door end, where the wrought-iron chimney was fixed; the fire-grate end of the tube was about 2 feet 6 inches in diameter and tapered down to about 1 foot 6 inches at the chimney end. It was a puffer, working 60lbs of steam to the inch; it worked very well. There were several others in the county at that time [or] something like it. It was made at the Neath Abbey Works in Wales.*

One drawback to Trevithick's licensing ideas was that he had no control over the actual building of these engines and several firms seem to have produced inferior products which gave the engines a bad reputation.[128]

Trevithick, who had quarrelled with many of the Cornish works, appears to have been on good terms with the Neath Abbey works for a considerable period. In 1810 Trevithick proposed to smelt the poor copper ores of Dolcoath and other Cornish mines by, 'borrowing Fox's and Neath Abbey blast furnace in which they used to smelt iron ore'.[129] Trevithick seems to have been satisfied with Neath Abbey's work for in 1813 he offered the works the contract for building his engines for Peru. However, Neath Abbey was unable to undertake the work and these engines were constructed by Hazeldine and Rastrick of Bridgnorth.[130] Trevithick's friendship with Neath Abbey came to an end when his later innovation of the high-pressure pole engine was criticised by Joseph T Price. Trevithick put to work the first example of a plunger pole engine at Herland Mine in 1816 (alongside a new 76in engine erected by Arthur Woolf).[131] Of a competition between the two engines, the quick tempered Trevithick writes:

> *I could not help at the meeting threatening to horsewhip J[oseph] Price for the falsehoods that he with others had reported. I hear that he is to go to London to meet the London Committee on Monday. I hope that the Committee will consider J. Price's report as from a disappointed man. It is reported that he has bought very largely in Woolf's patent, which is now not worth a farthing, besides losing the making thy castings which galls him very sorely.*

The engine had an inverted cylinder over the mine shaft and its' piston was coupled directly to the pump rods, as in the design of a Bull engine. The piston was moved by the force of high-pressure steam ranging from 60 to 120psi. After showing early promise, this type of engine was found to be of a basically unsound design.

The partners of the Neath Abbey Iron Company gained the lease of the Dyffryn estate minerals in 1806 and coal mining operations began with the pits supplied with beam engines built at the works. Soon Neath Abbey was building engines for other customers

A small Neath Abbey table engine built in the 1830s for the Vale of Neath Brewery.

too, and one early example was sent to Cornwall.[132] Engines could be manufactured at Neath Abbey at a far cheaper rate than in Cornwall and the company, with its extensive Cornish connections, exploited the market to its full. The works was to have valuable assistance in the Cornish trade through its friendship with the Cornish engineer, Arthur Woolf.

Woolf worked in London for several years during which time he took out a patent for the use of high-pressure steam generated in a cast iron tubular boiler. He applied his patent in the construction of high-pressure compound engines. These were beam engines with two cylinders placed at the same end of the beam. Steam expanded in the two cylinders in succession, a revival of an idea patented by Jonathan Hornblower in 1781.[133] Woolf returned to Cornwall in 1811, a time when there was a growing interest in increasing the efficiency of steam engines. A great number of engines were being employed in the expanding Cornish copper and tin mines and an interest in efficiency was being stimulated by *Lean's Engine Reporter*, a monthly publication which compared the efficiency of Cornish steam engines. The unit of work used was a foot-pound and the unit of coal consumed was the bushel. The number of millions of foot-pounds raised per bushel of coal was termed the 'duty'.

Woolf's first engines to be erected in Cornwall were used for winding purposes and it is possible that some of these were made at Neath Abbey, certainly Woolf's first compound pumping engine was built there. This engine was erected at Wheal Abraham in 1814 with 45in and 24in cylinders, the strokes being 7ft and 4ft 3in. A second Woolf compound pumping engine built by the Neath Abbey Iron Company was erected at Wheal Vor in the same year. This engine had 53in and 28in cylinders with 9ft and 6ft strokes. The cast iron beam weighed 15 tons 19cwt and the engines was supplied with two cast iron boilers. These Woolf compounds were two years in the making and were the first engines to be built in Cornwall with iron beams.

The Wheal Vor engine had the distinction of being the first Cornish engine to pass the 50 million 'duty' mark, which occurred in June 1816. On 4 December 1815 it was certified:

> *...that the duty done by Woolf's engine on the mine exceeds that of the other engine which is on Boulton and Watt's plan of erection, on an average of 116 to 34, that is to say that Woolf's engine performed the same duty by consuming 34 bushels of coal as the engine of Boulton and Watt does on the consumption of 116.*[134]

Joseph T. Price forwarded a copy of this certificate to *Tilloch's Philosophical Magazine*, and he stated that:

> *Woolf's engine is doing the same duty as is usually done by good engines on Boulton and Watt's plan with less than half the quantity of coals...from the facts exhibited, particularly by the engines we [the Neath Abbey Iron Company] have made on Woolf's plan, we do not hesitate to give it as our opinion that these engines are by far the most eligible where a saving in the consumption of coal is the object.*

Parallel with the application of Woolf's compound engines was the development of the single cylinder beam engine working with high-pressure steam. Richard Trevithick built a 24in engine, a single acting beam engine built on an inverted plan working with steam at a pressure of 40psi, at Wheal Prosper in the summer of 1812. This engine carried many of the characteristics which were to be embodied in the development of the true 'Cornish' beam engine.[135]

Woolf also applied himself to the design of single cylinder beam engines and in 1820 he erected an engine with a 90in single cylinder beam engine with a 9ft 11in stroke to drain the very wet Consolidated Mines. This engine was built at Neath Abbey and was reported to be the largest and most powerful steam engine in the world.[136] A second 90in engine was constructed which started on the old Wheal Fortune section of Consuls in February 1821.

Each of these engines were furnished with six wrought iron boilers for producing steam of high-pressure, three boilers were connected so as to be heated by two fires, leaving three others to be used when cleaning or repairing. It was reported that these engines were, 'executed in a very beautiful manner', with the cylinders cast in one piece and weighing $12\frac{1}{2}$ tons and the beam and gudgeon weighing nearly 25 tons. A third 90in engine was started at Poldice Mine and erected by William Sims from parts manufactured at Neath Abbey. The *West Briton* of 14 November 1821 reported that:

> *No less than three large engines have been set to work, erected and the whole of the pitwork belonging to them carried underground and fixed within the short space of five months. The largest engine was set at work on the 9th instant – the whole of the immense engine with its bottom etc which weighs about 15 tons was landed at the Port of Padstow, a distance of nearly thirty miles from the mine, only 29 days before it was set to work - the nozzles and many other parts of it were at that time in Wales.*[137]

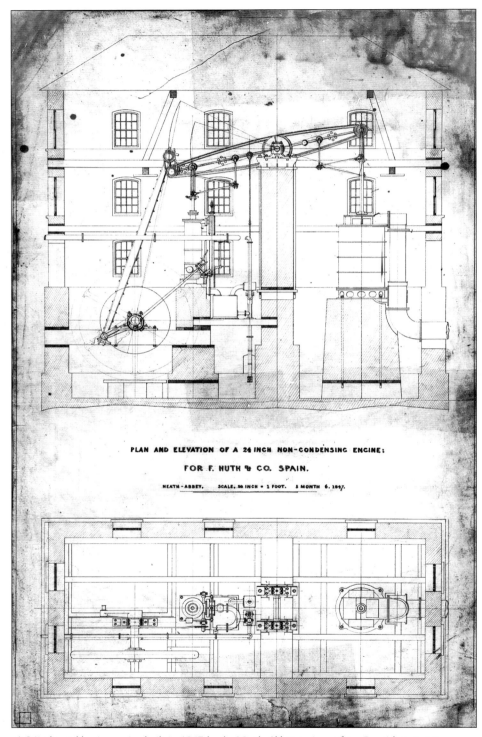

PLAN AND ELEVATION OF A 24 INCH NON-CONDENSING ENGINE:

FOR F. HUTH & CO. SPAIN.

NEATH-ABBEY.   SCALE, 3½ INCH = 1 FOOT.   5 MONTH 6. 1847.

A 24in beam blowing engine built in 1847 by the Neath Abbey engineers for a Spanish customer.

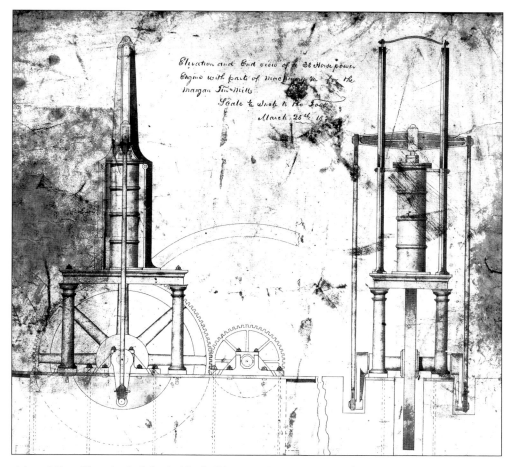

A large 38hp table engine built by the Neath Abbey Iron Company in 1828 for Margam Tin Mill.

To settle the argument concerning the efficiency of Woolf compound engines compared against single cylinder engines, two engines were erected at Wheal Alfred and their monthly duty figures compared. A 90in x 10ft single cylinder engine built by Neath Abbey was compared against a 40in/70in Woolf compound engine built by Harvey & Company of Hayle. The compound engine was supplied with steam from Woolf cast iron boilers and the 90in engine was fitted with typical Trevithick Cornish boilers.[138] The duty figures showed that neither engine was superior, but the single cylinder engine was far easier to maintain. This trial proved the advantages of the typical Cornish beam engine as an efficient pumping engine.

It appears that Neath Abbey built few engines for Cornwall after this trial. One of the last being a 60in engine started at Great Wheal Prosper in June 1837.[139] It is likely that Neath Abbey withdrew from the Cornish market to concentrate on building engines for the increasingly important industries of South Wales. Neath Abbey and the Cornish foundries existed in close co-operation and Neath Abbey could still obtain profits from Cornwall by selling pig iron to the Cornish works.

This co-operation continued over a considerable period with contracts and orders often being shared. A good example occurred in 1824 when John Taylor ordered six portable steam engines and pit work for the Real del Monte mines in Mexico and the order was jointly undertaken by Harvey & Company of Hayle and the Neath Abbey Ironworks.[140] At this time many orders were coming in from the developing South American mining market and in 1824 Perran Foundry was also building nine engines for the Real del Monte mines although, owing to a financial crisis, not all these engines were shipped. Neath Abbey's contribution to these orders appears to have been completed in March 1825 when the ship *Rosalind* left Swansea for Tampico and Vera Cruz in the Gulf of Mexico laden with mining machinery from the Neath Abbey Ironworks.[141] Further co-operation is illustrated by the routing of orders to the Cornish Foundries when Neath Abbey was operating at full capacity. Indeed, Harvey & Company kept a representative at Neath Abbey for this very purpose.[142]

Workers also appear to have moved freely from the Cornish foundries to Neath Abbey. An example of this is provided by Frank Pool who was trained at the Copperhouse Foundry, Hayle, then moved to Perran and then to Neath Abbey, returning later to Perran as a foreman.[143]

The Cornwall – Neath Abbey link was beneficial to both parties. Neath Abbey could benefit from the ideals of Cornish craftsmanship, exemplified by the work of Trevithick and Woolf, while Cornwall benefited from the advanced and skilful casting techniques of the Welsh works. The friendship between Woolf and Neath Abbey was particularly important in establishing Neath Abbey as a major engineering works. It continued even after Woolf had officially retired to Guernsey, for several orders came in which appear to have been steered to Neath Abbey from the Channel Islands.[144] Certainly in the period 1810-1825, the Neath Abbey Iron Company played a major role in the development of the Cornish beam engine.

Neath Abbey's withdrawal from the Cornish market meant that the works could concentrate their resources on building large steam engines for the developing coal and iron industries, the main type of stationary steam engine built to meet this demand being the beam engine. Neath Abbey beam engines were constructed for winding and pumping at collieries, for blowing iron furnaces and for driving rolling mills. In fact, the beam engine remained the staple product of the works until the introduction of other types in the late 1840s.

Although Neath Abbey played a significant part in the development of the single acting condensing beam pumping engine, they also built double acting rotative beam pumping engines. It was building several beam engines in the year 1845 and two of these illustrate the two dissimilar designs for beam pumping engines manufactured at Neath Abbey. One was supplied to Henry Crawshay's Lightmoor Colliery in the Forest of Dean. It was a 78in x 9ft Cornish beam engine and was still working in 1881 making seven strokes per minute, using steam at a pressure of 25psi and raising 605 gallons each minute.[145] The other engine was a double acting rotative beam engine supplied to C.H. Leigh of Pontypool. This engine had a 30in cylinder making a 6ft stroke and worked at a pressure of 50psi. It is one of the few Neath Abbey engines to survive and now stands sadly derelict at Glyn Pits, near Pontypool.[146] The Glyn Pits' engine was designed ingeniously for both winding and pumping.[147] This type of engine appears to have been a speciality of the Neath Abbey engineers and later this combined design was also adopted with horizontal engines. Double acting rotative beam engines produced a more uniform action and were preferred for such uses as driving rolling mills, colliery and mine winding and blowing furnaces.

One of Neath Abbey's most popular products seems to have been a $52\frac{1}{2}$in x 8ft beam blowing engine. The earliest drawing of such an engine is dated 1819 and was in production until the mid-1840s.[148] Many of the major South Wales ironworks bought beam blowing engines from Neath Abbey and the French engineers Coste and Perdonnet in 1829 described these in some detail.[149] The $52\frac{1}{2}$in beam blowing engine was usually supplied with a blowing cylinder of 105in diameter, which weighed seven tons – although a larger cylinder of 112in could be provided if necessary. This engine could blow three blast furnaces and three fineries. In 1839 Neath Abbey began to supply slightly smaller beam blowing engines but with 122in blowing cylinders, these were the largest cylinders to be cast in one piece in Britain until 1843, when a 144in cylinder was cast by Harvey & Company of Hayle.[150]

Although Neath Abbey was now primarily building beam engines for South Wales, they also exported a large number of engines to South America, France, Ireland, Germany, Spain, India and Australia. The Cornish connection ensured the company a share in the lucrative South American market where mines were being developed by John Taylor who controlled many of the large Cornish mines. Often beam engines for South America were supplied without a beam, for the engine parts had to be transported hundreds of miles from the coast to the mines and, for convenience, the mine owner would supply his own wooden beam.

Several other types of engines were produced at the works but until the late 1840s, they represented only a small portion of the output. The company built table engines which were supplied to provide power for smaller industrial output from a design patented by Henry Maudslay in 1807. It was a very compact direct acting engine which had a vertical cylinder placed on a cast iron table. The flywheel was usually driven by return connecting rods which worked through slots in the table. However, the Neath Abbey examples had a larger crosshead which allowed the connecting rods to move outside the table.[151] A Neath Abbey table engine with a $5\frac{3}{8}$in x 1ft 8in cylinder is preserved at the Welsh Industrial and Maritime Museum, Cardiff. This was probably built around 1836-1838 and was supplied to the Vale of Neath Brewery.

The works also built grasshopper beam engines. These had the beam suspended upon a swinging link at one end and the cylinder at the other, the crankshaft and connecting rod being between these two points. The first patent referring to grasshopper motion was taken out by William Freemantle in 1803 and the design was also utilised by the American, Oliver Evans, in 1804.[152] This compact design found favour as a power source in such enterprises as mills and small workshops.

The late 1840s saw a further change in output when the Neath Abbey Iron Company began to build horizontal stationary engines. A horizontal engine was used as early as 1801 in the steam boat *Charlotte Dundas* and a horizontal cylinder was used by Trevithick in his early high-pressure engines. Taylor and Martineau began to make horizontal engines in the early 1820s but prejudice was shown against this type because of a fear of excessive and uneven wear to the cylinder. Even so Neath Abbey had built an early example of a horizontal engine for the Nantyglo Ironworks in 1826.

Although Neath Abbey had previously built Trevithick engines with horizontal cylinders, they did not widely adopt the horizontal stationary type of engine until the late 1840s. The compact horizontal engine soon found favour and Neath Abbey built them in cylinder sizes from 12in to 30in. These were produced as power units for many different industries and also as winding and pumping engines for colliery use.

The output of Neath Abbey became even more mixed when the inverted vertical engine was added to the designs offered. The inverted vertical design had been used in Naysmith's steam hammer from 1845 and its compact design made it a popular unit for powering screw vessels. Neath Abbey constructed inverted vertical engines for the screw steam ships they built and this particular design was first adapted for stationary use in 1852.[153]

Such was the impact of these compact modern engines that of the 119 stationary steam engines produced at Neath Abbey in the 1850s only twenty can be identified as being of the beam type. Of the 103 stationary engines built in the 1860s only fourteen were beam engines, the horizontal design clearly dominated output. The demand for the larger beam engines at this time had declined due to recession in the Welsh iron industry and these figures must be compared with Neath Abbey's output in the 1840s when no less than fifty-seven beam engines were produced at the works.

The latter years of the company saw a reduced output of mainly horizontal engines, but one of the last stationary engines built was a fitting reminder of the products of the company at the peak of its success. This was a 70in x 13ft rotative beam engine built in 1882 for Henry Crawshay's Shakemantle Pit in the Forest of Dean. The engine was designed by P. Teague and pumped a 600ft deep pit with three lifts of pumps. The main beam was 36ft long and at the centre was 6ft deep and weighed over thirty tons. The 20ft diameter flywheel weighed thirty-two tons. Steam was supplied from six Cornish boilers at 25psi and the engine discharged 2,700 gallons of water per minute.[154] The Forest of Dean had been a rich market for Neath Abbey products from 1860 onwards and this had partially offset the declining orders from the troubled Welsh iron industry. No doubt the influence of Henry Crawshay had much to do with Neath Abbey's success in this area.

During its years of operation, the Neath Abbey Iron Company built up a reputation for producing expensive but reliable and well made engines. Many of the engines built by Neath Abbey were still giving excellent service forty years after the closure of the works. It was recorded in 1925 that:

> *At the Lightmoor Colliery in the Forest of Dean there is a Cornish condensing pump made at the Neath Abbey Ironworks in 1845. It is a 70in cylinder and will work with as low pressure as 10lbs per square inch and is very efficient delivering two tons of water per minute. The engine is still in its original state and is of beautiful design and workmanship and brightly polished. It works as well today as it did when the present manager, Mr Meredith started 43 years ago. The colliery has also winding engines working, which were made at the Neath Abbey works.[155]*

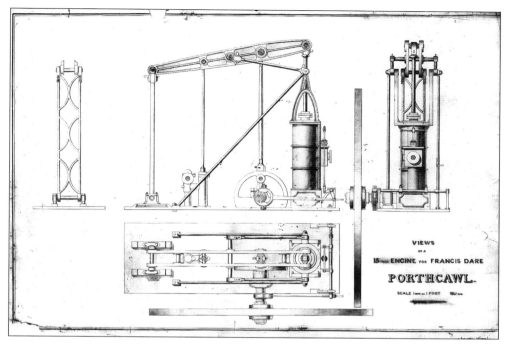

A 15in grasshopper beam engine built by the Neath Abbey Iron Company in 1841 for Francis Dare of Porthcawl.

When the works closed down in 1890, it did so in virtual obscurity. It is true to say that it had been out of the main stream of stationary steam development for many years, but the works should be remembered for its important contributions in the field of steam power. The Neath Abbey Iron Company was in the forefront of the development of the Cornish beam engine and the vast number of engines produced for the expanding industries of South Wales coalfield meant that the works provided most of the power for the development of the area in the early and mid-nineteenth century.

The Neath Abbey Iron Company first became involved in marine engineering work in 1817 when the 112 ton paddle steamer *Britannia* called at Neath Abbey for attention to her machinery.[156] The *Britannia* had been built in 1816 by James Munn of Greenock for the Holyhead to Howth mail service and fitted with a 20hp engine by James Cook of Glasgow. The vessel was heading for Bristol when it was found necessary to put into Neath Abbey. The Neath Abbey engineers must have been excited and interested by the sight of this steam ship for they were comparatively rare at this date, only sixteen years after the building of the pioneer steam ship *Charlotte Dundas*. They made detailed drawings of the Britannia's engine and this marked the beginning of preparations to build marine engines at the works.

The company set about collecting information concerning steam propulsion and it appears that Neath Abbey engineers were sent to examine and report on the engines of various vessels. Indeed, the Neath Abbey collection contains reports sent back from Dover in January and February 1822 concerning the machinery of the paddle steamer *Arrow*.[157]

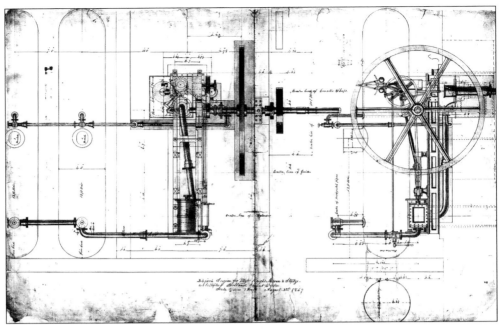

A 24in horizontal Neath Abbey engine built in 1859 for Knight, Bevan and Sturge of Northfleet, Kent.

The Neath Abbey Ironworks were well placed to enter into the marine engineering trade, being situated close to the estuary of the River Neath and on the tidal River Clydach. In this way Neath Abbey had ready access to the Bristol Channel where an important mercantile trade existed between the west of England and the Welsh ports. The proximity of the works to the developing copper importing port of Swansea was also an added advantage in the development of marine engineering at Neath.

The first marine engines from Neath Abbey were constructed for the paddle steamer *Glamorgan* in 1822. These were two simple side lever engines with 27in cylinders. The side lever design had been widely adopted for powering paddle steamers. It was a modified beam type design with a vertical cylinder and a connecting rod working upwards to a crankshaft, the beam being carried at the side of the engine. A sister vessel to the *Glamorgan* was also equipped with engines constructed at Neath Abbey. These ships at first traded between Bristol and Swansea and were owned by a number of partners which included Joseph T. Price and Henry H. Price. The Neath Abbey Iron Company took over the vacant Cheadle Copper Works in 1824 to cater for its marine engineering work for this works was ideally sited in position close to the confluence of the Rivers Neath and Clydach. It came to be known as Gwaith Bach (Little Works).

The building of marine engines was successful and a series of side lever engines were built in the 1820s and 1830s, mainly for wooden paddle steamers built at Bristol. The majority of these ships operated on the Bristol Channel routes carrying passengers and cargo.

The early 1840s was a period of expansion and innovation for the company, reflected in the marine engineering department with the building of their first iron ship. The very first iron boat had been made by John Wilkinson in 1787 for canal use but the first iron vessel to be operated at sea appears to have been a small pleasure boat launched on the Mersey in 1815. Another early successful iron ship was the *Aaron Manby*, completed in 1821 and the first iron ship to sail from London to Paris.[158] The growth of iron shipbuilding was slow and in 1842 when Neath Abbey launched their first iron ship, an eminent ship builder commented:

> *Many, therefore, still view the subject [iron shipbuilding] with distrust and regard it as one of the visionary schemes of this wonder working age which will soon be relinquished and forgotten.*[159]

Certainly there were many advantages in building ships of iron, the most important one being the all round strength of iron construction. The early contribution that Neath Abbey made to iron shipbuilding has justly earned the works a description as, 'one of the cradles of iron shipbuilding'.[160]

Neath Abbey's first iron ship was the *Prince of Wales*, a paddle steamer of 182t gross, built for Joseph T. Price. The first iron ship built for an outside customer was the *Henry Southan*, completed in 1845 and also the first screw propelled steamer to be built at Neath Abbey.[161]

Smith and Ericsson had taken out patents for screw propulsion in 1836 but the viability of the system was proved by a series of trials with the screw steamer *Archimedes* in 1840. The *Archimedes* paid a visit to Bristol in that year and the builders of the steamship *Great Britain* invited its designer to report on the advantages and disadvantages of screw propulsion. Brunel's report favoured the adoption of this new system for his ship for six basic reasons; a saving of weight, the simpler form the vessel would take, the operation of the screw would be unaffected by rolling, regularity of motion and freedom from shocks to the engine, increased power of steering given to the vessel and a great reduction in breadth.

The marine engineering work of the Neath Abbey Iron Company was closely linked with the port of Bristol and the company must have been aware of the developments in the building of the *Great Britain*. Influenced perhaps by Brunel's decision to adopt screw propulsion, the Neath Abbey Iron Company largely switched from building paddle to screw steamers. The company adopted two designs of steam engines for their screw steamers. Low power engines were of the single cylinder inverted vertical type with cylinders ranging from 10in to 24in in diameter. The larger sets were V-twin engines with two inverted diagonally mounted cylinders driving downwards to a centrally placed horizontal shaft.

Although much information is available concerning the marine engines of the Neath Abbey Iron Company, only one Neath Abbey engineering drawing relates to the actual construction of the iron ships.[162] It appears from descriptions of the ships that Neath Abbey products were clinker built with plates of adjacent strakes overlapping each other and riveted together.

The Neath Abbey drawings indicate that, apart from ships, the company was also heavily involved in the building of dredgers. An early dredging engine was completed in 1817 and these drawings record the building of three dredgers, two in 1848 for Wexford and Whitehaven Harbours.[163]

Further developments took place at Neath Abbey in the late 1840s when the works completed their first iron sailing ship, *La Serena*, a 373 tons barque built for a Swansea partnership which included Robert Eaton and Henry Bath. She was employed in bringing copper ore from South America to Swansea. There were some initial problems with her bottom, but after remedial work she proved to be a most successful vessel and was one of the first iron ships to round the Horn.

This pioneering sailing ship was to have a long and varied life. In 1865 she was owned by Hutchinson of Sunderland and was sailing between Sunderland and China. The following year saw her sailing from Liverpool to Japan and in 1874 she was owned by Ellis of London.

The success of *La Serena* brought in further orders for iron sailing ships and two of these were to be the biggest ships built by the Neath Abbey Iron Company. The first of these was the *Ellen Bates* which was completed in 1853 for Edward Bates of Liverpool. Edward Bates operated a service of sailing ships between Liverpool and Bombay and was one of the earliest Liverpool ship owners to adopt iron sailing ships. His first iron vessel was the brig *Panic* built in 1848 by Cato and Miller of Liverpool.[164]

The *Ellen Bates* was a sailing vessel of 1,098 tons and the building of this huge ship must have posed many problems for Neath Abbey's engineers as it was 211ft in length and launching the vessel into the muddy Rivers Neath and Clydach must have been a major undertaking. A second ship was built for Bates in 1856, a three masted sailing vessel of

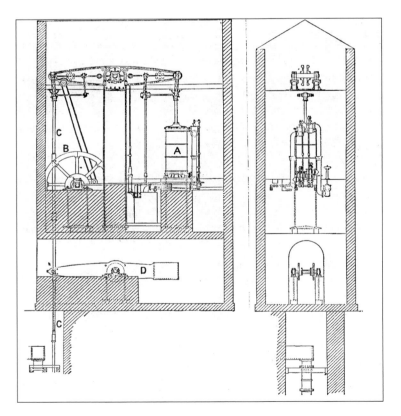

The last beam engine built by the Neath Abbey Iron Company. It was a 70in rotative pumping engine constructed in 1882 for the Shakemantle Iron Ore Mine in the Forest of Dean.

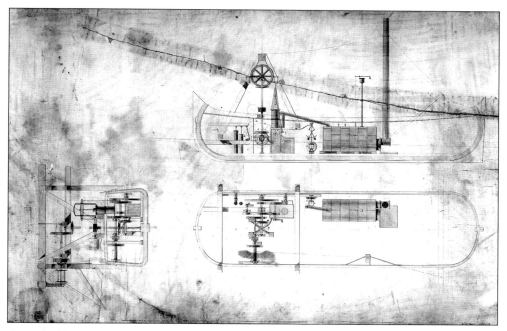

A Neath Abbey drawing of a 19in table engine built in 1817 for dredging.

1,175t called *Fearnought*. For the building of these vessels a large dry dock was constructed at Gwaith Bach. After completion both ships were towed to Liverpool for fitting out.[165] The Neath Abbey engineering drawings indicate that the 1840s and 1850s were the most successful years for the shipbuilding activities of the company. The 1840s saw eight ships built at Neath Abbey and no less than twelve ships were completed during the 1850s. The success of the marine engineering department of the company during the 1850s meant that Neath Abbey was at full capacity even though there was some decline in stationary steam engine building at the works in this period.

Neath Abbey experienced a recession in their shipbuilding department during the 1860s with only three ships built during the decade. Certainly at that time Neath Abbey was lagging behind modern engineering practice through their failure to innovate during the late 1850s and 1860s. The works had not adopted the modern design of high-pressure compound engines that had found favour in other areas. The limited possibilities of their shipyard also denied them a chance to tender for the larger ships then in vogue and the Quaker nature of the partnership did not allow the company to take any of the lucrative Admiralty contracts then being offered.

Although Neath Abbey was badly affected by this recession, the new partnership formed in 1876 attempted to revive the industry and a vessel was duly launched on 22 August 1876. This was the paddle tug *Flying Scud* built for Captain Rosser Rosser of Swansea.[166] The ship's lines were taken from a model of John Lewis, the shipwright of the company, and she was classed A1 at Lloyds having been constructed under the personal supervision of a Lloyds surveyor. The ship was fitted with a second-hand side

The Neath Abbey-built iron screw steamer John. *The ship was built in 1849 and was photographed working on the River Avon near Bristol.*

lever engine built in 1863 by W. Scott of North Shields. The company put great store in the production of the *Flying Scud* and a further revival in shipbuilding but orders were not forthcoming. The general engineering of Neath Abbey certainly could not compete with firms specialising in marine engineering although the shipyard at Neath Abbey continued to be used into the 1880s for boilering and repair work.

From 1829 onwards, when the Neath Abbey Iron Company began to build railway locomotives, the company constructed the whole range of steam products. The Neath Abbey Iron Company had early experience of railways for the ironworks was served by a railway when a drawing was made of the plant in 1792 and became further involved when they started their own coal and iron ore mines. The Neath Abbey partners would have been aware of the potential of the locomotive for they were closely involved with Trevithick during the time he was building his pioneer steam locomotive and would have known of its successful run on the Penydarren Tramroad in 1804.

Indeed, Joseph T. Price must have built up a great knowledge of railways for in 1818 Edward Pease, who was to be the leading figure in the setting up of the Stockton and Darlington Railway, wrote to him concerning his views on tramroads, railways and canals.[167] Price was also asked about the character of George Overton who was to be employed in making the first survey for the railway.

The contract for the cast iron rails for the Stockton & Darlington Railway was awarded to the Neath Abbey Ironworks, almost certainly because of the Quaker friendship that existed between the Price and Pease families. The chairs for the rails were to weigh 6lbs each and the cast iron rails were to be 4ft long, the depth at the ends to be 4in and the depth in the middle to be 6in.[168] Great care was taken in the work and George Stephenson himself visited Neath Abbey to view the production of the rails. During 1822 several cargoes of rails were shipped from Neath Abbey. On 22 July the ship *George Watt* left for the north-east with 113 edge rails, twenty cross rails, 1,700 one hole chairs for wrought iron rails and 7,800 two hole chairs.[169]

In 1825 the Stockton & Darlington Railway became the first public railway to employ steam power. The success of steam traction in the north-east had been plainly demonstrated to the Quaker partners of the Neath Abbey Iron Company who had played an important part in equipping the railway.

Steam traction was an attractive idea to the industrialists of South Wales valleys for many of the works were already connected to the canals of the area by horse tramroads and speeding up the transport of their products had definite economic advantages. The development of steam traction in South Wales took an important step in 1829 when two locomotives were delivered to the principality from Stephenson's Newcastle works. One was employed on the internal Penydarren Ironworks' line, while the other was delivered to Samuel Homfray of the Tredegar Ironworks.[170] This engine started running at the Tredegar works in October 1829 and once ran along the Sirhowy & Monmouthshire Tramroad into Newport, a distance of twenty-eight miles.

The success of this locomotive must have encouraged other traders on the Sirhowy tramroad to experiment with steam locomotives. One of these traders was Thomas Prothero and in late 1829 the Neath Abbey Ironworks began to build their first locomotive for him. Neath Abbey had built a stationary steam engine for Prothero in 1825 and this must have encouraged him to approach Neath Abbey concerning a locomotive rather than endure the lengthy wait associated with placing an order with Stephenson. This first locomotive built

A contemporary oil painting showing the Neath Abbey-built sailing ship La Serena. *She is depicted laying off shore at Coquimbo, Chile and undergoing loading with copper ore.*

The Neath Abbey-built tug Defiance *photographed at Hull Docks. This ship was built in 1862 as* Charley. *She originally worked on the Neath river and docks and was renamed after her sale to London owners in 1874.*

at Neath Abbey was probably delivered in 1831. The locomotive was named *Speedwell* and was built to a 4ft 2in gauge. It was a 0-4-0 locomotive with vertical 10½in x 2ft cylinders. The pistons worked through bell cranks through stirrup crossheads. An interesting feature was the heating of the feed water by passing it through a jacket around the exhaust pipe. A second bell crank locomotive was supplied to Prothero in the same year. Several other bell crank locomotives were built for various gauges. This Neath Abbey design shows little similarity to any other builder at this time although Sharp Roberts & Co. of Manchester commenced building locomotives in 1833 with vertical cylinders and bell crank drive.[171]

In some cases the cylinders were inverted and directly drove the bell cranks. The *Royal William* was of this type. It was supplied to the Gloucester & Cheltenham Railway in around 1831-1832.[172] This locomotive was a 0-6-0 built to a gauge of 3ft 6in. Like many of the early locomotives built at Neath Abbey, *Royal William* was used on a plateway and not on edge rails. The tramroads of the time were not strong enough to support several tons of locomotive and great difficulty was encountered in their day to day running. Thomas Phelps gave an eye-witness account of the first running of *Royal William* which shows the difficulty that these locomotives experienced on tramroads:

> *I ran alongside him – sometimes he was on and sometimes he was off. We started from the coal yard…It took some time to make the water bile to get the steam up and get un to move. He did at last and he ran along till the metals kicked up and the engine was off. It was hard work to get un to Barnwood but he spinned away at a good speed from Barnwood pike to*

opposite the turnpike on the Cheltenham Road. It was as much as I could kip up with un that distance. Then he stuck and he would not budge one inch further. They had a terrible bother to get un back home again. Coal was getting short and hardly water enough inside him to bile. The Cheltenham people was looken out for un at t'other end but he never got to Cheltenham and the Cheltenham folks went home disappointed saying 'twas all humbug'. They made a last trial and crowds of Gloucester people went to see the show. They was sartin sure he would run to Cheltenham and would be there in an hour or so. The Cheltenham folks again went out to meet un. They lit the fire in him, filled his belly full of water, puffed at the fire with bellows, and made him bile and bubble. They brought un out of the coal yard a boiling and a bubbling, a roaring, a blazing and a blowing off clouds of smoke and ashes; he coughed, groaned, grunted and snorted; by and by he began to run and we run after un. Before he got to Barton Pike he kicked and scouted on the metals, he groaned, he squealed and grunted, the fire rushed out, the sparks fled out and the steam and smoke rolled above in clouds and in a moment a terrible noise was yurd. We all fled back. We soon found out what was the matter. The blessed thing had busted. The driver got off just in time or he would have been roasted to cinders or biled or scalded to death. No, he never lived to reach Cheltenham. [sic][173]

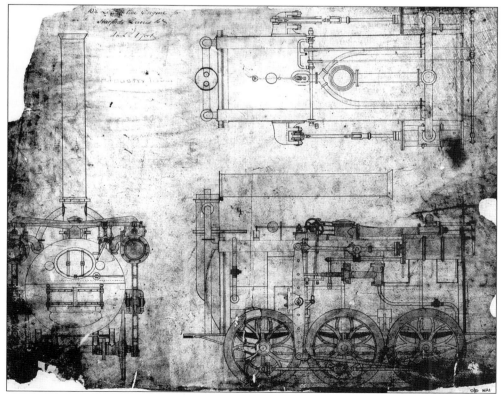

Industry, *an early Neath Abbey locomotive built in 1832 for the Ebbw Vale Ironworks.*

Caesar, a 0-6-0 saddle tank locomotive built by the Neath Abbey Ironworks for the Morfa colliery of Vivian & Sons.

An interesting series of locomotives was built for the Dowlais Iron Company with preparations for making the first underway in 1831.[174] This locomotive was of a novel design being a 0-4-4-0 articulated geared rack engine with inclined cylinders at the front. This was an interesting development as rack engines had previously been restricted to the Blenkinsop and Murray types. The novelty of the design was that Neath Abbey planned to use the rack as an auxiliary drive for steep sections. The original design of this locomotive appears to have been rejected by the Dowlais Iron Company but a second design was accepted and the locomotive was completed by June 1832. This was *Perseverance*, a geared 0-6-0 locomotive with 3ft 1in diameter wheels. The 10½in x 1ft 8in cylinders were inclined and positioned at the back of the boiler. This locomotive was delivered in June 1832 at a cost of £762 8s 7d but later reduced by £10.

The Dowlais Iron Company must have been well pleased with their purchase for further locomotives were delivered during the 1830s. The locomotives built for the Dowlais Iron Company were the result of co-operation between the engineers at Dowlais and the Neath Abbey designers. The Dowlais engineers provided detailed specifications for the locomotives which were incorporated into the designs produced by Charles Jordan. These designs were later submitted to the Dowlais Iron Company for criticism. No doubt the interest of the Dowlais Iron Company in steam traction had to some point been generated by their consulting engineer, the well known J.U. Rastrick, who was also a builder of locomotives.

The expansion and innovations that the company enjoyed during the 1840s are again reflected in their locomotive building activities. The 1840s saw Neath Abbey producing 0-6-0s with inside frames and horizontal cylinders, a design similar to a type produced by E.B. Wilson & Co. of Leeds. The marked similarities included a centrally domed boiler with a spring balance safety valve and a raised fire-box with safety valve on top.[175]

An important development took place in 1853 when Neath Abbey built its first saddle tank locomotive. This was a 0-6-0 with horizontal 14in x 1ft 8in cylinders built for J.&C. Bailey of the Nantyglo Ironworks.[176] A series of tank locomotives were constructed for various customers and by the early 1860s the Neath Abbey designers had arrived at a standardised design.

The Neath Abbey Iron Company sent one of its saddle tank locomotives to the International Exhibition in London in 1862. This was *Abbot* built to a gauge of 2ft 8in with 8in x 1ft 4in cylinders The locomotive had four coupled cast iron wheels of 2ft 4in diameter each being 4ft apart centre to centre. The boiler had $3\frac{1}{2}$ft^2 of grate and 59 tubes of $1\frac{1}{2}$in diameter and they were 6ft long (a total heating surface of 181ft^2). Abbot was 6.85 tons in weight and was carried on volute springs.[177] It is highly likely that at the end of the exhibition it was purchased by the Blanzy Mines in France. The locomotive proved its worth in France and so the Blanzy Mines had more narrow gauge locomotives made for them by Schneider & Cie who used the Neath Abbey locomotive as their model.

The side and saddle tank locomotives built at Neath Abbey were a very successful product and their building continued into the 1870s.[178] In fact the locomotives appear to have been the most successful product of the company during the final years of decline for the evidence indicates that the Neath Abbey Iron Company built approximately twenty-four tank locomotives between the years 1853 and 1880. The majority of these were purchased for use in the ironworks, collieries and copper works of South Wales. The

The newly completed 0-6-0 side tank locomotive Abercrave, *1870, in the works yard of the Neath Abbey Ironworks.*

67

decline during the 1860s and 1870s of the South Wales iron and copper industries robbed the company of these valuable markets for their locomotives. The railway market was highly competitive and it would have been difficult to promote sales in other areas. The old fashioned and cramped works was at a disadvantage against newer companies with modern equipment who could concentrate on locomotive buildings with the resulting economies of scale. Although Neath Abbey's locomotives were competitively priced, the contraction of their local market marked the end of locomotive building at the works.

The Neath Abbey Iron Company came into being at a time when many new and varied products were being introduced. Certainly the works was a pioneer in many of the new engineering fields and so became one of the great engineering concerns of the industrial revolution. The Neath Abbey engineering drawings show a remarkable variety of products. As well as the main steam engineering products, the works could supply structural ironwork, mill work, weighing machines, sawing machines, small aqueducts and even the occasional machine tool. The works' products clearly justified the listing of the company in an 1865 directory as 'Neath Abbey Iron Co., Engineers, Iron and Brass Founders, Iron Ship Builders, and Manufacturers of Every Description'.

One important non-steam product built at Neath Abbey was gas making plant, which began in the early 1820s. Although this is an early date, gas making equipment had been made by several other firms in the early 1800s. An early pioneer in gas manufacture was William Murdock, Boulton & Watt's engineer in Cornwall.

Murdock's experiments date from 1792 when he lit his house at Redruth with gas made by the distillation of coal with apparatus consisting of an iron retort with tinned copper and iron tubes. He also made experiments in gas lighting during a short stay at the Neath Abbey Ironworks. Murdock continued his experiments when recalled to the Soho Foundry and in 1802, to celebrate the Peace of Amiens, the factory was illuminated using gas.

The construction of gas plant for sale began in 1805 when a gas lighting system was installed by Murdock at the cotton factory of Phillips and Lee in Manchester. This was completed in 1807. It used 150 tons of coal in a year and provided 2,500 candle power. In 1808 Murdock installed further systems at factories for Burleigh of Manchester, Gott of Leeds, Kennedy of Manchester and one for a Glasgow firm. However, Boulton & Watt opposed the setting up of public gas companies and by 1815 had ceased making gas plant.

Another early builder of gas plant was Samuel Clegg who had assisted Murdock with his gas engineering work at Soho. Clegg left the employ of Boulton & Watt in 1804 and set himself up as a gas engineer. Several other builders of gas plant entered the field and by 1820 gas was being used as lighting for industrial premises, halls, schools and for street lighting.

The partners of the Neath Abbey Iron Company would have known, through their association with Boulton & Watt, of the gas engineering developments at Soho. Henry H. Price was clearly aware of this area of engineering through his friendship with William Bruton who, after working at Soho, had introduced the construction of cast iron gas pipes at the Butterley Ironworks.

The making of gas plant would certainly have been an attractive proposition for the Neath Abbey Iron Company given that the main material used in its construction would have been iron. The first plant built by Neath Abbey was for W. George junior of

A Neath Abbey side tank locomotive photographed in the early years of the twentieth century. The locomotive is pictured working on the Skewen incline of the Main Colliery Company's line.

Pontypool around 1820. An appreciable trade developed with complete gas plants being built for industry, schools and small towns. The company was able to supply gas holders, purifiers, retorts, mains and lamp posts.

The principal engineer involved in this trade was Edwin O. Tregelles. The Neath Abbey Iron Company seems to have been a main supplier of gas plant to three areas, namely South Wales, Southern Ireland and the West of England. The 1830s and 1840s were the years of maximum output, but the trade appears to have come to an end by the early 1860s which coincides with the date when the company ceased their own production of iron.

As general engineers the company became involved in the building of many different products. The works built much equipment for collieries and played an important part in the development of mine ventilators. The company was certainly building Struvé mine ventilators in the late 1840s and early 1850s. William Price Struvé was an engineer and viewer to the Governor and Company of Copper Miners at Cwmavon and had patented his machine on 12 March 1846. It consisted of two large bells (aerometers) activated by a beam engine moving up and down in water. Struvé's first ventilator was employed at the Eaglesbush Colliery near Neath where a few months earlier an explosion occurred killing twenty men. The Neath Abbey collection contains a drawing of a Struvé mine ventilator dated 1852 and it is highly likely that this ventilator was constructed by the Neath Abbey Iron Company. This 1852 drawing was for a product intended for the Middle Dyffryn Colliery at Aberdare and had two 20ft aerometers.

6

The Quaker Industrialists
of Neath Abbey

During the period 1801-1851, which coincided with the most successful years of the Neath Abbey Iron and Coal Companies, the population of the Neath Abbey and Skewen district multiplied by four and a half times and for 1851–1901 by three. The industrial development that encouraged this growth of the Clydach valley owes much to the drive and business acumen of the inter-related Fox and Price families.

The Quaker aspect of the partnership certainly gave the company an advantageous start. The Society of Friends had moved from being predominantly craftsmen and artisans in the seventeenth century to middle class traders in the late eighteenth century. Members were drawn from the more literate sections of the population, from those who asked questions of the traditional church and would not blindly follow its teachings. The Quakers were very much an educationally oriented group and most Quaker schools carried a strong bias to the practical, subjects such as geography, arithmetic and aspects of the study of nature; all subjects of some use to the budding businessman. There was no access for Quakers to universities or military professions and this meant that enquiring minds were mostly devoted to the affairs of the Society of Friends and the task of daily work.

Quakers regarded the desire of wealth a sin and the main outlet of profit appears to have been ploughing back money into business. Strength in business was further cemented by inter-society marriages of which the Fox family were an excellent example with their marriages into the important banking families of Backhouse and Lloyd. The constant persecution and harassment to which Quakers and other dissenting groups were subjected made them strive to demonstrate their real integrity and trustworthiness, traits clearly illustrated in the business history of Quaker companies.

The achievements of the Quaker industrialists were many. The Lloyds were dominant figures in the Midlands Association of Ironmasters and the Darby family established coke smelting of iron at Coalbrookdale. Many of the Quaker industrialists became involved in banking and Quaker merchants were to be found in most trades. To this list must be added the achievements of the Neath Abbey Iron and Coal Companies under the guiding hands of the Price family.

Peter Price was the one original partner of the Neath Abbey Iron Company that had experience of the iron and engineering industries. He was born in Madeley, Shropshire in 1739 of a strong Roman Catholic family.[179] At fifteen, Peter and his sister were taken ill with a fever; his sister died while he was unconscious for thirty-two days. His experiences whilst ill made him abandon his religion.

Henry Habberley Price (1794-1839).

Julia Struvé Price.

Deborah Waring, née Price (1785-1867).

Price was trained as a moulder in the Coalbrookdale Ironworks and in 1759 was recruited by Dr John Roebuck for his Carron Ironworks at Falkirk. At Carron Price became a foreman of the boring mill and must have worked with James Watt on the building of his experimental engine, particularly the attempts to bore an accurate cylinder. Watt was later to describe Price to Boulton as '…a man of character and a great deal of knowledge in the foundry way'.[180]

In 1769 Price left Carron for America where he spent five years putting up blast furnaces in Pennsylvania, Maryland, North Carolina and Virginia. While in America he dabbled in freemasonry and belonged to the Philadelphia Lodge.[181] It was quite likely that at this time he injured his back, had to give up heavy industrial work and joined the army in America, but on the outbreak of the War of Independence he returned to Britain. While returning to Britain he was engaged in conversation aboard ship by a member of the Society of Friends and their discussions led him to become a Quaker.

For a time Price was agent for the Dale or Ketley Company in London. Later he became a corn factor in Stourport and then in Cornwall. In 1781 he married Anna, sister of Samuel Tregelles, and in 1791 he joined his many relatives in setting up the Perran Foundry. In 1801 he came to the Neath Abbey Ironworks as manager of the concern. Price and his family were an addition to a fairly large community of Quakers living in the Vale of Neath. Price continued to be active in the affairs of the Neath Abbey Iron Company until his retirement in 1818. He died in 1821. One action that Peter Price has come to be remembered for is the founding of a free school for the poor children of the neighbourhood of Neath Abbey.

Lydia Redwood, née Price (1788-1863).

Peter and Anna Price had nine children and five directly or indirectly made a contribution to the industrialisation of the Neath area. In 1818 a new Fox/Price partnership took over the Neath Abbey Ironworks and Peter Price's shares were taken over by his sons, Henry Habberley Price and Joseph Tregelles Price.

Henry H. Price was to greatly influence the progress of engineering at the Neath Abbey Ironworks. Born in 1794, he was brought up in the Quaker tradition. However, he left the Society of Friends, probably at the time of his marriage to Julia Struvé of Guernsey. Henry H. Price's involvement in the building of locomotives and marine engines filled him with interest in the spread of the new methods of transport. He soon set himself up as a civil engineer living at the Rhyddings, Swansea. When Telford was working on the improvement of the Bristol-Milford Mail route, he employed Price to build new ferry piers on the old passage between Beachley and Aust on the Severn estuary.[182] Steam boats were introduced at both New and Old Passage ferries from 27 August 1827 onwards. In 1829 Henry H. Price was engineering a scheme to straighten the River Tees [183] which was achieved with the use of jetties as described by the engineer:

> *The River Tees from Stockton downwards, has been improved on this principle for several miles under my direction with the most perfect success, the main piles which are all firmly braced together and supported by diagonal trussing form two parallel rows of dolphin piles, all rise above high water and have beacons fixed on the outer ends of the jetties...*[184]

Henry H. Price was particularly interested in the development of harbours and was a pioneer of the Swansea Harbour Trust Development.[185] He also worked on harbour schemes at Waterford, Cork, Swansea, Neath and Llanelly. His engineering work was important to the Neath Abbey Ironworks for he attracted many orders to the concern. In 1837 a Neath Abbey locomotive was assisting Price in an abortive scheme to build a harbour at Sidmouth.[186] Price's harbour work explains the presence of drawings of dock gates for Montrose Wet Dock in the Neath Abbey Collection.[187] The works also benefited from Henry H. Price's travels for he was able to keep Neath Abbey in touch with the progress of engineering in other parts of the country. Price was later a partner in the Landore Coal Company and was involved in heating engineering. He died in around 1839.

However, it was Joseph Tregelles Price who had the greatest influence on the Neath Abbey companies. He was born in Penryn, Cornwall on 20 January 1784.[188] When he reached the age of eight he was sent to a Quaker school at Compton and left at fourteen to assist his father in business.

Joseph T. Price's years as managing partner were to coincide with the boom years of the Welsh iron industry. Not only was Price an effective manager but also he was an engineer of note with two patents to his name. While under Price's management the Neath Abbey Ironworks produced a wide range of steam products. It is no surprise that his activities were recorded by a Quaker poet in the following way:

> *Joseph Price, Joseph Price,*
> *Thou are mighty precise,*
> *Me thought t'other night in a dream*
> *That thou really walked,*
> *Slept, ate, drank and talked,*
> *And prayed every Sunday by steam.*[189]

With the increasing scale of operations Price must have faced many problems in keeping the works running efficiently. In many respects the rational and methodical management of labour was the central problem in the Industrial Revolution. An important aspect of this problem was the recruitment of labour. The pool of skilled men was very small and the absence of a single man could hold up major work. The ironmasters of South Wales were so conscious of this shortage that they dare not put out their furnaces in slack times for fear of losing their men. Poaching of workers and defences against it became necessary activities and this was a constant source of friction within the iron industry. Neath Abbey, not only being a bulk ironworks, but also a precision engineering establishment, often suffered from the poaching of skilled men. On 10 April 1824, Joseph T. Price wrote the following letter to Josiah John Guest of the Dowlais Ironworks:

> *I conceive thou canst not be aware that someone from your works has been down here twice enticing our men away by offers of high wages, that one man named, Griffith Hopkin has been employed by you in that way and that recently another named Yorath has been seduced in the same way. I cannot imagine that thou wouldst approve such a system. Its tendency is to occasion the worst effects. I only beg thou wilt enquire into it and discourage it. The latter*

named person has agreed with me not to quit our employ, and if your agent in that business has any claim in consequence of any engagement of his, or thou thinks it right to demand a month's notice, I will pay it for him. I did think of calling on thee about it, but when I passed Dowlais lately thou wert absent.[190]

In July 1826, Joseph T. Price was again forced to write to Dowlais:

Permit me to congratulate thee on thy parliamentary appointment. It cannot be known to thee that a lad named Henry Mansel, an apprentice of ours, is in thy employ, a fitter. In turning him back have the kindness to give him a magisterial reprimand. We were going to advertise him till I heard he was at Dowlais.[191]

Another major concern for the managing partner would have been the creation of discipline within the work force. Although the works at Neath Abbey had a Quaker aspect, the work force would have been a very mixed bunch. In South Wales it was estimated as late as the 1840s that the workers lost one week in five, and that in the fortnight after pay day only two thirds of the time was being worked. In 1820 Edwin Octavius Tregelles, Joseph T. Price's cousin, commenced work at Neath Abbey and recorded the following:

In the ninth month I went to work in the carpenters shop in connection with the foundry at Neath Abbey. Here I lost ground as a Christian, being exposed to the rehearsal of vice, though there was not much open sin. True it is that evil communication corrupt good manners; yes, and lay waste the serious impression of youth. I soon deviated from my habits of piety, but was preserved from descending to the depths of iniquity...[192]

Joseph Tregelles Price (1784-1854).

Elijah Waring (1788-1857).

The working man had to be made into a respectable and stable worker. To achieve this Joseph T. Price continued the tradition of school-founding instituted by his father.[193] Education could have two effects; it could instil discipline and also teach the requisite knowledge and skills for later employment in the neighbouring works. The works' school was described in detail in 1848:

> *These works and the houses round them form a suburb of Neath. Joseph Price Esq., who is managing partner of the Company, told me that the schools attached to them had the most beneficial effect upon the working classes of the neighbourhood, who used to be notorious for their black guardism. The School was formerly held in premises which were part of the works. Previous to the erection of the present school-rooms, which are separate buildings surrounded by a wall, Mr Price instituted some enquiries respecting the effects of the school which had been in operation for about twenty years. Cadoxton is a large parish, extending the entire width of the county from Swansea Bay to Brecknockshire and containing eight or nine hamlets. Of all the scholars who since its commencement had been at the school, two only had become charge-able on the parish…Mr Price was one of the first proprietors of works who introduced the custom of weekly stoppages for the support of the school. The plan has been already in successful operation for providing medical attendance. Mr Price considered that the masters in South Wales had the power by these means to provide effectually for the education of their*

Christiana Abberley Price (1792-1879).

Maria Louise Price (d1854).

people without further assistance. It is understood that, should the surplus arising from the stoppages in good times fail to meet the expenses of the schools in bad times, the company will still keep the school open. The present superintendent of the Bristol Company's Steamers, the chief engineers of the Gt Britain *and* Gt Western *and a great many of the engineers of the river boats in London had been educated in the Abbey school. Mr Price considered the mechanical employment in the adjoining works to be useful in promoting and carrying out the rudiments of education acquired in school; and he attributed the general success of the Neath Abbey people in the world to the tout ensemble of the influences with which they were surrounded and not to those of the school only.*[194]

The transfer from school to works could take place at an early age. In 1841 the numbers employed at the Neath Abbey Ironworks were listed as:

Adults	*175*
Under 18 years of age	*47*
Under 13 years of age	*11*

Charles Waring, the works' agent, described the concern to the Children's Employment Commission in the following terms:

*Edwin Price
(1828-1856).*

The Neath Abbey Iron Company is an engine Manufactory and contains a department for iron ship building & C. Our works have no special ventilation but they are sufficiently airy, and the usual temperature is from 58° to 70° , nor is there any great degree of heat required in those processes where children are employed...we have about 170 adults at work, but when we are full of work we employ about 260 to 300. Our two blast furnaces are not at work.[195]

Joseph T. Price as a humanitarian is best known for his part in the case of Richard Lewis (Dic Penderyn). There was much unrest in industrial South Wales with rising prices and the unjust truck system being used by some masters and Lewis had been condemned for his part in the Merthyr Riots of 1831. Joseph T. Price took an interest in the case and, after investigating the evidence against Lewis, decided he had been falsely accused. Price rode to London and was interviewed by the Home Secretary.[196] A reprieve was granted for a time but the innocent man was not saved from the gallows.

The unrest of the Merthyr ironworkers spread even to Neath Abbey. Forty or fifty workers had joined a 'union club' and the works' agent had served them with notice to quit. The men began to talk of strike action. Joseph T. Price invited his workmen to discuss dispassionately the advantages and disadvantages of union clubs. One hundred and fifty workers accepted and Price, having read the rules of the society, proceeded to enumerate the several merits and demerits of membership. Several employees addressed the meeting which lasted an hour and when a vote was taken everyone moved against the formation of a union in the works. [197] Edwin O. Tregelles records in his journal some of the events at Neath Abbey in June 1831:

> *These are momentous times. Riots at Merthyr. Cavalry constantly passing, and reports of many persons being killed. This has been a day of considerable excitement. I felt it required of me to address our workmen on adopting the peaceable spirit of the Redeemer, and I feel thankful that I was strengthened to declare the counsel of the Lord. Our men at Neath Abbey Ironworks were assembled in one of the large Smith's shop; cousin J.T. Price, my brother Nathaniel, the clerks and I went to them. Before much was said, I felt a sudden impulse to address them seriously and taking off my hat I said, 'Christ suffered for us, leaving an example, that ye should follow his steps; who did not sin, neither was guile found in his mouth; who, when he was reviled, reviled not again; when he suffered he threatened not, but committed himself to them that judgeth righteously'. This was followed by a respectful silence; and from that day forward, never again was any semblance of insubordination apparent. The men quietly dispersed and we heard no more of the strike.*[198]

Edwin O. Tregelles' religious zeal was later to clash with Joseph T. Price's more balanced views of religion and business, and Tregelles left the works. He recorded the incident in his journal in October 1831:

Left: *Charles Struvé Price (1831-1915) and his wife Anna.* Right: *Charles Struvé Price photographed with his sons Joseph and Charles.*

...a person called at the Neath Abbey Works' office to show some plans and requested a tender for some machinery. The matter was referred to me as an engineer to calculate the cost and give an estimate. I soon learnt that the engine and machinery were for a brewery in Newport in Monmouthshire. In a moment, I recollected that the liquor brewed at that place had been instrumental in causing murder in Abersychan, which came to my notice when I was there in 1826. I felt that I could have nothing to do with supplying machinery for such concerns. I therefore wrote a letter to my kind cousin Joseph T. Price, telling him that if I had to engage in such work, I should prefer leaving my situation in twelve months.[199]

Joseph Tregelles Price had steered the Neath Abbey Iron Company into one of the most versatile and respected engineering concerns in Britain but his last years had seen much sadness. One of his nieces was married in 1853 and departed with her sister and husband for Philadelphia and neither they nor their ship were heard of again. His health took a downward turn and his eyesight began to fail him.[200] Although suffering from a cold he attended an anti-slavery convention and the funeral of a friend. The cold turned to bronchitis and he died, unmarried, on 25 December 1854. *The Cambrian* commented:

Mr Price has been familiar to the public of South Wales during very many years as a leading man of business and an indefatigable philanthropist. His character was one of singular energy, cool discrimination and inflexible integrity. Few men could be so greatly missed in his own immediate neighbourhood; but his loss will be more extensively felt, not only in the religious community of which he was a member, but in various associations for benevolent objects and moral progress. Over the deep sorrow of his family connections, we reverently draw the veil but the public need no other evidence of an emotion spreading far more widely than the countenance and language of his numerous subordinates and workmen, who tearfully solicit a last look at all that now remains of their long venerated employer.[201]

Joseph T. Price was not only a very successful industrialist, but also a philosopher and social reformer. He was deeply involved with the Society of Friends and this work took him around Britain where he befriended other notable Quakers such as the Backhouses and Peases of the north-east. Many members of the Society of Friends periodically travelled in ministry and important trading as well as religious links were built up. The Quaker founders of the Stockton & Darlington Railway awarded the Neath Abbey Ironworks the contract for supplying cast iron rails. The link between the Pease and Price family would account for the award of the contact but in general Quaker firms allowed very favourable terms when dealing with fellow members of the Society of Friends.

Joseph T. Price was well known as a humanitarian. He was a man of great personality and was described as:

...a man of mark, and cannot be forgotten by any who ever knew him. He was more than six feet in height, of a powerful build, with a strong voice and hearty manner; one whom you would judge at first sight rather fitted for martial exercises and athletic sport, than for an elder of the Society of Friends.[202]

Charles Struvé Price pictured with his domestic staff and daughters Amy Isabella, Christina and Evelyn.

In 1816 Joseph T. Price with fellow Quakers founded the Peace Society in London. The society campaigned for the end of wars of all kind. Evan Rees, another Neath man, was a founder member and served as corresponding secretary and editor of the journal *Herald of Peace*. By 1834 the society had twenty-six auxiliaries, one being the Swansea and Neath Peace Society.[203] In June 1843 the International Peace Convention was held at Freemason's Hall, Lincoln's Inn Fields, London, a conference at which Joseph T. Price played a prominent part as chairman of one of the sessions. The work of the society broadened out during the 1840s, beyond the propagation of non-resistance on religious grounds, through its involvement with the anti-corn law campaign which was much supported in nonconformist journals.

Joseph Tregelles Price's sisters were also to play an important part, directly and indirectly, in industrial matters. Christiana Abberley Price (1792-1879), like her brother, was heavily involved in the work of the Society of Friends and was also a partner in the Neath Abbey Coal Company and the Perran Wharf Foundry in Cornwall. Lydia Price (1788-1863) married Isaac Redwood who became one of the largest shareholders in the Neath Abbey Coal Company. The Redwood family came from the Vale of Glamorgan and Isaac started up a currier's business in Neath.

Deborah Price (1785-1867) married Elijah Waring and this union was to produce a son who took an important part in the management of both Neath Abbey companies. Elijah Waring was born in Alton, Hampshire on 14 April 1788, the son of a manufacturer of silk and worsted shifts. As a young man he accompanied his cousin Edward Waring of Bristol on a tour through South Wales. It was on this tour that he became acquainted with the Quakers of Neath Abbey and he became engaged to Deborah Price. He settled in Neath and became a miller and corn

Charles Waring (d1887).

factor with his main business being in selling corn to the ironmasters of Merthyr, Aberdare and Hirwaun. Waring was also involved in establishing a branch of the West of England and South Wales District Bank at Cardiff during the early 1840s.[204] He was also an investigator for the Children's Employment Commission. He was a well-read man with an enquiring mind and he later left the Society of Friends and became a Wesleyan preacher.

Through his relations the Redwoods he met and befriended Edward Williams (Iolo Morganwg) and this fostered an interest in the Welsh language and history. Elijah Waring befriended Lady Charlotte Guest at Dowlais and he encouraged her interest in Welsh literature, leading to her translation of *The Mabinogion*. She recorded one conversation with Waring in the following terms:

> *...our conversation turned much upon the superstitions and legends of Wales - I think it might be desirable to make a collection of them. His love for ancient literature is quite refreshing to me who have been so long deprived of everything like fellow feeling in that respect.*[205]

Elijah Waring later wrote a book of recollections of Iolo Morganwg. He died at the Darran, Neath Abbey, 29 March 1857.

Charles Waring (1818-1887) was the oldest son of Deborah and Elijah Waring and was a manager at different times for both Neath Abbey companies. We are lucky in that Charles Waring wrote down a most interesting account of his life and moreover he was a keen photog-

Edwin Price Waring (b1824).

rapher and has also left a unique photographic record of the Price family in the early 1850s. Charles Waring was almost ten when he was sent to a Quaker school in Fishponds, near Bristol, where he was taught subjects that included Latin, Greek and mathematics. However, he was later bullied by some older boys and removed to another school at Thornbury. He recorded that there his education was feeble with the children not really being made to understand the work and much time was spent on going through Latin and English grammar like parrots.

In 1832 Charles Waring became an apprentice mechanical engineer at the Neath Abbey Ironworks. He started by working in the carpenters shop where he was taught pattern making. The shop was a large room which had windows on two sides and two rows of benches with lathes. Twenty to thirty pattern makers worked in this room and Charles Waring learnt carpentry under a pleasant man called Rees Rees. He later went on to learn the art of fitting and blacksmithing. The finishing department for the apprentices was the drawing office

With his apprentices Joseph T. Price would never take a premium and always paid a small wage. Waring's wage was 2s 6d per week and as an apprentice he should have worked in the morning from six o'clock to half past eight, then breakfast for half an hour, then nine to one o'clock with an hour for dinner and then two to six o'clock. Waring did have some special treatment for he was allowed to come in during winter at 9 o'clock and at 7 o'clock during summer. Waring's apprentice companions included Christopher Dickenson of Coalbrookdale and Samuel Bevan the son of Paul Bevan the London banker.

Robert Were Fox (1789-1877).

Soon Waring was working for the Neath Abbey Coal Company and was injured in an explosion at the Main Colliery in February 1834. He was sent down into the pit by an overman who he had seen cheating the company and it was he who directed Waring to a gas filled area in the mine and an explosion took place. The man was discharged but later committed a similar offence in the Aberdare valley.

Robert Barclay Fox (1817-1855).

It took six months for Waring to recover from his injuries but was soon working for the coal company again, which entailed riding some twenty to thirty miles each day. During the period 1845-1851 he was a managing partner of the Neath Abbey Iron Company and recorded that 'The Neath Abbey ironworks was celebrated for goodness and strength where people would pay 10% over other works' price'. Waring also recorded the following incident to show the quality of Neath Abbey work:

> *At the works was built the* Prince of Wales, *so strongly constructed that once on the River Avon coming from Bristol she was caught and left by the tide, jammed with no water below and a full cargo and her boilers full. She was undamaged. A modern Glasgow built boat would have crumpled like paper.*

Waring later sold his shares in the Neath Abbey Iron Company and during 1845-1868 was managing partner of the Abernant Iron Company. He also acted as a managing partner of the Neath Abbey Coal Company during the period 1854-1874. He became a full member of the Institute of Civil Engineers and one of his main interests lay in the development of coal cutting machinery. He died on 9 September 1887 after a long and painful illness.[206]

His brother, Edwin Price Waring, was also apprenticed and worked at the Neath Abbey Ironworks. After being employed by the Neath Abbey companies he went into the employment of Charles Lambert at Coquimbo in Chile.

After the death of Joseph Tregelles Price it was the three sons of Henry Habberley Price who were to be the main managers of the Neath Abbey companies. They were brought up at Neath Abbey in the Quaker tradition after the early death of their father. Edwin Price (1828-1856) died in his twenties and it was left to the other two brothers to guide the concerns. Henry Habberley Price (1825-1894) became the manager of the Neath Abbey Ironworks while Charles Struvé Price (1831-1915) became one of the managing partners of the Neath Abbey Coal Company.

Charles S. Price was in South Africa in 1854 and while there was robbed of all his possessions. He eventually found work with a mining company in the Cape of Good Hope and was sent 400 miles north of the Cape to help open the Concordia Mines. However, after five months of a six month contract he had a dreadful premonition that tragedy had struck his family and he quickly returned home.[207] He returned to find the family in mourning.

His sister, Julia L. Price had married Edward Tothill in 1854 and with her husband and sister, Maria Louisa Price had travelled to America on board the ship *City of Glasgow*. The ship, owned by the Inman Line, left Liverpool for Philadelphia on 1 March 1854 with a total of 480 people on board including crew. She was never heard of again. A sister ship later reported finding a large field of broken ice drifting around the course that the stricken ship would have taken.[208]

Charles later married Hannah Isabella Richardson, the daughter of Joshua Richardson. Richardson was from the north-east and had moved to Wales to pursue his career as a colliery engineer and was consulted on may occasions by the Neath Abbey Coal Company. Hannah Isabella Price was not a strong woman but she did have a life-long interest in homeopathy and spent many hours visiting and helping in the homes of the Neath Abbey workers. She died in 1898 and a friend at her funeral remarked:

> *There is hardly one amongst this sorrowful crowd who had not in some way been helped or cheered by her loving ministries, or had not been the better for having known her.*[209]

After the closure of the Neath Abbey Ironworks the Price family tradition in engineering was continued by Charles Edwin Price (b. 1859), the son of Charles Struvé Price. He formed a new company in February 1906 as Edwin Price & Co. to operate an engineering works at the Mill-Lands, Neath.[210] Price & Co. had been in business during the 1890s and had built several steam engines for local tinplate works.

The Fox family was also to make a major contribution to the development of the Neath Abbey area. The family was based in Falmouth but several of the partners travelled from Cornwall and spent extended periods helping with the management of the Neath Abbey companies. The brothers Robert Were Fox (1789-1877) and Alfred Fox (1794-1874) were important members of the Quaker partnerships. Alfred Fox was an important businessman in Cornwall with interests in shipping, mining and Falmouth Docks. His son Theodore Fox became one of the managing partners of the Neath Abbey Iron Company. Robert Were Fox's son Barclay Fox (1815-1855) was also a partner in the Neath Abbey Iron Company and like other members of the family he spent several weeks on visits to the concern to learn the trade and help with management.[211] One of Alfred Fox's son, Charles W. Fox died at Neath Abbey in 1866 at the age of twenty-three.

7

The Nineteenth Century
Coal Mining Industry

The early years of the nineteenth century saw Richard Parsons firmly in control of the coal mining activities around Neath Abbey. However, there was some coal mining activity on the Dyffryn Estate and this took on an important aspect when the partners of the Neath Abbey Iron Company were granted the mineral lease for this land. The lease was dated 12 August 1806 and was between Jane Magdaline Williams, Elizabeth Williams, Maria Catherine Williams and Walter Jeffreys on the one part and Robert Were Fox, Thomas Were Fox, George Fox, Edward Fox, Samuel Tregelles, John Gould, John Williams, Thomas Wilson, John Matravers and Peter Price on the other part. This lease was drawn up to run for a total of sixty-three years.[212] The Quaker partners had been mining iron stone at Pwllfaron at the head of the Neath valley but coal mining was a completely different venture. This move would allow the Neath Abbey partners to expand their iron making activities and to embark on a new career as coal merchants.

One of the first actions by the partners in this new venture was to sink a pit on the Dyffryn Estate which was known as Pwll Mawr. This was reported as being the deepest pit in the country at 200yds. Other collieries were developed on the estate using steam engines made at the Neath Abbey Ironworks. Brynddewy was a drift mine which entered the side of Mynydd Drymma to work the Brynddewy or Graigola seam. Pwll Mawr and Dyffryn Main were pits exploiting the Bryncoch, Dirty, Wernfraith and Greenway seams. In 1817 it was recorded that these mines were using four steam engines. The mining activities of the Quakers must have met with success for on 26 June 1819 a separate company was formed to operate the coal mines. The Neath Abbey Coal Company was formed with $\frac{5}{12}$ of the shares in the hands of the brothers Joseph Tregelles Price and Henry Habberley Price and $\frac{7}{12}$ in the hands of Thomas Were Fox, Alfred Fox, Joshua Fox, George Croker Fox and Charles Fox.[213] By this time the Quakers were also mining anthracite coal at Pwllfaron, on the Aberpergwm Estate.

In contrast to the exploits of the Neath Abbey Coal Company the business empire of Richard Parsons was experiencing great difficulty. In 1816 Parsons was declared bankrupt and a contributory factor must have been the very keen coal contracts he had offered in the late eighteenth century to attract new industry to the area. It appears that Parsons's coal mines were taken over by his son John. This initiated a period of co-operation between Parsons's pits and those of the Neath Abbey Coal Company. The result of this co-operation was a joint tramroad from the pits and the joint working for a period of the Graigola Colliery in the Swansea valley.

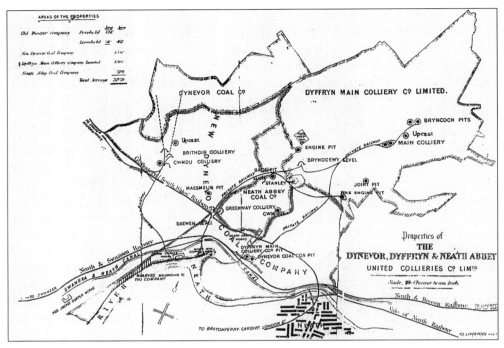

The mineral ground of the Dynevor, Dyffryn & Neath Abbey United Collieries Co. Ltd. The map shows the assets of the company in 1874 and also the mineral estates of the former companies.

The development of the Neath Abbey Coal Company's pits was not without danger. Problems existed in many of the mines of the Clydach valley including excess water and gas. Pwll Mawr was the site of an accident in 1839 with one fatality and fifteen or sixteen men injured. An explosion occurred before the men had stripped for work because a door in the workings had been left open through the negligence of the last man coming up the night before. This caused an accumulation of gas to take place and this was ignited by the later reckless actions of a young miner.[214]

The Neath Abbey Coal Company was prepared to exploit minerals in other areas outside the Clydach valley; mention has already been made of the Pwllfaron Colliery. During the late 1830s land was leased at Briton Ferry for coal mining purposes and it was planned to erect rolling mills and furnaces to use this coal to full advantage. The land was leased from the Earl of Jersey for ninety-nine years from 1 January 1839.[215] The lease consisted of the right to work minerals under land in Briton Ferry and Baglan to the north of the turnpike road from Aberavon to Neath. This amounted to two square miles plus permission was also given to work minerals in land under the River Neath. There was a dead rent of £500 and a payment of 4d per ton for the first two years after which the payment rose to 6d per ton. There was a wayleave payment of 6d per wey for any coal not consumed on the premises but all coal sent to the wharf on the property from the Main, Brynddewy and Pwllfaron Collieries was to be free of wayleave charges.

The lease also stipulated that no copper, spelter or brass works were to be erected on the land. The company exploited the lease by constructing several drifts and collieries including Blaen Baglan and Tormynydd. The most valuable seams on the property was the Tormynydd which produce excellent quality coal which could be cut large and the Jonnah seam which could be worked with the Tormynydd. Some of the lesser coals mined on the property found a ready buyer in the Briton Ferry Iron Company.[216]

A small ship canal was built on the property. It was 700yds long, 60ft wide at the top and 45ft wide at the bottom. It usually contained 16ft of water during spring tides and 18 to 20ft at very high tides. No ironworks was built on the property but the exploitation of the area was brought to a halt when the South Wales Railway intended to build their line across the land. A report was drawn up in March 1850 estimating that damage amounting to £19,605 would be done to the property if the line went ahead. This estimate was based on the plan to build an ironworks on the property. [217] By April 1851 this figure had been reduced to a more realistic figure of £7,796. The difficulties of working this mineral area with the construction of a new railway going on above ground persuaded the Neath Abbey Coal Company to give up the lease. On 8 February 1853 the company surrendered their leases to the Earl of Jersey for a consideration of £2,000 with the Earl having the option of buying the plant and machinery at the collieries after a valuation.[218]

1850-1860 was a period of great change for the coal mining industry of the Clydach valley. In the early 1850s the Longford and Neath Abbey Estates' mineral leases expired. The Neath Abbey mineral agent was dissatisfied with Parsons's activities in supplying the Neath Abbey copper works partly with coal from his Graigola Colliery. To answer this criticism Parsons sank a new level at Cwrt Herbert to supply the needs of local industry. Later when new leases were issued the Longford Estate and part of the Neath Abbey Estate's minerals were granted to the Neath Abbey Coal Company. In the north of the area important developments were being heralded by the purchase of the Dyffryn Estate by the local politician Howel Gwyn.[219]

In 1854 the Neath Abbey Coal Company was operating Pwllfaron, Bryncoch and Brynddewy Collieries with Parsons working his new drift at Court Herbert. In the following year the Neath Abbey Coal Company reopened the Main Colliery after pumping out the flooded workings. Water was a continual problem for the collieries along the valley and on 6 April 1859 a sudden inrush of water drowned the Main Colliery for a second time. Eighty men and boys were employed in this pit at the time. Headings were being bored towards an old pit called the Fire Engine Pit when the old workings were pierced and water entered the colliery like a river. The headings were being made to provide a second shaft at the pit and with only one shaft escape was difficult. The accident claimed the lives of twenty-five men and water rose to over 80ft in the pit.[220]

The death of John Parsons in 1855 opened a new chapter in the coal mining saga of Neath Abbey. Parson's mineral interests were purchased by John Thomas, the mineral agent of the Dyffryn Estate, and the Rev. David H. Griffiths. A new partnership called the Dynevor Coal Company was formed to work the mineral area previously owned by the Parsons' family. The partnership consisted of Thomas Griffiths and Edward Acland Moore, the brother-in-law of Howel Gwyn. In the year ending 25 March 1857 the Dynevor Coal Company raised just over 27,219 tons of coal from the Neath Abbey Estate mainly from the Greenway Pit, the Great Level (Brithdir), Wernddu Level, Ynismond Level, Gilfach Pit and the Lonlas Level. During the same period the Neath Abbey Coal Company took 18,707 tons of coal from the Neath Abbey Estate using workings that extended from Brynddewy, Main and Bryncoch.[221] So this total only represents a proportion of the coal won at these pits. The true output of the Neath Abbey Coal Company is recorded for the late 1860s. In 1866 the Main Colliery produced 87,368 tons of coal and Brynddewy 56,896 tons. In the following year the Main Colliery produced 93,479 tons of coal with Brynddewy producing 89,744 tons.

However, the Dynevor Coal Company during the same period was struggling to survive and in 1866 it failed. Part of the problem originated with the company's lease with the Neath Abbey Estate. By the lease the Dynevor Coal Company had bound itself to take 6,000 weys of coal from the estate. In the year ending 25 March 1857 the company only managed to raise just under 2,500 weys and for the year ending 25 March 1866 the company raised just over 4,816 weys.[222] It is obvious that the company could not sell this amount of coal as set out in the lease and was paying for coal not taken from the ground.

The collieries were then sold to John Newall Moore, the nephew of Howel Gwyn. John Thomas then instituted proceedings in the Court of Chancery and the sale was set aside. In February 1868 it appeared that another Neath colliery company, Evans & Bevan, would purchase the assets of the Dynevor Colliery Company giving creditors 12s 6d in the pound. However, Moore and Gwyn stepped in to offer more money and another bill in Chancery was threatened to set aside the sale. E.A. Moore later confirmed that the creditors would be paid in full and he and J.N. Moore then took over the collieries and the creditors were duly paid. A New Dynevor Coal Company was formed with the partnership being made up of E.A. Moore, J.N. Moore, Michael Lewis Brown and John Treffery The new company's main producing unit appears to have been the Brithdir Colliery. It is easy to discern the hand of Howel Gwyn behind these changes in the Clydach valley coal industry. He does appear to have had the foresight to see that if one company exploited the whole mineral area of the Clydach valley then real progress could be made in the local coal industry. It would, of course, also increase the value of the Dyffryn Estate mineral leases.

The Neath Abbey Coal Company in the late 1860s was also going through a testing time. The company knew that it would lose the Dyffryn Estate mineral lease in August 1869 and the output from Brynddewy and Main which supplied high quality coal at a low cost. Details of how the company reacted to this change are preserved in a series of accounts and reports that survived dating mainly from the late 1860s and early 1870s.[223] The reports are a record of a series of weekly meetings held by the company. The main local partners at this time were Charles Struvé Price, Charles Waring and Isaac Redwood. The other partners were members of the Fox family. Using these documents it is a fairly easy task to outline the closing years of the Neath Abbey Coal Company.

In the month of December 1867 the Main Colliery produced just over 6,000 tons of coal at a total labour charge of £665 7s 6d or £1 2s 1d per wey. This total was achieved despite encountering several faults which caused problems and additional expense. In the same period Brynddewy produced nearly 5,818 tons of coal at a labour cost of £355 12s 1d or 12s 3d per wey. Pwllfaron Colliery produced 1,717 tons of coal at a labour cost of £244 9s 3d or £1 8s 6d per wey. Even at this early date preparations were being made to find alternative sources of coal on the mineral ground that the Neath Abbey Coal Company would be left with in 1869. To this end a colliery was being sunk on the Longford Estate. This was called the Stanley Colliery and in January 1868 it had reached a depth of 33yds but the partners were dissatisfied with this slow progress. They blamed the contractor who was sinking the pit for being tardy in paying his men wages which resulted in several stoppages.[224]

During 1868 the Neath Abbey Coal Company attempted to raise and sell as much coal as possible before the end of their Dyffryn Lease. During that year the monthly totals for the Main Colliery varied between 3,994.65 and 7,418.25 tons. Brynddewy's monthly output during the year varied between 3,926.25 and 8,856 tons. Pwllfaron at the top of the Vale of Neath contributed monthly totals varying from 415 tons to 4,272 tons.[225] The year did not start well for selling coal and the Main colliers had to accept a reduction of a penny a ton for cutting coal. In February 1868 the company was waiting for the Brynddewy colliers to accept a similar cut.[226]

In an effort to find more coal on their property old workings at Cwm Clydach were opened up. By March the partners received a report that the Stanley Colliery had been sunk to a depth of 44yds and that Robert Smith the contractor had withdrawn from the contract having insufficient money to complete the task.[227] The sinking of this colliery had been hampered when in January a heavy feeder of water had been encountered.[228] Water at this time was a problem also at Pwllfaron where the colliers had pierced some old workings and this had brought in water that the engine could not deal with. The problem was solved but production was hit.

By the end of February 1868 the partners' policy of intensive mining had resulted in large stocks of coal being built up at the collieries and wharves. The stock of culm was assessed at over 11,000 tons and this gave the partners some concern.[229] Spring brought an improvement in the company's position in May at a meeting held at Falmouth the partners agreed to a new lease of Pwllfaron.[230] Rufus Buckett, the company's agent was sent to Ireland to seek fresh orders and he returned with an order to supply a large spinning factory in Belfast.

During 1868 the rapid exploitation of the coal reserves on the Dyffryn Estate continued. In June there was a stock of 2,500 tons of coal at Brynddewy and between 2,000 and 3,000 tons at the wharves which forced the partners to reduce the working of the colliery.[231] The company continued to cultivate new sales in Cornwall which had always been an important market for Neath Abbey coal. A successful outcome of this policy was announced in June when the company was awarded a contract to supply the Clifford Amalgamated Mines at Devoran with a thousand tons of Main Colliery coal at 11s per ton.[232] This was at a time when the coal trade in Cornwall was described as dull although coal shipments were generally brisk. Work to open out the old Cwm

Clydach Colliery continued and in August men were sent in to explore the workings. Reports at this time came to the company from Cornwall that somebody had been spreading rumours that the lease of the Neath Abbey ground had been taken from the company and the partners had no coal to sell. To answer these damaging rumours Rufus Buckett was ordered to send circulars to their customers to deny these reports.[233]

During the latter half of 1868 the company continued to urgently extract coal from the Dyffryn Estate while looking for fresh reserves under the Neath Abbey and Longford Estates. In October a worker was killed at Cwm Clydach. Foul air had come up from the workings and put his light out. Instead of immediately coming to the surface until the pit cleared he sent a companion to get a fresh light, when the man returned with the light he found his colleague insensible and past recovery.[234]

Specimens of coal found in Cwm Clydach were thought to be good and exploration there continued. The slow progress of the Stanley Colliery continued to disappoint and in November the sinking was down to 98yds and was still in soft ground.[235]

Fresh orders were still being pursued and in October Charles Waring had attended the Ironmasters' Meeting at Birmingham and had tried to persuade several owners to use a proportion of anthracite coal in their furnaces. However, little success was achieved from this trip.[236]

In December the tenure of the coal company's reports show a great haste and impatience as the time of the loss of the Dyffryn lease approached. The company pinned its hopes on the reopening of the Cwm Clydach Colliery. The colliery was connected to the workings of the old Wernfraith Pit and W.H. Bell, the company's general manager was, requested to get a portable engine to open out this section. 'We have no time to spare,' is recorded in the reports, as Bell was encouraged to increase the efforts at Cwm Clydach.[237] However, problems were encountered in the old workings, in December there was a waterfall in the pit all month and large quantities of foul air had been drawn in although this was being reduced.

The development of the Cwm Clydach Colliery continued during 1869 and in November a new railroad had been completed from the pit and locomotives had been tested running over the rails.[238] That August the Neath Abbey Coal Company lost the Dyffryn Estate mineral lease. The collieries were taken over by a new partnership called the Dyffryn Main Colliery Company which included members of the Moore family. The managing partner was Bartholomew Parker Bidder. The Dyffryn Main Colliery Company and the New Dynevor Coal Company had Moore and Gwyn representatives on both boards and this produced close co-operation between the two companies. An agreement was immediately signed to sink the Joint Pit, 'for the joint benefit of the Neath Abbey and Dyffryn Estates until such pit or shaft shall strike the Graigola or five foot seam of coal'. The object of this venture was to help to drain this very wet mineral area. The New Dynevor Coal Company's main activities were concentrated at Brithdir Colliery and at the Court Herbert Level. In February 1870 the New Dynevor Coal Company took out a fresh lease of Neath Abbey mineral ground for fifty-five years at a sleeping rent of £2,958. This lease bound the company to complete a pit at Maesmelin by 9 September 1870 and to sink a new pit near the Court

Herbert Drift to meet the Graigola seam.[239] These activities seem to have over-stretched the resources of the company and at least two new sums of money had to be gathered through mortgages.[240] By 1873 it was obvious that the New Dynevor Coal Company was financially struggling.

The Neath Abbey Coal Company was also facing huge problems during this period in winning enough coal to supply its customers. The loss of the Dyffryn lease had severely curtailed the company's operations. In addition the sinking of the Stanley Colliery had produced little workable coal and the company were now relying on the successful development of the Cwm Clydach Colliery. In January 1870 the company's workers were busy erecting engines at Cwm Clydach but at the end of the month the miners struck into old workings and this brought a considerable amount of water into the pit.[241] Work continued and preparations were being made to win coal from Cwm Clydach from the beginning of March. It was at this point that W.H. Bell, the general manager, was dismissed and replaced by John Graham.[242] The Neath Abbey Coal Company continued to search for new reserves with some coal being obtained from the Skewen Level and Tir Edmond Colliery. In early March Cwm Clydach Colliery was producing between 113 and 170 tons of coal each day and during the year output reached up to 1,500 a week. Output of coal each week from the Skewen Level varied between 225 and 489 tons during 1870. The July labour figures for 1870 shows how more expensive it was to win coal on the Neath Abbey and Stanley Estates compared with the Dyffryn Estate. The company was working at this time Cwm Clydach Colliery and the Skewen Level and the figures were:

	per wey this month	per wey last month
Cwm Clydach		
cost to surface	24s 8d	22s 7$\frac{1}{2}$d
mechanics' wages	2s 2$\frac{1}{2}$d	1s 9d
labour & locomotive	3s 6d	2s 10$\frac{1}{2}$d
TOTAL	30s 4$\frac{1}{2}$d	27s 3$\frac{1}{2}$d
Skewen Level		
cost to surface	16s 2d	16s 1$\frac{1}{2}$d
labour & loco	3s 6d	2s 10$\frac{1}{2}$d
TOTAL	19s 8d	19s 0$\frac{1}{2}$d [243]

Most of the company's efforts were now targeted at Cwm Clydach. Transportation was improved around the pit in the Spring of 1870 with a new railway. In April it was thought that an improved railway would mean Cwm Clydach could produce over 300 tons of coal each day.[244] This increase was difficult to achieve because the old headings at Cwm Clydach Colliery were narrow and awkward for the hauliers. Although the new railway had been built to and around the pit, there were problems with the company's locomotives which were not up to this work. It was recorded that the old locomotives *Stag* and *Dyffryn* were not suitable for the Cwm Clydach work because '…they are far from being suitable for working upon gradients that we now have as they have too little boiler room and are as well too light'.[245] The company then decided to order a new locomotive from the Neath Abbey Iron Company. This 0-6-0 locomotive was built to a gauge of 2ft 8in with 8½in x 16in cylinders. It was delivered in the following year at a cost of £550.

It was at this time that Howel Gwyn brought an action against the Neath Abbey Coal Company for dilapidation and breach of covenant whilst working the Dyffryn Estate Minerals. This was an annoying diversion for the company as the partners struggled to find and exploit fresh reserves of coal on their property. In September 1870 the reports record that, 'We shall have no difficulty in selling in Cornwall any quantity of coal we can raise'.[246] But this statement can be compared with one in the August reports which dolefully records, 'Our great want is of free coal.'[247] Further explorations for coal were taking place and the company reserved between £400 and £500 for work in uncovering the Maesmelin seam. Towards the end of the year output at Cwm Clydach was held back by influxes of water and the building of an underground railway. The year closed with the Neath Abbey Coal Company starting to sink a borehole at Coedffranc. The sinking of this borehole continued during the early months of 1871 and soon it had nearly reached the Hughes seam. The workings from Cwm Clydach were then being extended to try to connect with the company's headings from the Main Colliery which entered the Neath Abbey Estate.

Cwm Clydach Colliery seems to have been intensively developed for at times during the summer over 2,000 tons of coal was being raised each week from this pit. However, valuable time and effort had to be used by the partners in fighting Howel Gwyn's action. His claim was for £50,000 which included £20,000 for wayleave in bringing Neath Abbey Estate coal through the Dyffryn Main Colliery. As an answer the Neath Abbey Coal Company filed a bill against Howel Gwyn in the Rolls Court.

Further disappointment was reported in March when the Tir Edmond output was described in the following terms, 'Tir Edmond coal is not good quality and gives off gas. This coal in the above estate in my opinion if shipped for any purpose whatever will produce serious damage to our trade.'[248] More explorations for coal by the company included a slant driven at Greenway to reach the Greenway seam which was recorded as very good coal with a 3ft 6in thickness. This new level was to be used to replace the output of the Skewen and Tir Edmond levels.

The major focus of the company's operations continued to be at Cwm Clydach where ninety men were cutting coal in April. The new locomotive manufactured by the Neath Abbey Iron Company arrived in May and could haul 300 tons of coal each day, double the load of the old machines.[249] A further setback occurred in June with the death of Evan Owen. He was the Neath Abbey Coal Company's coal shipper at Briton Ferry and had served the partners for thirty-three years. It was recorded that, 'from his knowledge of the shipping business and energy of character his loss will be much felt by us'.[250]

The following month saw permission granted for the company to build a tramroad from the Skewen office to Maesmelin and Drymma. Later the company was asked to provide a set of gates where the tramroad crossed the Skewed road and this area was known as White Gates as late as the 1970s. This was a part of the general development of this western part of the company's mineral ground shown by instructions to John Graham to purchase winding engines for the Greenway Colliery. These were bought second hand at Longton, Stoke-on-Trent. They were a pair of 22in x 4ft engines made by Parkinson of Bolton.[251] The Greenway and Cwm Clydach Collieries were providing enough coal for the partners to record that, 'the output of the collieries is now more than up to our present trade'. This good news was balanced by information from Cornwall where the Falmouth partners wanted to retire altogether from the company when some of the leases expired.[252] The year closed with the company subscribing £25 towards building a local cottage hospital as a smallpox epidemic took hold in the district.[253]

Although the company's efforts to secure enough coal for their contracts were successful in 1871 and 1872, problems still persisted. In January 1873 Graham described the activities at Cwm Clydach in the following terms: 'We are working a colliery under the greatest disadvantage that could exist, viz that of producing coal from an old colliery which had previously been considered worked out'.[254]

Additional ventilation was achieved at Cwm Clydach by using a furnace but during 1873 production dropped to below 1,000 tons per week. In April the company began to discuss what would happen in eleven months time on the expiration of their Neath Abbey leases. Their experiences of working this mineral ground must not have encouraged the partners in thinking about negotiating for further leases. The problems associated with this mineral ground are vividly illustrated by what was taking place at the Greenway Colliery workings on the Stanley Estate. The difficulties were summed up in one of the weekly reports:

> *In this estate the Greenway seam has been opened by means of a slope driven from the crop on the rise of the seam near to the western boundary of the property and an engine and other buildings erected on the company's freehold, but as we afterwards found out that the seam had been tampered with by workings made without any record or plan to show their existence.[255]*

The partners were disappointed in not being able to increase production at the Greenway Colliery and resorted to working a double shift at Cwm Clydach.[256] However, output at Cwm Clydach was disrupted when a man who was put down the pit was discovered not to be a collier and the workers went on strike.

The difficulties of winning enough coal from the company's property must have taken its toll on the managers, particularly Graham, the general manager. He resigned in June to take up a position with the Mid Cannock Coal Company and was replaced by Herbert Kirkhouse.[257] By 19 July the benefits of working intensively the Cwm Clydach Colliery had not been proved and the night turn was abandoned. A drift at Bath Pit was also opened in May but this proved a failure and was closed down in August.

For the last quarter of 1873 coal production at Cwm Clydach varied from 1,219 to 1,639 tons per week with the Greenway Colliery producing from 242 tons to 349 tons per week. During the year the long running dispute with Howel Gwyn was settled with Gwyn withdrawing his writ. One result of this was that the company had to pay a substantial legal bill for fighting the action.

A further blow to the company was the death in November of Isaac Redwood the principal shareholder. This was followed in the next year by the death of Alfred Fox the most experienced businessman amongst the Falmouth partners.

The death of Redwood, the wishes of the Falmouth partners to retire from their Welsh companies and the expiration of the Neath Abbey leases in 1874 prompted the Neath Abbey Coal Company to close down their operations and sell the assets. The company had made profits even after the loss of the Dyffryn lease, as the early 1870s were a period of rising prices and great demand for coal. Indeed, in 1872 the company made a profit of £8,460 but time would have brought a great reduction to profits as coal would have progressively been more difficult to find on their reduced holding. Pressure had been mounting from the three mineral estates along the Clydach valley to have one operating company to exploit the resources. This idea was certainly forthcoming from the Moore/Gwyn faction but the other landlords were also unhappy concerning the situation. Workings from one mineral estate had moved into another estate and this had caused difficulties over assessing the amount of coal taken from the differing estates. It had also caused problems concerning the charges made for bringing up coal from one estate through a pit built on another estate. These wayleave payments had been difficult to police and resulted in part of Howel Gwyn's writ against the Neath Abbey Coal Company.

Problems also existed when a coal company pierced the boundary between estates bringing in water from one mineral area into another. In 1870 the Neath Abbey Coal Company was repeatedly warned not to extend the headings at Cwm Clydach through the Cwmfelin fault which would have brought water from the Stanley Estate into the Neath Abbey Estate.

The Neath Abbey Coal Company's property was sold to Bidder & Co. better known as the Dyffryn Main Colliery Co. When the assets of the Neath Abbey Coal Co. were realised the partners received £56,312 19s 3d, later increased by £8,000 although £3,882 7s 3d was deducted as the cost of the Gwyn legal action. The partners hoped to recoup these costs from Gwyn but this was not subsequently the case.[258] Other assets not wanted by the Dyffryn Main Colliery Company were disposed of in 1875. These included the valuable Glanbrane Estate and the Pwllfaron Colliery.

The Dyffryn Main Colliery Company and the New Dynevor Coal Company were both controlled by members of the Moore family and a new company to operate both undertakings was floated. This was the Dynevor, Dyffryn and Neath Abbey United Collieries Company Limited. The new company was to have a capital of £25,000 divided into 10,000 shares each with a value of £25.[259] Although the company was successfully formed it seems likely that not all the shares were taken up. The new company took over many and varied assets including the lease of the Mines Royal Copper Works and three steamships, *Cid*, *Eagle* and *Pioneer*.

So, the mineral resources of the Clydach valley had at last come under the control of a single company. However, problems existed for the new company from the outset of the merger. To achieve the merger all the assets of the Neath Abbey Coal Company and New Dynevor Coal Company were taken into the new company. This included several pits which were exhausted and a few which had been complete failures like the Stanley and Bath Collieries of the Neath Abbey Coal Company. The last account sheet of the Dyffryn Main Colliery Co. Ltd shows that for the four months ending 30 June 1874 the Neath Abbey collieries had been run at a loss of £623 15s 1d. In the sixteen months ending 30 June 1874 the Dyffryn collieries had made a profit of £11,373 8s 6d. The Neath Abbey and Dyffryn Collieries were then sold to the new company for £190,500.[260]

The new company had to start operations at a serious disadvantage and several collieries had to be closed down. During the period 1874-1881 the united company operated the following collieries, Brithdir (1874-1881), West Brithdir (1876-1881), Brynddewy (1874-1881), Dyffryn Main (1974-1881), Fire Engine (1874-1876), Greenway (1874), Cwmddu (1875-1881), Tyr Edmond (1875) and Court Herbert (1879-81). The official new company name was named the Dynevor, Dyffryn and Neath Abbey United Collieries Company Limited, however, official statistics for the period show how little corporate identity existed within the organisation. Individual colliery managers sent in details of their pits to the government using a baffling number of titles. The collieries of the company were listed as being owned by the Dynevor Coal Co., the Dynevor, Dyffryn and Neath Abbey United Collieries Co. (Ltd) and the Dyffryn Main and Neath Abbey United Collieries Co.(Ltd).[261]

The new company continued to exploit the markets cultivated by the Neath Abbey coal owners during the nineteenth century the most important being France, Cornwall, Ireland and the local copper and iron industries. However, the company was soon in financial trouble and in January 1880 an agreement was reached with the Neath Abbey Estate over rent arrears.[262] In the previous year the company had lost its steamer *Eagle* when it sank twenty-five miles north of Bishop Rock and by this time the other two steamships had been sold off.

Problems continued during the 1880s. In December 1884 shipments of the company's coal were seized to pay outstanding bills. It is no wonder that the company failed in 1889 and it seemed that the story of coal winning along the Clydach valley had come to an end. Although the united company was making profits, a large share capital had to be serviced. The company had been handicapped by the large amounts of disused plant and redundant pits they had been forced to take over in unifying the mineral ground under one company. An optimistic forecast of profits had also led the company to take on leases under difficult terms. When the company collapsed it appeared that coal mining in the area could not pay its way.

However, one of the liquidators recognised that coal mining in the Neath Abbey area was still commercially viable and a new company was formed to take the industry well into the twentieth century.

8

The Main Colliery Company

The Dynevor, Dyffryn and Neath Abbey United Collieries Company Ltd was liquidated in the spring and summer of 1889 by Francis Pavy and Lord Claud John Hamilton. It was Pavy, chairman of the Railways Share Trust & Agency Company Ltd of London who had enough foresight to see that mining in the Clydach valley was still feasible given the correct leases and financial backing.

Soon an agreement was reached between the defunct company, the mineral landlords and the new undertaking called the Main Colliery Company Ltd. Pavy was a director of the new company and he managed to attract a varied and experienced group of men to join him in the enterprise. The other directors were James Inskip of Bristol, chairman of the Taff Vale Railway Company, John Cady JP of Swansea, a director of the Glamorganshire Banking Company Ltd, John Crow Richardson JP of Swansea, Henry B.O. Savile JP of Bristol, Chairman of the South Wales Railway Wagon Co. Ltd, and William Hole Williams, chairman of the Lewis Merthyr Navigation Colliery Company Ltd.

The capital of the new company was set at £100,000 divided into £10 shares. The new company believed that it would hold 1,000 acres of unworked coal and 150 acres of freehold minerals of which 40 acres were untouched. The Main Colliery Company was able to attract shareholders by informing them that the collieries had been supplying between 50,000 and 60,000 tons of coal each year to just one customer, namely to the local smelting works of the Cape Copper Company, and also that they had persuaded the estate owners to alter the terms of their previous mineral leases. The colliery property of the previous company had been purchased at a cost of £63,000 plus some legal costs and they made profits of £10,000 in the last twelve months of its existence. In 1883 these collieries had been valued at £64,275 and within three months a new valuation of £68,819 had been obtained.[263]

The prospectus seems to have attracted enough interested investors for a successful launch of the Main Colliery Company Limited. James Inskip was appointed chairman with the company's offices being situated in Bristol where it was to be firmly rooted for the whole of its existence. During 1889 meetings were held in London, Cardiff, Bristol and Neath Abbey as policies for the new company were formulated and John Newall Moore was appointed as commercial manager in charge of sales at Neath Abbey.

The progress of the company can be easily charted through the preservation of a huge body of the company's records. These unique records cover every aspect of the company's operations but particularly important are the minutes of the general meetings, the minute book of the directors and the annual reports and statement of accounts given each year on 30 June.[264] Using these documents the following detailed chronological account of the company has been built up:

30 September 1889

Dyffryn rent arrears settled at £3,000, Neath Abbey estate arrears at £10,500.

Mr Moore was authorised to enter into a new contract with the Cape Copper Company for the supply of coal.

29 October 1889

Mr Rees was authorised to improve the ventilation of Brithdir Colliery; he was also authorised to accept the tender of £198 for a new boiler and fire box for the locomotive *Dynevor.*

13 November 1889

Mr Thomas Evans was appointed as manager in place of Mr William Thomas Rees from 1 December at a salary of £420 per annum.

Three new boilers were needed for Main Colliery. Mr Evans was offered three second hand Lancashire boilers.

It was resolved to give a truck of coal to Swansea Hospital and also to subscribe three guineas to Swansea Hospital and two guineas to Porthcawl Rest.

18 December 1889

An increase in yearly salaries has was agreed:

	from	to
J.F. Williams, shipping clerk	£150	£175
William Richards, bookkeeper	£120	£150
F.G. Lloyd, invoice and pay clerk	£84	£120
John Cole, Skewen shops	£64	£90
Ernest Grant, shorthand clerk	£130	£150

It was resolved that arrangements be made for the sale of the company's wagons to the Bristol & South Wales Wagon Company with a view to them being let to the company on the hire purchase system, the rate of interest not to exceed 6%.

15 January 1890

It was reported that the company owned 536 iron trams of which fifty needed repair and a further 276 wooden trams. Tenders were invited for the supply of fifty additional trams. Tir Edmund Colliery to get a ventilating fan.

19 February 1890

J.N. Moore's report into chartering steamers was considered. It was decided to charter the *Marie Fleurie* for six fortnightly terms at a total cost of £1,000.

19 March 1890

A strike occurred of the hauliers at Court Herbert and Brithdir Collieries. It has been brought before the association and the company was supported. A meeting of the sliding scale was called by Sir W.J. Lewis to consider the matter.

Twenty trams were ordered from Jones of Neath and a further twenty subject to approval of the first batch.

The board was considering opening out the old Skewen pits at a cost of £4,500 or investing in a new 450yds deep sinking near the Main Colliery.

The Primrose Colliery was pumping water into the Main seam, and it was resolved that they should be prevented from doing this.

The SS *Marie Fleurie* was chartered for three months at £1,080.

A new contract was made with the Tharsis Company. The terms were 13s 6d per ton with a wages clause providing for an additional 3d a ton on every increase of $2\frac{1}{2}$% in wages.

23 April 1890

Contracts were expiring at Warrenpoint, Dublin, Penzance and Granville Mines.

For any quotations and fresh sales the company adopted a price of 10s 6d a ton fob Neath Abbey for thro coal. For large coal they were hoping for 13s 6d at Neath Abbey. The above prices for the Irish market were arrived at by 'consulting with our principal competitors, Vivian & Son'.

14 May 1890

Notice was given to the hauliers at Court Herbert, Brithdir and Tir Edmond.

11 June 1890

Mr Moore was authorised to renew the Cornish contracts but not to go below 10s 3d per ton without the chairman's sanction.

Sir William Thomas Llewis met the board and the position of the proposed new pit was fully discussed and reports from Mr Evans for various schemes considered.

It was probable that the Joint Pumping Pit would be sunk as a ventilating shaft.

Boilers for the locomotives *Abercarne* and *Queen* were to be purchased.

Repairs were needed on the old pumping engine at the Main Colliery.

30 June 1890 Annual Report

At the outset the collieries were purchased for £63,000, with initial expenses of £1,524 14s 8d.

The output of coal for the year was 267,099 tons and net profits £16,623 5s 11d.

The original issue of the shares was limited to 5,250 but now 2,625 new shares were issued bringing the subscribed capital to £78,750.

23 July 1890

It was ordered that a steamer was to be chartered.

The following estimates were calculated:

sinking the Joint Pit from the Main seam to the Graigola seam, a total of 260yds making a total depth of 410yds, plus boilers and engines	*£24,934*
sinking a pit for ventilation only	*£12,400*
sinking a new pit near Main Colliery	*£32,110*
railway from joint pit to Court Herbert Yard	*£4,750*

13 August 1890

It was resolved to increase the commission payable to Mr Thomas Smith at Warrenpoint from 2d to 3d per ton.

Mr Moore was authorised to charter the SS *Marie Fleurie* for one year at £330 per month as recommended by him.

17 September 1890

The company was authorised to seek tenders for new plant at Main and Joint Pumping Pits.

15 October 1890

Directors discussed and signed a lease for Tennant Minerals, with a dead rent of £200, a royalty of $5\frac{1}{2}$d and wayleave at 1d per ton.

12 November 1890

£20 was contributed to Cadoxton schools.

There was stock in hand despite stoppages at some of the collieries.

The directors were anxious to increase the areas of sales.

17 December 1890

The company considered altering the gauge of the tramway.

28 January 1891

It was agreed to purchase a lathe, steam hammer and planning machine for the Skewen shops at a cost of £290.

18 February 1891

The contract with the Cape Copper Company continues.

It was agreed that the gauge of the company's tramroads was to be altered.

Thirty-five trams are purchased from Davis Brothers at £7 17s 6d each.

Estimates were calculated for work at the new pits:

> *No.1 Main to be 18ft diameter, 460 yards deep and will cost £33,541.*
>
> *The Joint Pumping Pit to be deepened to become No.2 Main, 16ft diameter and to go down a further 260 yards at a cost of £14,678.*
>
> *This will give a total of £48,219 to which can be added £1,094 for increase in labour charges. This work should be completed in two years.*

18 March 1891

It was decided to quote 14s 6d per ton for the Tharsis Company subject to a rise and fall in wages.

22 April 1891

The board urged Moore to dispose of more coal and find additional customers.

Mr Moore reported that 5,000 tons of coal had been sold to the Tharsis Company at a price of 14s per ton and the board authorised him to accept 13s 6d if the price would secure an order for an additional 5,000 tons.

Mr Evans was authorised to accept Harvey & Co.'s tender of £1,445 for a pumping engine for the new sinking.

13 May 1891

The board considered working the Victoria seam.

The SS *Marie Fleurie* was chartered for a year from 1 July at £320 per month.

12 June 1891

Moore was told to accept 9s per ton for mining coal and 10s for Main Colliery coal.

The company had increased stocks of coal on their hands, standing at 9,411 tons on 23 May.

The SS *Marie Fleurie's* charter was to run from 14 August at £320 per month.

30 June 1891 Annual Report

The output of coal for the year was 250,596 tons and the net profit was £20,290.

22 July 1891

John Crow Richardson resigns from the board but it was hoped that he would return to it one day.

Cornwall coal was sold at 8s 6d for mining coal and 9s 6d for Main coal.

Moore had sold coal at prices equal to 8s 6d and 8s $7\frac{1}{2}$d per ton for France and was instructed not to accept French orders below the average of 8s 6d per ton.

The board urges Moore to secure fresh customers in new markets.

The Cape Copper Company contract coal was sold at 12s for large coal, 8s for furnace coal, 9s for thro and bituminous coal and 10s 6d for coal supplied to workmen.

Mr Evans authorised to purchase the hauling plant offered by the Uskside Engineering Company for the Waunceirch Drift, the price not to exceed £350.

4 August 1891

A second ship was chartered, the SS *Harley* at £290 per month.

Preparations were made to work coal under the Tennant Estate.

The closure of Brithdir Colliery was considered.

Moore was told to attend to the large stock of unsold coal and the loss caused by deterioration.

14 October 1891

Moore urged to open up every available market.

25 November 1891

The results of working the Dyffryn Main Colliery were carefully considered with reference to the necessity of either continuing the working or pumping the water for the protection of the new sinking. It was determined to give notice to the workmen at the colliery on 31 December.

Mr Evans reported that the new pit was completed to a depth of 86 yards.

Moore was authorised to charter the SS *Henry Fisher* at £320 per month until the end of January.

23 December 1891

It was resolved to experiment by raising only 120 tons of coal per day from Main.

Moore was urged to take immediate steps to dispose of large stocks of coal lying on the wharf.

20 January 1892

It was decided to renew the Cape Copper Works' contract at the following prices, being a reduction in the prices paid per ton in December:

furnace coal	7s 6d
bituminous	8s 6d
thro steam	8s 6d
workmen's coal	10s
large coal	11s 6d

These prices were not to be subject to a sliding scale.

A strike of hauliers had kept the collieries idle since 31 December; the Colliery Owners' Association supported the company in the dispute.

10 February 1892

The strike of the hauliers ended on 27 January.

The charter of the SS *Henry Fisher* was reduced by £20 per month.

Workmen were given notice for 1 March at Brithdir because of its imminent closure.

16 March 1892

It was decided to continue Brithdir for another month.

No.1 Main was sunk to 185yds. It was hoped coal would be struck in December.

Pumping at Main Colliery cost £340 per month and it was advised to stop this colliery but pumping had to continue on account of the new sinking.

13 April 1892

Moore was authorised to quote 11s 6d a ton for the Tharsis contract in the hope of securing the full quantity of 15,000 tons.

Some salaries increased, J.N. Moore's wages rose from £250 to £275 per annum.

xxxviii

THE . . .
Main Colliery Company
LIMITED,
NEATH, SOUTH WALES.

PROPRIETORS OF
DYNEVOR DYFFRYN WELSH
SMOKELESS STEAM COAL.

LARGELY USED IN LONDON BY CONSUMERS OF BEST SMOKELESS STEAM COAL.

Also extensively used for Electricity Generating Purposes in England, Ireland, and France, and for all classes of Mill and Factory work, for Breweries, Paper Works, Copper Works, and Tin Smelting and for General Steam-Raising Requirements.

HIGHLY DURABLE, CLEAN, AND ECONOMICAL.

Supplied to **The Peninsular and Oriental Steam Navigation Co.** and various other large Liners, and for General Bunkering Purposes, for which it is specially recommended.

A Stock of Bunker Coal is always ready at Dublin, Belfast, Cork, and Rouen.

Also Proprietors of **Hughes Vein Dry Coal,** extensively used on the Continent for house purposes and for the manufacture of Patent Fuel.

SHIPPING PORTS.

HEAD OFFICE.	POSTAL ADDRESS.	TELEGRAPHIC ADDRESS.
NEATH	Main Colliery Co., Ltd.	" Main," Skewen.

AGENCIES.

CARDIFF	Fifoot, Ching & Co., The Exchange.	" Footing."
SWANSEA	J. R. Davies & Co., Albion Chambers.	" Dynevor."
PORT TALBOT	Main Colliery Co., Ltd., Neath.	" Main," Skewen.

FOREIGN AGENCIES.

TROUVILLE & HONFLEUR	G. Lecourt, 42, Rue d'Orbec, Lisieux.	"Lecourt, Char-bons," Lisieux.
HAVRE and FECAMP	Auger Freres, 44, Rue Jacques Fauquet, Bolbec.	" Auger Freres," Bolbec.
DIEPPE	Thoumyre Fils.	" Thoumyre," Dieppe.

IRISH AGENCIES.

BELFAST	McElroy & Son, Granville Buildings, 43a, High St.	" Bunkers."
DUBLIN	Flower & McDonald, 14, D'Olier Street.	" Donald," Dublin.
CORK	J. H. Rutter & Co., 91, South Mall.	" Rutter."

LIVERPOOL.

LIVERPOOL	R. W. Hall & Co., 49, Oriel Road, Bootle.

A 1914 advert describing the products of the Main Colliery Company.

A 1910 view of the pumping engine house at Main No.6. This house and the inverted beam Cornish engine was erected in 1855 for the Neath Abbey Coal Company.

15 June 1892
There was an explosion at Brithdir, one man injured.

30 June 1892 Annual Report
The output of coal for the year was 239,794 tons and the net profit was £10,220.

30 July 1892
Two second-hand Lancashire boilers were purchased for the Brithdir Colliery.
The SS *Count* was chartered for £270 per month for one year.
Forest Goch Pit was leased to William Daniel Thomas and Daniel Thomas of Alltwen for a royalty of 10d per ton and a dead rent of £120.

21 September 1892
No.1 Pit was sunk to 309yds from the surface and No.2 Pit 66yds below the Main Colliery seam. Expenditure on this project stands at £3,000 to date.
It was decided to donate 20 guineas to the Park Slip Colliery Fund.

19 October 1892

Sales of coal had to be increased.

Company solicitors wrote to the Bryncoch Colliery Company with regard to arrears of royalties.

The board approved of the proceedings taken by Mr Evans against hauliers and others for refusing to work at Court Herbert and thus stopping the colliery.

23 November 1892

Two men were killed at Brithdir Colliery on 20 July.

A telegram was sent to Fisher, Renwick & Co. offering to continue the charter of *Henry Fisher* from 1 November for four months at £265 per month, if this was declined the owners' terms of £290 would be accepted.

150 tons of steel rails were purchased.

15 December 1892

A serious loss of £1,416 was made on chartering steamers for the year ending 30 June.

Sales to Devon firms quoted at 6s 3d per ton fob Neath Abbey.

11 January 1893

Death of Mr Hopkins, the resident manager. The board decided to donate £80 to his wife and allow her to occupy the company's house as long as 'can be conveniently arranged' and provide her with coal.

The chairman arranged a reduction in royalties of 2d a ton on the Glanbrane property and at the Main Colliery a reduction from 4d to 3d per ton.

15 February 1893

The Graigola seam was struck at No.1 Pit on 28 January. No.2 Pit would have to sink a further 70yds which would take six months.

A Capell ventilating fan was purchased from the Bowling Iron Company for £1,490. An office in Rouen was opened. Mr Edward Coots was to represent the company there at a salary of £160 a year.

14 June 1893

Moore was authorised to sell in Cornwall at the best prices he could obtain.

30 June 1893 Annual Report

The output of coal for the year was 266,126 tons and the net profit made was £3,152.

The chairman commented that a large part of the company's capital was unproductive because the expense of sinkings. This fact, and the state of the coal trade in general, meant that the company's operations were not satisfactory.

19 July 1893

The minutes reported that:

> With regards to the order secured by Messrs Harvey and Messrs Bain for 20,000 tons of this company's mining coal for the Carn Brea and Tincroft Mines, the contract terms will leave the company with 5s 7$\frac{1}{2}$d per ton net.
>
> Mr Moore reported that Messrs Radford had contracted to supply 10,000 tons to these mines and he thought he might be able to secure an order for 5,000 tons from them. The matter was left in his hands with the understanding that he would endeavour to obtain 5s 9d per ton and not accept less than 5s 7$\frac{1}{2}$d per ton.

The gauge of the tramway at Brithdir was to be altered from 4ft 4in to 2ft 7$\frac{1}{2}$in so as to have a uniform gauge at all the collieries.

20 September 1893

There was a burst pipe in the new pit with a large pump. Harveys was deemed liable.

10 October 1893

Mr Evans informed the board that in about a month he expected the output from the new pit to increase to 100 tons a day.

15 November 1893

The board approved a new furnace and airway for improving the ventilation of Tir Edmond Colliery.

13 December 1893

The Victoria seam at Court Herbert was to be reopened.

Moore was to quote the following prices for coal to local works for the three months ending 31 March 1894:

furnace coal	7s 9d per ton
binding coal	9s 3d per ton
steam coal	9s 3d per ton
house coal	11s 9d per ton
large coal	13s per ton.

The board approved the following letter that was sent to Mr J.N. Moore from the chairman on 11 December:

> I am sorry to write this letter which may probably cause regret or even pain to you, but a review of all the circumstances leaves me no alternative and I hope you will take the matter into your calm and careful consideration.
>
> It appears that in July and August last you entered into contracts binding the company to a greater extent than was known to the Board or myself. For instance at our August meeting you reported a margin of 10,000 tons per month for sale at current prices – I have no doubt that you fully believed this estimate when you gave it to us, but the discrepancy

between the estimate and the facts is such as to show a want of watchfulness in making contracts and in reporting to the board.

My view, repeatedly passed on to you is that there ought to be contracts for a quantity representing from one half to two thirds of the output, with a free hand for the sale of the remaining part thereof. Further when you were authorised to sell 5,000 tons to Messrs Radford at a certain price you sold 24,000 tons and accepted a condition empowering the buyers at their option to obtain a considerable portion of that quantity at more than 6d per ton below the authorised price. Contracts were also made in France and an estimate of net results was submitted to the board which appears to have been based on inaccurate data concerning freights and other expenses. You also gave some of the Cornish buyers an option of increasing the quantities to be taken by them at low prices, which of course they exercised when the markets turned in their favour. This is a case of 'heads I win, tails you loose' [sic]. Finally upon this point, you appear to have made a contract as late as the 29th August when prices were very high, at a low figure having regard to the circumstances then existing, and you have also made a contract to run over two years forward, which in my judgement is imprudent when low prices are prevailing. In connection with the subject of contracts, I do not like our continental business as now conducted. We seem to be entirely in the hands of parties on the continent, and to have all the disadvantages of forward contracts when the markets are in favour of buyers, with some of the disadvantages of consignments when the markets are against buyers. Altogether there is a hybrid character to these transactions, with an element of uncertainty which ought to be removed.

The letter went on to state that the company was not gaining enough spot sales and wondered if the sales department needed to be managed from Swansea.

10 January 1894
Moore was authorised to sell large coal fob Swansea over the year at 12s 3d per ton.
The company was discussing entering the bunker trade.

14 February 1894
The SS *Henry Fisher* ran aground and the company claimed from the ship owners for the jettisoned coal.
The board urged better terms for sales particularly for the continent.

14 March 1894
It was decided to close the old Main Colliery, provided that, after consulting with Mr Moore, sufficient smelting coal can be worked at Waunceirch to enable the Main Colliery to be dispensed with.

18 April 1894
With regards to contracts for the coming year, Mr Moore was authorised to quote on the basis of 7s 3d per ton fob for natural thro coal and he was not to accept less without consulting the chairman.

The winding engines at No.1 Main Colliery, D. Evans winding man.

19 May 1894

It was proposed to close down Brithdir Colliery which would mean discontinuing the working of Glanbrane coal through this colliery.

A tender of £3,000 was accepted from Harvey & Co. for winding engines for the new pit.

Mr Moore was authorised to quote the following to the West India & Pacific Steam Ship Company:

> 8s 1½d for 10,000 tons over twelve months to 30 June 1895.
> 8s for 5,000 tons over six months to 31 December 1894.
> 8s 3d for 5,000 tons over six months to 30 June 1895.

He was also authorised to sell natural thro coal to Cornwall or Ireland at 7s per ton fob wharf or in truck and France at 7s 3d.

30 June 1894 Annual Report

The output of coal for the year was 301,473 tons and a profit of £6,241 was made.

Coal was now coming on the market from the new pits at a rate of 500 tons a day.

The operations of the company were halted for a month because of a strike by the hauliers.

18 July 1894

The board approved the proposal to start a branch of the Miner's Provident Fund and agreed to subscribe at the usual rate of 3d for each shilling contributed by the men of the company.

1 August 1894
Harvey's winding engines were to be paid for in three instalments.

26 September 1894
The charter of the SS *Henry Fisher* was not to be renewed unless the owners considerably reduced the hire cost of £290 per month.

21 November 1894
Complaints were made about the quality of the bunker coal supplied by the company. It was stated that copper coal should not be sent out with this coal.
The SS *Henry Fisher* chartered at £270 a month.

12 December 1894
The complaints about bunker coal continued to come in. It was decided that coal from the new pit should be supplied without any admixture of Tir Edmund coal.
A contract for 20,000 tons of bunker coal for Swansea had been won at 8s per ton over the year.

9 January 1895
Workmen at the Skewen shops asked for a reduction in working hours from ten to nine.

13 March 1895
Natural thro coal from the new pit was giving great satisfaction as bunkering coal.

15 May 1895
Discussions took place over the working of the Brithdir and Tir Edmund Collieries.

12 June 1895
The chartering of the SS *Henry Fisher* and the SS *Count* was approved at £263 15s and £250 per month respectively.

30 June 1895 Annual Report
The output of coal for the year was 315,542 tons with a profit made of £6,213.
It was noted that the coal trade was depressed and it was good that under these conditions the company could work at a profit.

24 July 1895
J.N. Moore was paid $2\frac{1}{2}$% of profits as commission.

14 August 1895
Sir W.T. Lewis recommended the closing of the Brithdir Colliery.

9 November 1895
A report on the company's collieries was received from Henry T. Wales:

The mineral taking at this time comprised 3,800 acres. The three principal seams in this part of the coalfield are the Wernfraith, the Graigola and the Hughes'. The company is working the Brithdir Drift, the Tir Edmond Level, the Court Herbert Colliery, the New Main Colliery and the Waunceirch Slant. Hughes' seam not yet worked on the property although an adjoining colliery to the south of the property is working this seam success-fully.

Brithdir and Tir Edmond are working the seam known as the Brithdir or Four Feet Seam lying 24yds above the Graigola seam.

Brithdir Colliery

This consists of a drift which follows the Four Feet Seam for a distance of 1,500yds in a northerly direction at which point the boundary is met. There is only one district at work which lies to the west side of the main drift. Here there are twenty-five places working in a southerly direction and the daily output of coal amounts to 125 tons of which 35 tons are worked by a night shift. The Four Feet Seam at this colliery shows a section of coal varying from 3ft 10in up to 5ft 11in in thickness.

The coal is hard but there are several layers of stone running through it causing the seam to be dirty and it does not possess good reputation in the market. The coal contains a high percentage of sulphur and because of this the small coal is liable to spontaneous combustion.

The following is an average section of the Four Feet Seam taken in this district:

	Feet	Inches
Roof, grey stone		
Little stone		10
Coal		$8\frac{1}{2}$
Shale		
Coal	2	0
Smooth		
Coal	2	6

The area of coal remaining in front of the present workings consists of eight acres only. The roads were very narrow and low because little attention had been given to the colliery because at any time it was thought the working could be discontinued. The working cost is excessively high owing to the small output and the great lengths of roads requiring to be maintained to reach the present working. The cost of haulage, both underground and on the surface, is also enormously high.

It was recommended that the colliery should be closed at once.
  The report continued:

Tir Edmond Colliery

The same seam is worked here as at Brithdir with a daily output of 200 tons. Here, the Four Feet Seam is sub-divided by a larger number of layers of shale than at Brithdir and the quality of coal is no better than at Brithdir. The area remaining to be worked is sufficient to maintain the present output of coal for another four years.

The working cost is not excessive but, having regard to the undoubtedly inferior quality of coal, and also to the way in which the output of the New Main Colliery is interfered with by the traffic of this colliery, it is recommended that this colliery closes at the end of the year.

Court Herbert Colliery

This colliery is situated on the lower side of the Dyffryn Fault and works the Victoria and Graigola Seams. There are two pits sunk to the Graigola Seam which is met with at a depth of 142yds. These are equipped with proper winding, pumping and ventilating appliance. The daily output of this colliery is 400 tons, of which 50 tons are obtained from the Victoria Seam and 350 tons from the Graigola Seam. The Victoria Seam is identical with the Four Feet Seam at Brithdir and Tir Edmond, but it is not so much split up and the analysis indicates a better quality coal.

The following is the average section of the Four Feet Seam at this colliery:

	Feet	Inches
Roof, shale		
Coal	2	2
Clod		11
Coal	2	0

The Graigola Seam is also worked here at a distance of a mile to the dip from the pits. The seam contains three beds of coal. The lowest, which is one foot thick, contains small bands of shale. This bed is worked and filled separately and is sold to copper works under the name of Copper Coal. The following is the average section of the Graigola Seam at this colliery:

	Feet	Inches
Roof, strong clift		
Coal	1	2
Rashings	1	4
Coal	2	4
Copper Coal	1	0

The working cost of the Court Herbert Colliery is practically the same as at New Main Colliery. The most northerly workings in the Graigola Seam at this colliery have communicated with the southernmost working from the New Main Colliery, and a line has been decided upon as the boundary between the two collieries. Under this arrangement the Court Herbert Colliery would last for another four or five years in the Graigola Seam.

Nos 3 and 4 Main in 1912.

New Main Colliery

This colliery consists of a pair of pits sunk to the Graigola Seam at a depth of 430yds. The winding shaft has been sunk from the surface and is of an 18ft diameter. The No 2 or upcast pit has been deepened from the Wernfraith seam, the diameter of the new portion of the shaft being 15ft. The Graigola seam is of good quality at this colliery and the measures are almost flat in every direction from the bottom of No.1 or winding pit. The roof above the seam is excellent and consists of hard rock with the yield of large coal being about one third. The average section of the seam is:

	Feet	Inches
Roof, rock		
Coal	*1*	*2*
Clod	*1*	*2*
Coal	*2*	*2*
Copper Coal	*1*	*0*

The method of working which has been adopted is a suitable one under the circumstances, large pillars being left so as to prevent damage to the coal from the pressure from above. The output of the colliery is at present 550 tons per day but sufficient headings have been driven in all directions from the pit to yield a considerably larger output than this. On the surface at this colliery the engine house has nearly been completed for the permanent winding engines which are ready to be delivered. A Cornish pumping engine has also been fixed on this shaft and deals with the water down to the Wernfraith Seam, a depth of 180yds from the surface.

At the No.2 Pit a Capell Fan with engine is now at work. The winding engine at No.2 Pit is engaged in drawing water from the Graigola seam by means of a tank and works continuously through twenty-four hours. The workings in the Graigola Seam have now reached a sufficient distance from the bottom of the pit to require the application of some system of mechanical haulage such as the endless rope system.

Water

The subject which calls for early attention is the method of dealing with the water at the Court Herbert and New Main Collieries. At present there are several pumps in use at both collieries, some worked by steam and others by compressed air and at the No.2 Main pit water is wound up by means of a tank. The cost of pumping and winding the water at these pits exceeds £4,000 per year. This is a heavy item and by expending about £5,000 on new pumping plant a saving of £2,000 a year might be effected. All the water should be collected at one shaft where modern pumping plant would deal with the problem.

Surface Haulage

At present coal from the collieries is conveyed to the tipping stages at the river wharf in the same trams which are used underground. There are six small locomotives in use for drawing the trams and the roads over which they pass are well laid and kept in good order. The output from the New Main and Tir Edmond Collieries is conveyed along a fairly level road for a distance of about two miles to the top of the Skewen Incline. The trams of coal are lowered down this incline which is self-acting and from the foot of the incline the trams are again drawn by means of small locomotives to the tipping places on the river wharf.

There are serious drawbacks to such a system as this. The coal is much broken in transit on account of the jolting and bumping together of the trams. Another very great objection is that the capacity of the system is limited to about 800 tons of coal per day and the cost of repairs to the trams is a heavy one. Upon the advice of your late engineer it was decided to convert the present tramway gauge into an ordinary railway gauge of 4ft 8½in. A considerable portion of this work has already been carried out both on the tramways and at the river wharf. The sleepers have been laid to suit the railway gauge and as the rails now in use on the tramways are heavy enough the only work remaining to be done is that of moving one rail so as to obtain the proper width. It is also part of this scheme to lower the railway wagons down the Skewen Incline by means of a stationary engine at the top of it. An engine which was already on the ground has been utilised for this purpose and is partly erected with the necessary boilers and chimney. The amount expended on this scheme already amounts to £15,000 and it is estimated that the further amount required to complete the scheme will be £16,000. When this scheme is completed the difficulties of dealing with a larger traffic than now exists will disappear and the New Main Colliery can be developed to its full capacity of about 7,000 tons of coal per week.

After the new system of haulage is completed, I do not anticipate that there will be a saving of more than 1d per ton in the actual cost of working, but there will be doubtless a considerable improvement in the condition of the coal, owing to the absence of the jarring which is inevitable under the present system.

Waunceirch Slant

It is unnecessary that I should make any lengthened remarks upon the Waunceirch Slant which is working out the old pillars left in the Wernfraith Seam. The output is 50 tons per day and the coal is of very good quality for house purposes. The colliery appears to be carried on at a moderate profit.

In conclusion I would express my opinion that, in your new Main winning there is the making of a fine and profitable colliery which should for many years to come be worked at a low cost.

After all the work necessary for the full development of this colliery has been completed and the cost of working placed upon a permanently low basis, it will be time to consider the advisability of working the Hughes' Seam, upon the western portion of your property, where the prospects are favourable for the establishment of a successful colliery to work these lower measures. [265]

13 November 1895
Brithdir was to be closed forthwith and Tir Edmond at the end of the year.

11 December 1895
H.T. Wales of Pontypridd elected as a director. He will take charge of engineering work at a rate of £400 a year.

12 February 1896
Sale of 8,000-10,000 tons of thro bunker coal at 7s fob Swansea.

15 April 1896
Problems arising with the owners of the chartered steamers over running aground and losses. Mr Wales paid the fee of £31 10s for the report on the collieries prior to becoming a director.

13 May 1896
Harvey's permanent winding engine completed.

10 June 1896
Moore authorised to charter the SS *Electra* at £250 per month in place of SS *Count*.

30 June 1896 Annual Report
The output of coal for the year was 283,624 tons and a profit of £670 was made. The managers have found great difficulty in working at a profit.

The Main Colliery Company's shipping wharves photographed in 1909 when they stretched for 1,500ft.

22 July 1896
New pumping plant to be built at No.2 Pit. A higher tender accepted but it should not cost more than £3,000 and the annual saving would be £1,700.

6 August 1896
Explosion at new pit with loss of life.
New pumping plant to be manufactured by Messrs Simpson & Co.

30 September 1896
Mr Lemoine to take charge of the Rouen agency at a commission of fifty centimes per ton. The winding engines are still at Harveys and they are complaining that the company is slow to pay total cost and slow in arranging the fixing of the engines.
Acceptance of tender announced for providing telephonic communications between offices, collieries and the wharf at a cost £108.

10 March 1897
New pumping machinery would be delivered shortly. It will take three months to fix and get working.

5 May 1897
The company is urging the harbour board to dredge around the wharf which would cost £1,000.

9 June 1897
SS *Henry Fisher*'s charter renewed at £260 per month.

30 June 1897 Annual Report
Output of coal for the year was 310,523 tons and a profit of £4,633 was made.

22 September 1897
New pumping plant at No.2 tested on the previous Saturday.

10 November 1897
Mr Moore could sell 20,000 tons of coal at 8s less $2\frac{1}{2}$% fob Swansea.

12 January 1898
Mr Wales submitted report on estimate of winning the Hughes' vein to the west of the Dyffryn fault.

11 May 1898
General strike in South Wales. The company's collieries have been idle since 1 April.

30 June 1898 Annual Report
Output of coal for the year was 254,941 tons with a profit of £9,350 being made. The quantity of coal mined was reduced by the strike. The company is now possessed of the Hughes Seam which is being worked to great advantage in the adjoining property.

7 September 1898
Strike at an end, work is resuming at the company's collieries.

12 October 1898
Report on winning Hughes Seam received. Cost would be £45,000, plus appliances and the cost of surface land. Upcast shaft to be completed in two years and another year for opening out shaft. The width of seam would be 3ft 6in and would yield an average profit of 1s per ton or £10,000 per year.

16 November 1898
Managing director to receive £600 per year.

11 January 1899
Two new locomotives from Messrs Peckett, Bristol, have been ordered at £1,475 each. Delivery to be made in five months.

15 March 1899
New contracts for 25,000 tons have been made since the last meeting. The company's coal has been found suitable for electric works.

30 June 1899 – Annual Report
During the year 298,995 tons of coal were produced and a profit of £28,093 made.

11 October 1899
Conversion of tramway gauge completed. Four narrow gauge locomotives to be sold.

16 November 1899
It was decided to sell off all six old locomotives which were worth £1,610.

13 December 1899
The remaining pillars of the Graigola Seam in the Court Herbert Colliery were expected to last six months and the present output of about 230 tons per day would gradually disappear. Some of this could be replaced from additional working of the Victoria Seam. The board was thinking about reopening Tir Edmond. It was proposed to buy two second hand locomotives in case of accidents to the new ones. It was thought that coal in the proposed new pit could be reached by September 1901.

4 February 1900
It was not safe to use the old winding engine for the new No.3 winding pit. The tender of Dalgleish & Co. of St Helens was accepted for a pair of 32in winding engines with a 10ft drum. The price was £2,050. It was proposed to ask the Great Western Railway for 6s per ton for the pillar coal left in the Graigola Seam for the support of the Skewen viaduct. The Great Western Railway agreed to pay £520 for the coal in the Victoria Seam and £1,800 for coal in the Graigola Seam.

25 April 1900
As Graigola Seam at Court Herbert was rapidly becoming exhausted it was proposed to drive a heading from the bottom of the pit for a distance of about 140 yards to the north or north west for the purpose of winning about 100 acres of the Graigola Seam between the Cwmfelin and Dyffryn faults. This would take nine months and cost £1,000. This unworked area forms part of the Stanley Estate.

23 May 1900
Company offices moved to Ghyston Buildings which were the offices of the Bristol and South Wales Railway Waggon Company. Stone for the new pit buildings would be obtained from J.N. Moore's Brithdir Quarry and a tramway would be laid to it. No.4 Pit sunk to a depth of 5yds.

30 June 1900 Annual Report
During the year 416,828 tons of coal were produced at a profit of £62,458. The sinking of the new pits to win and work the Hughes Seam is being pressed forward (These pits were sunk at Skewen).

The Skewen incline showing the Main Company's railway line descending from Bryncoch to the river.

24 July 1900
Ships chartered:

Player	£390 per month
Topaz	£450 per month
Fleswick	£430 per month

26 September 1900
No.4 Pit sunk to a depth of 63yds and 38yds had been walled. No.3 Pit had been sunk to 16yds.

17 October 1900
No.4 Pit sunk to 72yds and had struck strong rock. The pit frames had been erected at No.3 Pit.

12 December 1900
No.4 Pit sunk to 112yds with 40yds unwalled. No.3 Pit sunk to 49yds with 11yds unwalled.

16 January 1901
No.4 Pit sunk to 132yds, 70yds unwalled. Average speed of sinking was three feet per day. No.3 Pit is down to 55yds but a considerable feeder of water was met with at the lower Maesmelyn Seam which meant a suspension of work until a permanent winding engine was at work. At No.1 Pit the water in the Graigola workings was gradually increasing and it will be necessary to deal with it by some other way than winding it.

13 February 1901

It was recommended that electrical plant should be purchased for dealing with the water at the Graigola Seam at No.1 Pit and for producing the current for ninety-seven lamps, forty-two fixed at the bottom of No.1 Pit and fifty-five at the surface. The total cost is estimated at £850. No.4 Pit is down to 143yds and 133½yds are walled.

22 May 1901

The company accepted the tender of Walker Brothers, Wigan for a fan at the new pit costing £1,681. 10s.

30 June 1901 Annual Report

During the year 410,354 tons of coal were produced making a profit of £101,469. One of the new pits has reached the Hughes Seam.

24 July 1901

The Hughes Seam at No.4 Pit was met at a depth of 245yds. The average thickness of the workable coal is 3ft 7in. No.3 Pit is excavated down to 117yds. The Graigola workings at No.1 Pit are now so far from the pit that it is necessary to arrange for haulage by mechanical power. It was resolved to accept the tender from Qualter Hall & Co. for endless rope haulage at a cost of £1,070.

13 December 1901

Preparations were being made for working the pillars of coal in the Wernfraith Seam in No.6 Pit (formerly known as the Old Main Pit). A small output of coal would be obtained in six weeks time.

12 March 1902

Death of Captain Pavy. No.3 Pit hits Hughes Seam at 243yds.

16 April 1902

Fire in the Victoria Seam in Court Herbert Colliery has subsided.

Nos 3 and 4 Pits now connected and will soon be opened out.

Forty-five houses are to be built by the company for £140 at Cwrtyclafdy. The final cost was £153.

13 May 1902

£25,000 has been spent on new works and a further £14,000 would be needed to complete the projects.

More problems with water at No.1 Pit were reported.

30 June 1902 Annual Report

During the year 400,361 tons of coal were produced at a profit of £56,765. Trevor Lewis elected to board to fill vacancy on death of Captain Francis Pavy.

23 October 1902

At the Court Herbert Colliery the pillars in the Graigola Seam have been worked back as far as possible.

The endless rope haulage system at No.1 Pit has allowed the company to dispense with twenty-five horses.

12 November 1902

A dispute has occurred over the working of the Hughes Seam. The men have been offered 4s 2½d per day.

14 January 1903

The Great Western Railway has paid the company £3,123 for the Graigola coal under the Skewen viaduct.

15 April 1903

Wage dispute at Nos 3 and 4 Pits settled at the terms offered at the start of the problem. They will be the same as at No.1 Pit.

Tenders have been invited for the building of a steam ship for the company.

13 May 1903

The working of the Victoria Seam at Court Herbert Colliery was suspended for ten days because of a fire in the gob.

Trams of coal from Court Herbert Colliery were conveyed 100yds to the tipping stage of the sidings by one of the old small locomotives. It was desired to change this to endless rope haulage by a small engine. Qualter Hall & Co. quoted £202 16s for this. The old small locomotive was to be sold.

30 May 1903 Annual Report

During the year 380,893 tons of coal were produced making a profit of £49,889.

14 October 1903

The heading at No.1 Pit from the Graigola Seam to the Victoria Seam has reached coal. It is 4ft 1in thick and of good hard quality.

9 December 1903

The death of Mr John Crow Richardson has been reported.

A hauling engine for No.4 Pit has been ordered from Llewellyn & Cubitt at a cost of £309.

Mr Thomas Hobart Walker Hobart Inskip has been elected a director.

13 January 1904

The company's new steam ship has had its keel laid down in the first week of December. It will be called SS *Main*. Pumps for No.4 Pit have been bought from Hathorn and Davey and the Coalbrookdale Company.

No.1 Main Colliery photographed in 1913. At this time the shafts had been sunk to a depth of 1,360ft to work the Graigola and Victoria seams.

9 February 1904
Victoria Seam at No.1 Pit was being worked with an output of 50 tons per day.

10 March 1904
Cardiff was chosen as the port of registry of the new steamer. Captain McCorquodale appointed as master at £5 per week.

7 June 1904
The SS *Main* has made her trial trip and has since carried the company's coal.

30 June 1904 Annual Report
During the year 363,320 tons of coal were produced making a profit of £22,714.

17 October 1904
There have been numerous stoppages for want of trade and collieries were working irregularly throughout the district. There were continuous problems with wage levels for the new pits. The men suspended work because the working of the colliery was too irregular to enable them to earn a living.

9 November 1904
Arbitration taking place over prices for work on the Victoria Seam at No.1 Pit and at Court Herbert.

7 December 1904

Arbitration settled over prices for working the Victoria Seam by long wall at No.1 Pit and at Court Herbert.

11 January 1905

Strike of workers in Victoria and Graigola Seams.

22 February 1905

Strike at No.1 Pit (Victoria & Graigola Seams) came to an end on 11 January.

22 March 1905

Death of John Newall Moore on 27 February. T.G. Lloyd becomes head of sales department.

25 May 1905

Endless rope system in No.1 Pit extended into Victoria Seam. No improvement in trade with competition keen. Herbert Moore appointed agent for Devon and Somerset at £120 a year.

The Main Colliery Company's office at Skewen. The general manager's office, the surveying department and part of the colliery stores can be seen.

The Main Colliery Co.'s power station at No.1 pit. This was erected in 1908 and consisted of two Bellis and Morcom three crank triple-expansion engines directly coupled to two BTH three phase 3,300 volt 50 periods alternators each with an output of 1,000kWs.

30 June 1905 Annual Report
During the year 334,969 tons of coal were produced at a profit of £21,076. At this time prices still not settled for work at the new pits, problem in the hands of arbitrators.

20 September 1905
Damage reported to the pumping engine at No.1 Pit. Hathorn Davy to repair this at a cost of £624 and will charge £174 to change the engine adding their patent differential gear for regulating the working of the inlet and outlet valves.
The working of No.1 Pit has been interfered with by a large outburst of water in the Graigola workings. 10,000 gallons entered each hour and it was necessary to fix new pumps in the colliery. A temporary dam was built but this strategy did not work.

17 November 1905
Temporary pump idea abandoned for No.1 Pit. It was decided to get electrical equipment.

16 January 1906
The new pumping arrangements for Nos 1 and 2 Pits delayed so a three throw pump has been ordered from the Coalbrookdale Company for £227.

8 June 1906
A serious explosion occurred in the Victoria Seam at Court Herbert Colliery. Nine men were seriously injured, five of whom later died. The workings where the explosion took place were flooded for safety.

30 June 1906 Annual Report
During the year 356,967 tons of coal were produced at a profit of £20,788.

27 July 1906
Problems continued at Court Herbert. Another fire broke out in the road conveying air to the Main district and it was feared this might reach the pump at No.1 Pit.
Coal from the Victoria Seam was unobtainable from 9 to 17 July causing great difficulty in supplying contracts.

10 August 1906
Letter received from workmen giving the company a vote of confidence and exonerating the managers from any blame for the explosion. The letter was written on 4 August at the Smiths Arms, Neath Abbey.

27 September 1906
Underground fire at No.1 Pit with coal winding stopped from 27 August to 3 September. Robert McCorquodale the brother of the previous master appointed captain of SS *Main*.

23 November 1906
Workmen at No.1 Pit ceased work from 1 to 5 November because of non-unionist dispute.

12 January 1907
Court Herbert will take until May to get back to full output.

30 June 1907 Annual Report
During the year 318,976 tons of coal were produced at a profit of £15,801. The Court Herbert explosion involved a heavy expenditure to reopen workings. Arbitration award for new pit now signed and it was hoped that work would start there soon.

14 November 1907
Work resumed on Tuesday 29 October under the terms of the Arbitrators' award. 70 tons a day were being produced and this would gradually be increased.

17 December 1907
The output of the new pits was 130 tons a day.

3 April 1908
The Graigola seam at Court Herbert Colliery was producing about 450 tons of coal per week. The seam in these workings was noted as being 'much distorted by faults'.

20 June 1908
The Court Herbert Colliery needed to be deepened to win and work the Hughes Seam. The seam at Nos 3 and 4 pits was found to be unsuitable for the London market, but reports from the continent on this coal were not unsatisfactory.

30 June 1908 Annual Report
During the year 400,692 tons of coal were produced at a profit of £17,643. The working of the new colliery was started on 4 November.
Court Herbert Colliery was deepened to work the lower seams of coal on the eastern side of the Dyffryn Fault. This and the fitting of the company's collieries with electrical equipment to deal with pumping and other work increased expenditure and so the board decided to create new ordinary shares.

15 September 1908
10,000 new ordinary shares were issued at £10 each.

Rice Vaughan Price, general manager of the Main Colliery Company's pits, 1897-1918.

30 September 1908

At No.1 Pit the Graigola Seam was struck beyond the Cwmfelin fault, the seam looked good with hard coal and a strong roof. The area to be worked lay between the Cwmfelin and Dyffryn faults.

The Graigola Seam in the Court Herbert Colliery was closed down except for one heading.

A compressed air machine was purchased from Walker Brothers of Wigan for Nos 3 and 4 Pits.

17 October 1908

At Court Herbert Colliery good progress was made in the new airways being driven with the object of extinguishing the two fires in the main dip

SS *Glassford*, loaded with 330 tons of coal, was lost.

16 November 1908

In the Victoria Seam of Court Herbert Colliery one airway was completed and the other was six weeks away from being finished.

Notice was given to 305 men. This was to regulate the required output for which sale can be found. The reduction in weekly capacity would be around 2,300 tons.

7,900 tons of thro coal was sold forward at net prices ranging from 8s 9d to 11s 1d per ton. The Drumma minerals were to be leased from a Mr Paddon at a rent of £120. The company has not worked coal on this property since 1894 but the Hughes Seam here would not be reached for many years.

1 March 1909

H.T. Wales resigns as engineer and Managing Director, R. Vaughan Price was appointed colliery agent at £500 a year on the understanding that a consulting engineer would be called in when necessary.

Wages will be reduced by 5% from 1 March. The steamer *Carlston* was chartered for three months at £320 per month.

Colonel Savile resigns from the board because of age and is replaced by his son Charles C. Savile.

13 April 1909

Plans were being made to reopen the Skewen Pits.

8 May 1909

Three pumps were purchased from the Worthington Pump Co. Ltd to replace hydraulic ones at No.4 Pit.

Court Herbert Colliery needed a new hauling engine to deal with increased output. One was ordered from J. Wood & Sons.

11 June 1909

Wage reduction of $7\frac{1}{2}$% announced.

30 June 1909 Annual Report
During the year 450,936 tons of coal were produced at a profit of £13,464.

13 August 1909
One of the clerks (J.T. Davies) left and a rearrangement of staff and salaries took place:

	Present salary	New
J.H. Cole, book-keeper	£175	£200
J.T. Davies, sales accounts	£135	gone
W.D. Johns, colliery accounts	£120	£130
J.D. David, sales accounts	£105	£120
G.H. Weekes, assistant book-keeper	£104	£110
J.L. John, sales and accounts	£85	£100
D.J. Noot, colliery accounts	£70 4s	£90
Thos. Jenkins, shorthand and typewriter	£65	£75
W. Craig, colliery accounts	£90	gone
Oswald Rees, new clerk	£80	
O.T. Davies, general duties	£40	£50
P. Poley, telephones	£18 4s	£23 7s
B. Morris, boy	new	£15 12s

29 October 1909
The Company chairman, James Inskip, died after a short illness.

16 November 1909
Sir George White and his son Mr Samuel White were elected to the board. Sir George White became chairman.
In connection with the reopening of the Skewen Pits for winning coal between the Cwmfelin and Dyffryn faults, it was recommended that the company sink a new shaft. This would take twelve months at an estimated cost of £5,500.

24 January 1910
The company applied to the Neath Abbey Estate to cross the Cwmfelin fault for the winning of a portion of the Graigola Seam.

14 February 1910
A hauling engine was purchased for No.4 Pit from the Uskside Engineering Company at a cost of £140.

14 March 1910
A new hauling plant at Court Herbert was started up.
A tender was put out for a new steel pithead frame for the upcast pit at Court Herbert.

20 June 1910
The Skewen pit was sunk to 29yds and walling completed.

30 June 1910 Annual Report
During the year 439,712 tons of coal were produced at a profit of £13,464.

18 October 1910
The new pit (No 7) was sunk to 50yds.
It was resolved to apply to the Dyffryn Estate for consent to work the pillars of solid coal (120,000 tons of the Graigola Seam) which were left for the protection of the Main north headings in No.1 Pit when it was intended to work the Primrose Barrier.

21 November 1910
The output for the four weeks ending 12 October was 39,803 tons, a record.

12 December 1910
No 7 Pit was driven to open headings at Graigola Seam but a fault was encountered.

16 January 1911
Coal from the Graigola pillars in No.1 Pit was being gradually exhausted, so it was decided to reduce the output.

13 February 1911
Tender accepted from J. Wood & Sons for a haulage engine for No.4 Pit.

13 March 1911
On the company's property the output from the Graigola Seam was being gradually reduced. More coal was now worked from the Hughes seam which was more costly by about 1s 3d a ton.

	1908	1909	1910	1911
Graigola Seam	39%	31%	26%	19%
Victoria Seam	49%	49%	48%	48%
Hughes Seam	9%	17%	23%	30%
Wernfraith	3%	3%	3%	3%

Pillars from the Waunceirch Slant have been exhausted and would be abandoned.

12 June 1911
At No 7 Pit communication was made with the old Skewen Pits which were cleared and now formed the upcast shaft (No 8 Pit) for this colliery.

30 June 1911 Annual Report
During the year 479,080 tons of coal were produced at a profit of £8,471.
At the No.7 Pit, the Three Feet, Victoria and Graigola Seams were won and of excellent quality.

20 July 1911
It was proposed to work the Wernfraith Seam in the Tennant property from No.6 Pit and a lease was taken out.
A lease was also taken out on the Tennant property for the Victoria Seam. This was for 60 years from 25 December 1910, with a royalty of 4d per ton and a half yearly dead rent of £87 10s.
A further lease was arranged with Mr E. Price for Hughes Vein on his property. This was for forty years from 25 December 1910, with a royalty of 7d per ton and a dead rent of £200 per year for the first and second years and £400 each year after.

10 October 1911
The Graigola Seam at No.1 Pit was reported as not likely to last beyond June 1912. Permission to work the pillars in the north heading to the Primrose Barrier was not granted. At the No 7 Pit the Victoria Seam was intersected.
No.1 Pit was to go ahead and work the Hughes Seam.

17 January 1912
Two air compressing engines were bought for No.4 and No.7 Pits.

3 April 1912
A general strike commenced at all collieries on 1 March and lasted for nearly seven weeks.

5 June 1912
The company was in discussions with the Lords of the Abbey regarding a large reduction in royalty payments. They agreed but the Main Colliery Company had to:

(1)   Equip No 3 downcast so as to raise more coals
(2)   Extend workings in Hughes Seam at No.3 Pit
(3)   Complete equipment at No.7 Pit to increase output
(4)   Drive cross measure headings through the Dyffryn fault into
       Hughes Seam at No.1 and No.6 Pits.

The new five year royalties agreed were:

Victoria Seam   5d per ton
Hughes Seam   4½d per ton
Graigola Seam   5d per ton

Court Herbert Colliery workers, 1910.

The company calculated that these measures would cost £40,000 and so they wanted a fifteen-year agreement. In the end all parties signed a ten-year agreement.

Some of the company's other landlords also agree to these terms.

30 June 1912 Annual Report

During the year 410,510 tons of coal were produced at a profit of £278. All profits were absorbed by the expenditure caused by the two month strike.

18 November 1912

A tender was accepted from Walker Brothers of Wigan for a fan at No.7 Pit that cost £236 10s.

`

11 December 1912

The sum of £250 was to be spent to win an area from No.6 pit of about forty acres of the Little Bryncoch Seam lying to the south west of No.1 Pit. It was expected there would be 100,000 tons from which the profit would be 1s to 1s 6d per ton and winning would take only about two months. It was hoped the output of this coal could be increased to 100 tons a day.

A similar area of this seam was expected to be won on the north east side of the pit at an outlay of £300.

The Great Western Railway paid £2,250 for the preservation of pillars under the Skewen viaduct.

A second hand hauling engine was purchased from Thomas Johnson of Wigan for No.7 Pit costing £327 10s.

Trade outlook is encouraging and the selling price would probably rise from 11s to 11s 3d a ton.

9 March 1913

The number of men employed was increased but it was difficult to get them to work in No 7 Pit owing to the coal being 'stiff', which required increased labour to cut, and because of the steep inclination of the strata (1 in 4).

A tender for £1,875 was accepted for a coal screening plant for No.7 Pit.

23 June 1913

Alterations were being made to the pit bottoms at No.3 and No.4 Pits at a cost of £1,000 so as to increase output to 800-900 tons per day.

H.T. Wales continued as a director of the company.

30 June 1913 Annual Report

During the year 408,864 tons of coal were produced at a profit of £13,169.

12 June 1914

A tender was accepted for air compressors at No.4 and No.7 Pits at a total cost of £3,252.

30 June 1914 Annual Report

During the year 462,013 tons of coal were produced at a profit of £21,974.

28 October 1914

It was resolved not to charge rent for colliers serving in the armed forces. The families of these men were to be supplied with coal at a reduced rate.

11 November 1914

A small haulage engine was purchased for No.7 Pit from the Uskside Engineering Company.

Reports and meetings now become intermittent during the war years.

18 March 1915

No.7 Pit was to be electrified.

30 June 1915 Annual Report

During the year 398,613 tons of coal were produced at a profit of £21,669.

8 December 1916

The Board approved the purchase of railway carriages for taking the men to and from No.1 Pit.

Sir George White (1854-1916), Chairman of the Main Colliery Company, 1909-1916.

31 December 1916 Annual Report
During the eighteen months 574,613 tons of coal were produced at a profit of £14,174.
The £10 shares were divided into £1 shares.
The death of Sir George White was announced, with Samuel White succeeding him as chairman.
Sir G. Stanley White is elected to fill vacancy on the board.

22 June 1917
Drymma minerals were purchased by the company for £2,160.

5 October 1917
Court Herbert Colliery was reported as idle for two days because of a gob fire and a strike due to complaints of victimisation by managers.
Boring was taking place at Cadoxton for the Resolven Seam.
The price of steam coal for France was reduced by the Controller of Mines from 25s fob to 23s 6d.
The price for Hughes cobbles is set at 30s fob.

31 December 1917 Annual Report
During the year 285,014 tons of coal were produced at a profit of £10,030.
During this period the collieries have continued under the control and direction of the
Board of Trade, Controller of Mines.

11 January 1918
No.4 Pit was to be kept going after serious discussions but a reduction must be made on
the losses.

10 April 1918
The collieries are being irregularly worked. Losses of £40,000 were made from
7 September to February 27 and these could have been avoided 'if we could have
conducted our own business without interference of the Coal Controller.'

6 December 1918
R. Vaughan Price resigned to become the manager of Graigola Merthyr Collieries.

7 February 1919
H.T. Wales was appointed as consultant engineer.

31 December 1922 Annual Report
The delay in issuing a report was due to the fact that it had only recently been possible to
arrive at a settlement of accounts with the Mines Department of the Board of Trade.
Control ended on 31 March 1921 and was at once followed by a disastrous strike lasting
for three months. Collieries were flooded and an immense amount of damage was done
to the underground workings and machinery, the repair of which necessitated a very heavy
expenditure. The output of coal for the five years was 1,139,394 tons.

8 February 1923
Since the last meeting on 21 September George White & Co. had advanced the company
£15,000.

29 March 1923
George White & Co. advanced the company another £5,000.

30 November 1923
Plans were drawn up to close the Court Herbert Colliery.

31 December 1924
The output of coal for the year was 146,464 tons. A strike occurred on 2 July 1924 and
lasted until 9 August when the men indicated their willingness to return to work. By that
time however, the directors had reached the conclusion that, owing to adverse economic
conditions, it would be better to defer the re-starting of work at the collieries until a
brighter outlook presented itself. Consequently during the latter half of the year there was

only a restricted coal output and with the assistance of the company's officials operations have been directed chiefly to keeping the pits unwatered and ventilated. Debit balance stands at £36,171 1s 5d.

John Bicknell, the company secretary from the start of the enterprise, had to resign through ill health.

20 April 1924
The Graigola Seam at Court Herbert was worked out and this seam at No.1 Pit would be exhausted within a year.

26 June 1924
George White & Co. advanced the company another £15,000.

10 December 1926
The collieries started up again on 1 December, but No.4 Pit was not re-opened.
LNER has accepted the company's offer of £1,500 for their ovoid briquetting plant.

27 January 1927
William George Verdon Smith CBE joined the board.

25 February 1927
George White & Co. advanced the company a further £8,500, bringing the total advanced to £137,910 17s 5d.

31 March 1927
George White & Co. advanced £12,500, making a total of £150,410 17s 5d.
After the submission of Mr Wales' report it was decided that all operations at Nos 1 and 4 Pits should cease, other than pumping and ventilating. The four levels and Wernddu Colliery should also cease production.
The erection of the ovoid plant was deferred.

30 October 1928
George White & Co. advances to the company £5,000 which brings the total advanced to £246,660 17s 5d.

10 December 1928
The death of the chairman Mr Samuel White on 9 December was announced to the board.
The company secretary reported that on 4 December 1928 the company had been served with a notice of the appointment of Sir William Mclintock as Receiver. The appointment had been made by Messrs George White & Co. as the holder of the debenture in the favour in respect of the large advances made by them to the company.
On 4 December a distraint had been made on the company's effects at the colliery on behalf of J.G. Moore-Gwyn, the owner of the Dyffryn Estate.

From these records we can see that The Main Colliery Company was a far more successful concern than its predecessor. One reason for this was that not only did the company contain managers with local knowledge but it had also an experienced board of directors with a wide range of industrial and mining experience. The directors made a logical decision in working only five collieries in the company's early years; namely, Court Herbert, Brithdir, Tir Edmond, Waunceirch and New Main Collieries.

Another beneficial decision was to virtually close the Main Colliery which worked the Wernffraith Seam and sink a new colliery in the neighbourhood to win the Graigola Seam in the Bryncoch area. This decision was applauded in H.T. Wales' report on the company's mines which was published in 1895.

This report was a turning point for the company as it agreed with and wished to expand on the policy of deeper mining to win new seams of coal. The result of this was the sinking of No.3 and No.4 Pits to win the Hughes Seam in the western portion of the company's property. The sinking of these pits began in 1900 but difficulties in agreeing rates for working the new colliery delayed the beginning of coal production until 1907. A further effect of the report was in speeding up the change of the company's tramroads to a railway gauge.

The successful opening of the new colliery meant that the company could offer a range of coals for sale. These included coals that were suitable for a wide range of industrial purposes such as Hughes Dry Vein Coal which was used in Europe for house purposes and for the manufacture of patent fuel.

The company continued to develop the deeper seams during the period before the First World War. Nos 1 and 2 Pits, after exploiting the Graigola Seam, were later worked for the Victoria Seam. The Court Herbert Colliery also worked the Griagola Seam and was later extended to mine the Victoria Seam. Nos 3 and 4 Pits continued working the Hughes Seam where at times an output of 900 tons was achieved. No.1 Pit reached a daily output of 1,400 tons of coal a day. A new colliery called Nos 7 and 8 Pits was sunk in 1910-1911 at Skewen to work the Graigola and Victoria Seams. No.6 Pit was later used to exploit the remaining pillars of Wernffraith coal still left in the workings.

The importance of each of the collieries can be gauged from the size of the labour force used at each pit. At its greatest output the company employed about 2,000 men.[266] In 1915 Court Herbert Colliery employed 352 men, Nos 1 and 2 Pits employed 834, Nos 3 and 4 employed 560, No.6 had twenty-nine workers and Nos 7 and 8 Pits had seventy-two men.

The company operated before the First World War with good profits because of a large local market for their coal coupled with low production and haulage costs. The close proximity of the pits to a shipping place on the River Neath helped produce low quotes for coal delivered on board ship.

However, the years 1914-1918 were a period of great change in the fortunes of the Main Colliery Company. In 1914 a report on the company's mines highlighted several worrying problems with the new pits. Nos 3 and 4 Pits had over the previous four years only been returning a profit of 1d a ton and the report commented, 'There must be a substantial improvement if the colliery is to be placed on a satisfactory basis.' Problems that existed at the colliery included the high cutting price of coal paid to the colliers, the very high percentage of small coal obtained and an insufficient power supply for haulage and pumping. Nos 7 and 8 Pits weren't completely unsatisfactory but there was a problem developing because of the high inclination of the seams and the need for mechanical haulage.[267]

In 1915 another report on the state of the Dyffryn Mineral Estate also touched on problems with the Main Colliery Company's pits.[268] The Wernffraith Seam at No 6 Pit (Old Main) was virtually worked out, but coal was still being cut at a depth of 40yds in the Bryncoch Seam. However, it was estimated that only forty acres of this coal remained with a possible 100,000 tons of workable coal.

In Nos 1 and 2 Pits problems with the Victoria Seam were developing. It was stated that great doubts existed as to how far in a northerly direction the seam would be workable. Furthermore, the Victoria Seam was liable to gob fires and great care had to be exercised in working it. The Graigola Seam in No.1 Pit was also exhausted with only pillar coal remaining.

Despite these set backs the board of directors continued to have faith in the health of the company. In some ways the death of James Inskip in 1909 and the subsequent appointment of Sir George White of Bristol as chairman was beneficial to the company, if only in terms of its longevity. Sir George White was a pioneer of tramways in Bristol and the founder of the Bristol Aeroplane Company [269] and a most shrewd and experienced industrialist. He was also a business enemy of the Inskip family and the death of James Inskip had allowed White to take over part of their industrial empire. However, it was only through the drive and financial backing of the White family that the Main Colliery Company's story stretched into the 1920s.

Problems for the company were being compounded by the demands of the First World War. The company's first difficulty was to find enough workers to be able to run the collieries efficiently. The total number of men employed at the collieries on 30 June 1915 was 1,665 compared with 2,065 in the previous year. By 29 August 1915 a total of 425 men had joined the armed forces or left for munitions work. It was reported that in the first eleven months of the war the company's activities were severely hampered by a variety of outside factors. Unlike Rhondda coal, the Main Company's output was of a character which did not command any sale to the Admiralty, so they could not benefit from wartime orders like other companies. Also the war had disrupted two major markets for their coal. As much as 80% of the Main Company's coal was sold to France for use in domestic stoves of a type not used in the UK and much of the small coal was sold for the preparation of patent fuel for abroad. The war also caused the pits to be left idle for seventy-five days in the year.

Problems were exacerbated with Government control of the company's mines which started from 1 December 1916 and until 31 March 1921. The Mines Department of the Board of Trade then intensively worked the Main Company's pits for the benefit of the nation and not for the shareholders. This meant that by the end of Government control seams were approaching exhaustion and some machinery was ageing and worn out. The company bitterly complained later that although substantial profits were made in 1919, the Government department took $\frac{2}{3}$ of it and $\frac{1}{2}$ in 1920.

Telegraphic Address. "MAIN, SKEWEN".
LIEBER'S CODE USED.

Telephone: NEATH N° 221.
(2 LINES)

The Main Colliery Company, Ltd.

—— PROPRIETORS OF THE DYNEVOR DYFFRYN COLLIERIES. ——

COLLIERY OWNERS.
COAL EXPORTERS.
SHIP BROKERS
AND
SHIP OWNERS.

Neath Abbey.

Neath (Friday)
30th December 1932.

All offers are made subject to War, Strikes, Lockout and Accident clauses
& to acceptance by return of post unless otherwise stated.
PLEASE ADDRESS ALL COMMUNICATIONS TO THE COMPANY.

R.W. Mercer Esq.,
Clare Street House,
BRISTOL.

Dear Sir,

I thank you for your letter of the 29th instant enclosing Wages Cheque £6. 5. 5., and note you propose visiting Skewen next week.

With reference to the Plans asked for by Messrs. Warrens as far as I can see the only one missing is that of the Wernffraith Seam at No.6 Pit, and the following is a list of plans showing the workings of the various seams in the Abbey Estate which I have here.

No.1 Pit.   -   Graigola & Victoria.

No.6 Pit.   -   Little Bryncoch.

Nos. 3 & 4 Pits. Hughes Seam.

No.7 Pit.   Graigola & Victoria.

Court Herbert.   Graigola & Victoria.

GOSHEN HOUSE.

I will get an estimate for repairs to the above house and forward to you in a day or so.

Yours faithfully.

GDavies

One of the last letters sent by the Main Colliery Company, 30 December 1932.

The war impacted on the company in a more direct way when on 9 October 1917 the company lost its steamer SS *Main*. She was intercepted by a German submarine one and a half miles east of Drummore, Luce Bay, Wigtownshire; the submarine opened fire from the surface and sank the vessel with gunfire. Twelve men were killed but the captain was among the survivors. [270]

When the collieries were handed back to the company in 1921 preparations were made to restart activity on a large scale. However, in that year there was a three month strike by the workers which resulted in the flooding of the collieries and did an immense amount of damage to workings and machinery. This meant a large expenditure to get the collieries back in good order. The problem now facing the company was to produce enough coal to be profitable and in 1924 it was computed that this meant winning at least 300,000 tons of coal a year. Some of the old drifts were opened on the company's property to gain more output and the New Wernddu Colliery was taken back into the company's hands from a sub-leasing agreement with the New Wernddu Colliery Company.

The efforts to continue the company's activities were further set back by a strike of 320 men at No.4 Pit in July 1924. This dispute arose over the employment of firemen during a holiday week in place of the usual continuous workers which contravened the terms of a national agreement. Arbitrators were called in and the following recommendations were accepted: the question of a minimum wage affecting certain workers was agreed to, a new method was set up to deal with the minimum wage, continuous shift men were not to be replaced on holidays and stop days in the future and were to be compensated for loss of work during the Whitsun week. The question of yardage for heading water and tramming was to be enquired into by two arbitrators within twenty-one days from 11 August.

It was hoped that with the end of this dispute there would be a return to work. However, the workers were told that the strike was at an end but owing to fact that the economic conditions in the coal trade were in such a bad state, it was impossible for the company to open its collieries for the production of coal. The company continued to pump and ventilate its mines at a cost of £2,000 a month which later rose to £6,000.

One piece of good news was announced in June 1925 that a payment of £59,000 had been received from the Ministry of Mines. However, by this time the company firmly believed that its continental trade had been taken over by German and American suppliers. The company undertook no further serious mining of coal and the Main Colliery Company remained afloat only because of a series of loans from George White & Co.

Although some local bitterness was expressed at the closing of the collieries it was virtually impossible for the company to continue. There were several reasons for this. Some of the new pits sunk by the company were not as remunerative as expected. Also several important seams of coal exploited by the company had become exhausted and by 1926 the last of the large local copper works that bought Main Company coal had closed. Generally economic conditions from 1924 onwards also grew worse particularly in the coal industry. The problems worsened with the resumption of coal production in the Ruhr and reparation deliveries from Germany in the aftermath of the Dawes Agreement of August 1924 removed the large French market for Main Company's coal.[271]

From September 1924 to March 1925 more than half of the collieries in Britain ran at a deficit. The level of unemployment in the industry rose from 2.1% in March 1924 to 25% in June 1925. Reliant as it was on exports, South Wales suffered more acutely than other coal producing areas. Under these circumstances there was no way back to commercial profit for the Main Colliery Company and closure was inevitable.

However, from the 1930s to the present day some small scale mining of coal has continued in the area. On 10 May 1932 T.R & R. Davies, calling themselves the Wenffraith House Coal Colliery Company Ltd, took out a lease of coal mining land on the Dyffryn Estate.[272] This concern mined approximately 134 acres of the Little Bryncoch Seam and the lease was to run from 29 September 1931 for thirty years. The lease cost the company £125 per year plus 6d a ton for the coal mined and a wayleave of 1d a ton. It was thought that 100 tons of coal could be mined each week, a vastly different output for the estate compared with the heady early days of the Main Colliery Company.

Appendix One

Statement of Expenses of Making Iron at Neath Abbey, June 30th 1799 to July 1st 1800.

	Total	Per Ton
Wages at furnace No 1 & 2	£908 13 4	£0 6 0$\frac{1}{4}$
Coals at 4s per ton (17,000) 5.6 tons per ton of iron		
	£3,400 1 11	
coaking	£565 12 11$\frac{1}{2}$	
	£3,965 14 10$\frac{1}{2}$	£1 6 2$\frac{3}{4}$
Welsh mine at 14/ per ton (9,820) 3$\frac{1}{4}$ per ton of iron		
	£6,897 16 0	
Lancashire ore at 20/ (460) = 3 cwt per ton		
	£459 19 8	
	£7,357 15 8	£2 8 7$\frac{1}{2}$
Engine men (3)	£169 13 11$\frac{1}{2}$	
Materials used	£20 1 11	
	£189 15 10$\frac{1}{2}$	£0. 1. 3$\frac{3}{4}$
Agencies	£322 6 0	£0. 2. 1$\frac{1}{2}$
Limestone at 3/6 per ton (4,143) 11/3 per ton	£725 14 0	£0. 4. 9.$\frac{1}{2}$
Haulage or carriage paid to others		
	£239 8 11$\frac{1}{2}$	
Hay and oats	£293. 16. 8	
Harness	£37 6 3$\frac{1}{2}$	
Horses	£32 13 9	
Rent and taxes on Farm	£45 14 4	£649	£0. 4. 3$\frac{1}{2}$
Carpenters and Wheelwrights	£196 11 4	
Smith work £319 8 5		
Masons	£85 11 5$\frac{1}{2}$	£601 19 2$\frac{1}{2}$	£0 3 11$\frac{1}{2}$
Labourers	£403 5 2$\frac{1}{2}$	
Rent & taxes on furnaces	£134 14 0$\frac{1}{2}$	
Wrought iron & steel	£289 1 3	
Timber	£571 14 8$\frac{1}{2}$	
Hearth stones	£34 3 11	
Fire bricks	£40 8 8	
Postage stamps & stationery	£32 17 6	
Allowances & expences	£49 0 2	
Rope	£34 12 11	
Copper brass & lead	£22 5 2	
Insurances	£12 0 10	
Shovel & helves	£24 2 4	
Abatements on pig iron	£19 5 6	

Abatements on castings	£14 1 2		
Freight on iron	£38 2 6		
Barge	£6 13 0		
Castings	£22 19 9		
Tools at Neath and Mumbles	£13 3 9		
Refinery	£112 14 0		
Furniture in office & houses	£1 18 5		
Sundries	£95 3 8		
DEDUCT AS UNDER	£1,972 8 5½		
Machinery increased in value	£1,072 9 7		
Rail roads increased in value	£195 19 1		
For sundries included in the above			
to belong to last year	£350		
	£1,618 8 8	£353 19 9½	£0 2 4
TOTAL		£15,074 18. 10	£4. 19. 8

Total expense of making 3,025 tons pig in which is included 430 tons refined.

SOURCE - BRL, MB, Box 318/35.

Appendix Two

Stationary steam engines built by the Neath Abbey Iron Company.

Year Built	Details and Customer
1806	A Trevithick high-pressure whim engine for Wheal Crenver and Abraham, Cornwall. Possibly a Trevithick high-pressure engine for Swansea Pottery. 50in engine for Nailsea.
1807	16in beam engine for Dyffryn Main Colliery.
c1808	16in beam engine for Brinddewy Colliery.
1809	18in beam engine for Mr Stokes, Hean Castle near Tenby. 16in beam engine for Mr Williams, Scorrier House, Cornwall. 24in x 5ft beam engine for Dyffryn Main Colliery.
c1809	18in beam engine for Lord Milford, Kilgetty Colliery, Pembrokeshire.
1810	30in engine for Dyffryn Main Colliery.
1811	An engine for Joseph & Crawshay Bailey of the Nantyglo Ironworks. 36in condensing beam pumping engine for Park Mead Colliery, Swansea. 30in condensing beam engine for Kilgetty Colliery, Pembrokeshire.
1812	16in rotative beam winding engine for John Parsons, Neath.
1813	Woolf compound winding engines for Cornwall. 40in x 8ft rotative beam engine for rolling mill for the Nantyglo Ironworks.
1814	45in x 7ft, 24in x 4ft 3in Woolf compound pumping engine for Wheal Abraham, Cornwall. 24in beam engine for Wheal Vor, Cornwall. 40in engine for the Rhymney Iron Company. 53in x 9ft, 28in x 6ft Woolf compound beam pumping engine for Wheal Vor, Cornwall.
1815	76in beam pumping engine for Dolcoath Mine Cornwall. Part built at Neath Abbey and part at the mine. 53in beam pumping engine for the Allihies Mining Company, County Kerry, Ireland.

| 1816 | 19in x 3ft 6in beam engine for Herland Mine, Cornwall. |
| | 19in engine for Robinson & Fayle, Dublin. |

1817	33in blowing engine for Wayne, Williams & Co., Gadlys Ironworks, Aberdare.
	$3\frac{1}{2}$in A frame beam engine, rotative and condensing for Mr Shaw, Dublin.
	16in engine for David Walters.

| 1818 | 18in rotative beam engine for William Aitken, Rouen, France. |
| | $52\frac{1}{2}$in beam blowing engine for Cyfarthfa Ironworks. |

1819	$52\frac{1}{2}$in beam blowing engine for Blaenavon Ironworks.
	$52\frac{1}{2}$in beam blowing engine for Hill & Sons, Plymouth Ironworks, Merthyr Tydfil.
	50in blowing engine for the Dowlais Ironworks.
	Rotative beam engine for the Gandyrris Iron Company, Blaenavon.
	$52\frac{1}{2}$in beam blowing engine for the Penydarren Iron Company, Merthy Tydfil.
	Two 90in beam pumping engines for the Consolidated Mine Adventurers, Cornwall. These engines were erected in 1820.
	50in non-rotative beam blowing engine with 100in blowing cylinder for the Nantyglo Ironworks.

1820	18in engine for the Parys Copper Co., Anglesey.
	$52\frac{1}{2}$in beam blowing engine for the Cyfarthfa Ironworks, Merthyr Tydfil.
	$52\frac{1}{2}$in beam blowing engine for the Hirwaun Ironworks.
	19in engine for Mr Guerin, Guernsey.
	40in engine for the Taibach Copper Works.

1821	16in x 3ft 4in rotative condensing beam engine for winding coal and pumping water for Mr Thomas Edwards, Gaen House, near Newport.
	24in beam engine for Mr Bowen, Pembrokeshire.
	19in engine for France.
	24in engine for the Nantyglo Ironworks.
	45in engine for France.
	18in x 3ft 6in rotative condensing beam engine for Davies, Strangman & Co., Waterford, Ireland.
	90in x 10ft condensing beam pumping engine for Poldice Mine, Cornwall.

1822	Two 15in, 14hp beam engines for St Etienne, France.
	18in condensing beam engine for Kilgetty Colliery, Pembrokeshire.
	30in condensing beam engine for Mr. Smith.
	40in rotative beam engine for rolling mills for Boiguer & Co., Fourchambault, France.

1823   16in beam engine for Guant & Co., Pembrey.

72in single acting beam engine designed by Woolf for Wheal Alfred, Cornwall

30in engine for Mr Cox, Cwm Twy Colliery.

40in engine for Aberdare.

70in beam pumping engine for Wheal Sparnon, Consolidated Mine Adventurers, Cornwall.

30in beam blowing engine for Guant & Co., Pembrey.

1824   53in beam pumping engine for the Anglo-Mexican Mining Company.

40in engine for the Blaenavon Ironworks.

12in underground inclined plane engine for Jevons & Wood, Venallt.

24in high-pressure blowing engine for the Porto Novo Iron Company, Coromandel, East Indies.

45in double acting rotative engine for the Nantyglo Ironworks.

20in x $4\frac{1}{2}$ft beam blowing engine for Boiguer & Co., Fourchambault, France.

22in stamping engine and winding engines for the Anglo-Mexican silver mines.

90in x 10ft condensing beam pumping engine for Wheal Alfred, Cornwall.

1825   52in rotative beam engine for driving rolling mills for Shears & Co., Llangennech.

16in engine for Mr Prothero.

40in engine for Sir John Owen,

40in engine for the Landshipping Colliery, Pembrokeshire.

40in beam rolling engine for Vivian & Sons, Hafod Copper Works, Swansea.

30in engine and a 56in beam blowing engine with an 110in blowing cylinder for the Bute Ironworks.

24in engine for the Hibernian Mining Company.

26in engine and a 30in engine for the Sirhowy Iron Company.

18in rotative beam engine for Mr E.Martin, France.

18in rotative condensing beam engine for Flourn.

Three portable steam engines for the Real del Monte Mines, Mexico.

1826   Two $52\frac{1}{2}$in condensing beam engines for the Llangennech Coal Company.

12in horizontal engine for the Nantyglo Ironworks.

High-pressure rotative beam engine for John Bryant.

16in engine for Mr Brough.

40in x 8ft beam engine for Samuel Brown & Co., Newbridge.

16in x 3ft 4in beam engine for Mr Edward Thomas.

$52\frac{1}{2}$in rotative beam blowing engine for the Plymouth Ironworks.

18in x $4\frac{1}{2}$ft beam engine for a forge for the British Iron Co., France.

1827
18in x 4ft 6in, 10hp rotative condensing beam engine for the Basse Indre Co., France.

Two 52½in beam blowing engines for the British Iron Co., Abersychan.

34in beam blowing engine for Wayne, Williams & Co., Gadlys Ironworks, Aberdare.

33in condensing beam engine for B. Whitehouse.

40in beam blowing engine for the Maesteg Company.

40in blowing engine for the British Iron Company.

45in mill engine with a 20ft flywheel for the Abersychan Ironworks.

1827-30
Three 45in beam blowing engines for the Aveyron Mining Co., France.

1828
14hp engine for David Thomas, Neath.

28in condensing engine for Mr Davies, Abercwmboy Colliery.

53in engine for the Bolanos Mine, Peru.

45in rotative beam engine for the Morfa Copper Works. Swansea.

2hp table engine for David James, Merthyr Tydfil, Bark Mill.

28in high-pressure beam engine for the Ebbw Vale Ironworks.

38hp table engine for the Margam Tinplate Works.

38in engine for the Dowlais Ironworks.

Rotative beam engine for driving a rolling mill for Fox, Williams & Co., Perran Wharf, Cornwall.

52½in blowing engine for Leigh & George, Pontypool Ironworks.

1829
36in condensing beam pumping engine for the Landore Coal Company.

Two 40in beam pumping engines.

45in beam blowing engine for Asell & Co., France.

4hp table engine for Mr Reynolds Aubrey & Co., Cwmllynfill Colliery.

2hp engine for Vivian & Sons, Hafod Copper Works, Swansea.

4hp engine for J.M. Heath.

28in engine for the Penydarren Ironworks.

4hp table engine for Cwm Twrch.

60in beam blowing engine for the Sirhowy Iron Company.

1830
34in x 7ft rotative condensing beam stamping engine for Usborne, Benson & Co., Forest Copper Works, Swansea.

8hp engine for N. Perchard, Jersey.

11in high-pressure beam engine for Mr Strick.

36in x 6ft 9in beam pumping engine for the Cwm Pit of the Landore Coal Company, Swansea.

4hp table engine for Mr B. Gibbins, Chemical Works, Neath.

10½in engine for F. Dare, Bridgend.

30in beam stamping engine for the Allihies Mining Co., County Kerry, Ireland.

22in beam engine for winding and pumping for the Aveyron Mining Co., France.

1831	34in rotative condensing beam engine and a 52½in beam engine for C.H. Leigh, Pontypool.
	40in beam engine for Fourchambault, France..
1832	20hp engines for Joseph Claypon.
	Tipping engine for the Millbrook Iron Company.
	28in engine for the Sirhowy Iron Company.
1833	18in beam engine for T.S. Biddulph, Pembrokeshire.
	6hp engine for Mr Smith.
	9in pumping engine for George Insole, Maesmawr Colliery.
c1833	Two high-pressure engines for the Cyfarthfa Ironworks, Merthyr Tydfil.
1834	18in rotative beam engine for winding for the Allihies Mining Co., County Kerry, Ireland.
	40in engine for the Tredegar Ironworks.
	15½in high-pressure rotative beam engine for winding and pumping for George Insole.
	22in hammer engine for Morfa Copper Works, Swansea.
	50in beam blowing engine for Hunt Brothers, Pentwyn Ironworks.
	30in beam engine for T.S. Grubb, Clonmel.
	14in high-pressure engine for George Penrose, Neath.
	34in beam engine for the British Iron Company.
	45in blowing engine for the Dundyvan Iron Company.
	24in A frame rotative beam engine for the Pymore Mill Co., Bridport, Dorset.
	70in beam pumping engine for Lloyd Williams & Co., Hendra Mine, Flintshire.
	22in engine for Mr John Parsons.
	24in beam engine for Williams, Foster & Company.
	18in rotative condensing beam engine for C.H. Leigh, Pontypool.
1835	19in beam engine, 12hp, for James Ozanne, Guernsey.
	1hp engine for Charles Bewley & Co., Dublin.
	21½in x 6ft high-pressure pumping engine for G. Cox, Hendreforgan Colliery.
	16in high-pressure engine for Mr Crane.
	30½in high-pressure rotative beam pumping engine for William Crawshay, Cyfarthfa.
	Rotative engine for Henry Bath & Son, Swansea and Chile.
	30in engine for Cuba.
	12in high-pressure engine for the Allihies Mining Co., County Kerry, Ireland.
1836	60in beam blowing engine for the Nantyglo Ironworks.
	18in high-pressure beam engine for the Mersey Steel & Iron Company.
	4hp engine for Mr Christopher James, near Landore, Swansea.
	12in high-pressure engine for Mr Parsons.
	40in blowing engine for the Dowlais Ironworks (No 4).

30in high-pressure rotative beam blowing engine with 122in blowing cylinder for the Penydarren Ironworks.

18in high-pressure beam engine for William Crawshay, Cyfarthfa Ironworks.

24in high-pressure beam engine for the Clydach Iron Company.

c1836-38 $5\frac{1}{2}$in x 1ft 8in table engine for the Vale of Neath Brewery (now in Swansea Maritime Museum).

1837 $52\frac{1}{2}$in beam blowing engine for the Golynos Ironworks.

$38\frac{1}{2}$in beam blowing engine for the Penydarren Iron Co.

12in high-pressure beam winding and pumping engine for the Clydach Iron Company.

43in engine and 40in engine for George Insole.

52in condensing beam pumping engine for Harfords, Davies & Company, Sirhowy Ironworks.

60in condensing beam pumping engine for Great Wheal Prosper, Cornwall.

60in engine for the Ebbw Vale Ironworks.

40in engine for Morfa Copper Works, Swansea

19in rotative beam engine for Mr Llewellyn, Ynispenllwch Tinplate Works, Swansea.

12hp beam engine for D. Lewis, Stradey, Llanelly.

Two 34in rotative pumping engines for William Crawshay, Treforest Tinplate Mills.

45in beam blowing engine for Mr George Crane.

Parts of 24in drift engines for the Dowlais Iron Company.

22in engine for Budnick Mine, Cornwall.

1838   18in rotative high-pressure beam engine for Waun Wyllt Colliery.

$52\frac{1}{2}$in blowing engine for the Sirhowy Iron Company.

12in engine for inclined plane and underground mine works for the Clydach Iron Company.

$15\frac{1}{2}$in x 5ft A frame beam engine for winding and pumping for George Penrose, Neath.

40in beam blowing engine for the Dowlais Iron Company.

45in x 8ft beam blowing engine for the Yniscedwyn Ironworks.

12hp engine for Mr A. Fisher, Youghal, Ireland.

46in rotative beam rolling mill engine for the Rhymney Ironworks.

30in condensing beam engine for Germany.

Engine for Henry Bath & Son, Swansea and Chile.

$52\frac{1}{2}$in beam blowing engine for the Cambrian Iron & Spelter Co., Maesteg.

$21\frac{1}{2}$in high-pressure engine for Mr Llewellyn, Aberdulais, Neath.

$15\frac{1}{2}$ in high-pressure A frame beam engine for George Insole.

18in beam engine and two 15in x 2ft 6in high-pressure beam engines for the Rhymney Iron Company.

20hp winding and pumping engine for Joseph Claypon, Brecon Forest Tramroad.

1839 45in engine for Fox, Williams & Co., Perran Wharf, Cornwall.

16in high-pressure engine for the Swansea Coal Company.

$52\frac{1}{2}$in beam blowing engine for the Hirwaun Ironworks.

24in high-pressure non-condensing beam blowing engine for the Gwendraeth
Anthracite and Iron Company.

Two 72in beam pumping engines for the Glasgow Waterworks.

42in beam blowing engine with a 122in blowing cylinder for the Tredegar Iron Company.

34in beam engine for John Parsons, Neath.

43in engine for the Landshipping Colliery.

38in high-pressure rolling mill engine for the Penydarren Ironworks.

43in engine for George Insole.

2hp engine for David James, Merthyr Tydfil.

$10\frac{1}{2}$in slag engine for Vivian & Sons, Hafod Copper Works, Swansea.

40in beam engine for Vivian & Sons, Hafod Copper Works, Swansea.

Two $52\frac{1}{2}$in rotative beam engines and a 38in A frame condensing beam engine for
the Rhymney Iron Company.

38in high-pressure beam blowing engine for the Sirhowy Iron Company.

24in beam engine for the Ystalyfera Ironworks.

42in rotative beam rolling mill engine and a 42in blowing engine for the Cambrian
Iron & Spelter Co., Maesteg.

Two coupled 15in high-pressure beam engines for the White Rock Copper Co.,
Swansea.

Beam blowing engine with 122in blowing cylinder for the Victoria Ironworks, Ebbw
Vale.

60in engine for the Rhymney Iron Company.

1840 Two coupled 15in high-pressure beam engines for the Nant-y-Crynwith Colliery of
the Cambrian Iron & Spelter Company.

14in engine for Mr John Parsons.

12in engine for Henry Bath & Son, Swansea & Chile.

12in engine for Mansell Phillips.

18in x $2\frac{1}{2}$ft high-pressure horizontal engine for the Monmouthshire Canal and
Railway Company.

45in blowing engine for William Crawshay, Cyfarthfa Ironworks.

24in rolling mill engine and 40in engine for the Clydach Iron Company.

Two coupled 15in high-pressure beam engines for Parsons & Strange,
Tonmawr Colliery, Neath.

Two $52\frac{1}{2}$in beam blowing engine for the Blaenavon Ironworks.

30in engine for the Main Colliery, Neath Abbey Coal Company.

$52\frac{1}{2}$in beam blowing engine for the Clydach Ironworks.

40in rolling mill engine for the Margam Copper Works.

$52\frac{1}{2}$in beam blowing engine for the Cyfarthfa Ironworks.

12in engine for Henry Bath & Son, Swansea and Chile

36in high-pressure beam engine for William Crawshay, Forest of Dean.

1841 10½in engine for the Briton Ferry Colliery.

24in high-pressure engine for the Victoria Ironworks, Ebbw Vale.

15in engine for the Clydach Iron Company.

12in x 3½ft, 12hp rotative beam engine and an 8hp engine for Richard Blakemore & Company.

36in beam engine for the Swansea Coal Company.

21in x 6ft rotative beam engine for T.S. Grubb, Clonmel, Ireland.

1842 40in rotative beam rolling mill engine for the Taibach Copper Works.

26in beam engine for Fourchambault, France.

15in grasshopper beam engine for Francis Dare, Porthcawl.

40in expansive beam blowing engine for France.

2hp engine for Birmingham Spelter Works.

18in x 2ft engine for Cox Brothers, Court de Wyck.

13in and 14in high-pressure engines for Vivian & Sons.

10½in engine for the Cheadle Works.

20in beam engine for Mr Parsons, Neath.

12in crushing engine for Henry Bath & Co., Swansea and Chile.

c1842 30in mill engine for Banks & Co., Pontymister Works.

21in x 6ft rotative beam engine for the Aberdulais Tinplate Works, Neath.

1843 45in rotative beam engine for the Nantyglo Ironworks.

2hp engine for Charles Lambert, Coquimbo, Chile.

65in single acting beam engine for Starling Benson, Penclawdd Works.

40in engine for the Hafod Copper Works.

2hp engine for Evan Evans, Neath.

30in beam engine for the Briton Ferry Colliery.

18in engine for Port Tennant.

45in rolling mill engine for the Nantyglo Ironworks.

2hp engine for Evan Evans

12in high-pressure beam engine for Lucy Thomas, Waun Wyllt Colliery.

18in x 4ft high-pressure vertical engine for J.W. Lyon, Port Tennant.

45in rotative condensing beam engine for driving rolling mills for B. & N. Sherwood & Co.

1844 12in high-pressure rotative beam engine for Mr Taylor.

45in engine for France.

10½in high-pressure engine for Mr J. Hall.

24in high-pressure engine for Col. Cameron.

28in condensing beam engine for W.W. Young.

24in high-pressure engine for the Porto Novo Iron Company, East Indies.

7½in, 4hp grasshopper beam engine for Mr George Bedford, Baglan.

18in x 4ft beam engine for David Davies of Hirwaun.

1845 78in x 9ft condensing beam pumping engine for Henry Crawshay, Lightmoor Colliery, Forest of Dean.

12in table engine for the Abernant Ironworks.

24in high-pressure engine for Lucy Thomas, Waun Wyllt Colliery.

40in engine for the Abernant Ironworks.

38in engine for the Pentwyn & Golynos Iron Company.

30in x 6ft rotative beam engine for pumping and winding for C.H. Leigh, Pontypool.

38in high-pressure engine for William Llewellyn, Aberdulais, Neath.

45in rolling mill engine for the Llynvi Vale Iron Company, Maesteg.

12in engine for Briton Ferry.

60in rotative condensing beam engine to drive rolling mills for the Cwmavon Ironworks.

30in rotative beam engine for Morris Brothers & Morgan, Abercarne Iron and Tinplate Works.

28in rotative condensing beam pumping engine for the Aberdare Canal Company.

$52\frac{1}{2}$in beam blowing engine for the Ystalyfera Iron Company.

30in x 6ft beam engine for the Pontypool Ironworks.

13in engine for Mr Morgan Hughes, Thomas Chapel, near Tenby.

24in high-pressure beam engine for Crawshay Bailey, Nantyglo Ironworks.

4hp engine for the Melyncryddan Chemical Works, Neath.

24in beam engine for Mr Wayne, Aberdare.

Two coupled 15in beam engines for the Cwmavon Works.

2hp engine for D. Arthur, Neath.

1846 24in high-pressure engine for the Onllwyn Ironworks.

$10\frac{1}{2}$in engine for Adam Murray.

12in high-pressure engine for the Aberaman Ironworks.

$10\frac{1}{2}$in, 4 hp table engine and 7in, 4hp horizontal engine for Robert Bruton, Spain.

Two 32in, 35hp beam engines for Fox, Henderson & Co., London Works, Birmingham.

60in rotative beam engine to drive rolling mills for the Briton Ferry Ironworks.

12in beam engine for Francis Crawshay.

$10\frac{1}{2}$in engine for Mr William Thomas, Lletyshenkin Colliery.

40in beam engine for rolling mill for Vivian & Sons, Hafod Copper Works.

4hp table engine for Pinto Perez, Spain.

2hp table engine for Francis Crawshay, Hirawun.

16in engine for C.H. Leigh, Pontypool.

2hp table engine for Robert Crawshay, Cyfarthfa.

44in x 9ft beam blowing engine with 122in blowing cylinder and 44in rotative beam rolling mill engine for Crawshay Bailey, Aberaman Ironworks.

$32\frac{1}{2}$in beam blowing engine for Trimsaran.

44in rolling mill engine for the Golynos Ironworks.

1846-47 40in engine for Briton Ferry.

1847   24in x 7ft beam blowing engine for F. Huth & Co., Spain.

Two 45in x 8ft beam blowing engines for F.L. Riant & Langlois, Aubin, France.

22in beam blowing engine for F. Ade Elorza, Spain.

12in high-pressure beam engine for winding and pumping for the Graigola Colliery.

34in rotative beam pumping engine for Henry Crawshay, Cinderford.

30in beam blowing engine for the Pendroso Mining Co., Spain.

12in high-pressure engine for Mr Wayne.

7in x 1ft 8in vertical engine for the Swansea Iron Shipbuilding Company.

12in engine for John Parsons, Neath.

30in high-pressure condensing rotative beam engine for White Brothers, Waterford, Ireland.

36in engine for the Amman Iron Company.

30in x 4ft horizontal, non-condensing engine for W.H. Darby, Brymbo Colliery.

12in engine for the Gadlys Iron Co., Aberdare.

17in pumping engine for George Insole, No.1 Pit, Cymmer.

12in A frame beam engine for winding and pumping for Francis Crawshay.

1848   16in high-pressure engine for the Gadlys Iron Co., Aberdare.

27in rolling mill engine for Fred. Huth & Company, Spain.

30in x 6ft engine for the Briton Ferry Ironworks.

4hp engine for the Swansea Iron Shipbuilding Company.

16in high-pressure beam engine for pumping and winding for the Aberdare Coal Company.

1849   24in x 1ft high-pressure engine for the Hirwaun Ironworks.

24in x 1ft engine for Francis Crawshay.

22in blowing engine for Darthez Brothers, Sargadeloz Ironworks, Spain.

16in horizontal high-pressure winding engine for the Gadlys Iron Company.

12in horizontal engine for George Penrose & Co., Neath

14in engine for the Yniscedwyn Ironworks.

Beam engine for winding and pumping for Mr Calvert, Newbridge.

30in x 7ft rotative beam engine for David Williams, Ynyscynon Colliery, Aberdare.

20in high-pressure horizontal engine for Bow Common Copper Works, London.

16in horizontal engine for Vivian & Sons, Morfa Colliery, Taibach.

1850   30in high-pressure engine for Messrs Waynes, Gadlys Ironworks, Aberdare.

24in high-pressure horizontal blowing engine for Banks & Company, Pontymister.

28in rotative beam engine for Kidd & Company, Bristol.

18in x $2\frac{1}{2}$ft high-pressure horizontal engine for the Monmouthshire Canal & Railway Company.

24in horizontal engine for winding and pumping for Mr Thomas Shepherd, Merthyr Tydfil.

14in high-pressure engine for George Penrose, Neath.

1851 40in beam blowing engine for the Aberdare Iron Company.

12in horizontal winding engine for George Penrose, Neath.

24in high-pressure horizontal engine for Edward Jenkins, Pontnewydd Tinplate Works, Nr Newport.

24in x 6ft horizontal mill engine for N. Daniells, Redbrook Tinplate Works.

13in horizontal engine and 20in high-pressure horizontal engine for W.P. Struvé.

30in high-pressure horizontal engine for Banks & Company, Pontymister.

24in high-pressure engine for the Machen Coal Company.

22in high-pressure engine for Robert Crawshay, Cyfarthfa.

30in high-pressure horizontal engine for Major Phillips.

22in beam engine for Henry Crawshay, Cinderford.

18in horizontal engine for Thomas Powell, Newport.

1852 16in horizontal engine for Nash Vaughan Edwards Vaughan, Rheola, Neath Valley.

30in high-pressure horizontal engine for the Glamorgan Iron & Coal Co., Tondu Ironworks.

Two 12in horizontal engines for the Aberdare Iron Company.

32in high-pressure beam engine for the Lletyshenkin Colliery.

22in x 2ft 9in engine for Mr Sturge, Northfleet, Kent.

16in horizontal engine for Young & Allen, Neath Brickworks.

40in rotative beam rolling mill engine for Taibach Copper Works.

26in x 6ft horizontal winding engine for the Dowlais Iron Company.

52in beam blowing engine for the Corngreaves Ironworks, New British Iron Company.

$9\frac{1}{2}$in x 1ft horizontal high-pressure engine for the Abernant Ironworks of the Aberdare Iron Company.

31in high-pressure horizontal engine for the Ystalyfera Iron Company.

Two 12in horizontal high-pressure blowing engines with a 5ft flywheel and a 10in x 9in vertical engine for the Aberdare Iron Company.

26in x 5ft horizontal engine for T.W. Booker, Pentyrch and Melingriffiths.

50in beam blowing engine and a 24in rotative high-pressure beam engine for the Nantyglo Ironworks.

12in x 3ft horizontal pumping engine for the Gloucester & Berkeley Canal Company.

25in horizontal engine for Ford & Son, Pyle.

36in high-pressure horizontal engine for Cwmavon.

1853 16in horizontal engine for Vivian & Sons, Morfa Collery, Taibach.

12in x 2ft engine for the Gadlys Iron Company.

12in beam engine for grinding silver ore for Mr Vega Copiapo.

24in horizontal engine for winding and pumping for the Aberdare Iron Company.

32in high-pressure beam blowing engine for the Aberdare Iron Company.

34in horizontal engine for T.W. Booker, Pentyrch and Melingriffiths.

20in x 4ft horizontal engine for pumping for Plant & Cadman.

30in x 6ft horizontal engine for George Penrose & Company, Neath.

24in x 4ft horizontal engine for winding and pumping for the Glamorgan and Cardiff Coal & Coke Co., Trecastle Colliery, Llantrisant.

20in horizontal engine for Henry Bath & Son, Swansea and Chile.

20in x 4ft horizontal engine and a 50in x 12ft beam blowing engine with a 90in blowing cylinder for the Aberdare Iron Company.

1854   12in engine for the Neath Abbey Coal Company.

16in x 3ft horizontal pumping engine for Weston-Super-Mare.

24in x 4ft high-pressure horizontal engine for Messrs Guichet ainé & Russell, Metaux a Nantes, France.

7in x 1ft 8in horizontal high-pressure engine for bone mill for H. Gibbins, Neath.

12in engine for the Abernant Ironworks.

20in x 4ft horizontal engine with 12ft flywheel for David Davies, Blaengwawr Colliery, Aberdare.

24in high-pressure beam blowing engine (No 3) for the Aberdare Iron Company.

20in x 4ft high-pressure horizontal engine for Dr Wagstaff, Forest of Dean.

30in high-pressure horizontal engine for George Penrose, Eaglesbush Colliery.

15in hoist engine for Francis Crawshay.

4in x 1ft hoist engine for coal drop crane for Newport Docks.

Horizontal engine for winding and pumping for James Brogden, Tondu Ironworks.

20in x 3ft engine for Mr Vegas.

24in x 2ft horizontal engine for Francis Crawshay, Blaen Hirwaun Mine Works.

45in rotative beam engine for the forge for the Aberdare Iron Company.

1855   13in x 3ft horizontal engine for pumping and winding and a 16in winding engine for David Davies, Blaengwawr Colliery, Aberdare.

16in engine for Henry Bath & Son (for Chile).

51in x 10ft inverted beam pumping engine for the Main Colliery, Neath Abbey Coal Company.

22in x 2ft 7in horizontal engine for Risca Colliery.

42in beam rolling mill engine for the Llynvi Vale Ironworks.

28in beam engine for winding and pumping for David Davies, Blaengwawr Colliery, Aberdare.

12in engine for Henry Bath & Son, Swansea and Chile.

14in x 1½ft inverted vertical engine to drive shears for the Llynvi Vale Iron Company, Maesteg.

Two 26in vertical inclined engines for David Davies, Abercwmboy Colliery.

40in beam blowing engine for the Llynvi Vale Ironworks.

1856   24in x 1ft engine for Francis Crawshay, Treforest Tinplate Works.

45in beam rolling mill engine for Williams, Foster & Co., Morfa Copper Works.

34in rotative beam pumping engine for the Gloucester & Berkeley Canal Company.

41in mill engine and a 9in x 1ft feed engine for the Taibach Copper Works.

10in x 1ft inverted vertical engine for the Yorkshire Tire & Axle Company.

10in engine for the Aberdare Iron Company.

20in x 5ft beam blowing engine and a 20in winding and pumping engine for Gordon & Stuart, Calcutta, India.

16in engine for Vivian & Sons, Morfa Colliery,

Two 12in horizontal blowing engines for the Aberdare Iron Company.

13in x 2ft horizontal engine for David Davies, Blaengwawr Colliery, Aberdare.

30in high-pressure direct acting Bull pumping engine for Henry Crawshay, Cinderford, Shakemantle Pit.

12in horizontal engine for George Penrose & Co., Eaglesbush Colliery, Neath.

20in x 4ft horizontal high-pressure blowing engine for John Gero, Malaga, Spain.

Two 25in high-pressure engines for the Cwm Du Colliery, Dynevor Coal Co., Neath.

1857   24in x 4ft horizontal engine for Mr Russel, Cwmtileri Colliery.

30in engine for the Dynevor Coal Company.

40in beam engine for rolling mill for Vivian & Sons, Hafod Copper Works.

18in x 3ft horizontal engine with a 9ft flywheel and a 14in x $1\frac{1}{2}$ft high-pressure vertical engine for the Aberdare Iron Company.

54in x 8ft high-pressure beam blowing engine with a 120in cylinder for Francis Crawshay, Treforest.

12in engine for Henry Bath & Son, Swansea and Chile.

20in high-pressure horizontal engine for winding and pumping for Edward Thomas, Baglan.

60in x 10ft direct acting high-pressure Bull pumping engine for Henry Crawshay, Cinderford, Shakemantle Pit.

1858   16in winding engine for Brithdir Colliery, Dynevor Coal Co., Neath,

54in x 8ft rotative beam blowing engine with an 84in blowing cylinder for Cinderford Ironworks, Forest of Dean.

Blowing engine for an ironworks for William Bird, London (export agent).

24in x 4ft semi-portable horizontal engine for the Port Phillip and Colonial Gold Mining Co., Australia.

45in x 10ft beam blowing engine with 104in blowing cylinder for the Gadlys Iron Company.

Two 23in x 3ft horizontal engines for Yellow Metal Rolling Mill.

27in x 3ft horizontal mill engine for the Aberdare Iron Company.

9in x $1\frac{1}{2}$ft portable engine on boiler for Vivian & Sons, Morfa Colliery.

15in high-pressure horizontal engine for Henry Crawshay, Shakemantle Iron Mine, Forest of Dean.

30in high-pressure horizontal mill engine for Banks & Company, Pontymister.

23in high-pressure horizontal engine for the Llanelly Copper Works.

1859   Two 12in x $2\frac{1}{2}$ft horizontal haulage engines for Edward Thomas, Baglan.

27in horizontal engine for Middle Bank Copper Works, Swansea..

8in x 10in inverted vertical engine for Mr Houghton.

24in x 2ft 9in vertical engine for Knight, Bevan & Sturge, Portland Cement Works, Northfleet.

22in horizontal engine for Mr J.J. Jenkins & Company, Morriston.

20in x 3ft horizontal underground winding engine for the Gadlys Iron Company.

Two 25in horizontal winding engines with piston valves for the Neath Abbey Coal Company.

24in x 4ft horizontal engine for Hallam & Company, Upper Forest, Morriston.

12in engine for a crushing mill for Henry Bath & Son, Swansea and Chile.

1860   24in condensing horizontal engine for Knight, Bevan & Sturge, Portland Cement Works, Northfleet, Kent.

16in mill engine for Henry Bath & Son, Swansea and Chile.

39in direct acting Bull pumping engine for the Llynvi Vale Ironworks.

Two 22in x 4ft high-pressure horizontal engines for copper and silver mills for James Lewis

& Co., agents for Mr Logan.

$19\frac{1}{2}$in x 4ft beam engine for winding and pumping for the Landshipping Colliery, Pembrokeshire.

16in engine for Fredericks & Jenner, Pontneathvaughan, Neath.

Two 16in x $3\frac{1}{2}$ft horizontal engines for the Clunes Quartz Mining Company.

1861   Two 16in engines for Edward Thomas & Sons, Baglan Colliery.

Two 16in x 4ft 6in horizontal engines for Vivian & Sons, Morfa Colliery, Taibach.

22in x 4ft engine for copper mill.

12in x 3ft horizontal engine for Vivian & Sons, Taibach.

20in x 3ft horizontal engine for the Gadlys Iron Company.

24in x 5ft horizontal engine for Shepherd & Evans, Cwmaman Colliery.

22in x 1ft horizontal engine for the Blaenavon Ironworks.

12in x 9in vertical engine for Edward Thomas, Baglan.

30in engine for the Briton Ferry Ironworks.

1862   Two 15in horizontal engines for Mr Ferguson, London.

Two 22in x 4ft horizontal engines for winding and pumping for Messrs Morgan & Thomas, Primrose Colliery, near Alltwen.

45in x 5ft expansive condensing beam engine for Charles Lambert, Port Tennant Copper Mills.

Two 30in x 6ft engines for Cwmavon.

12in x$1\frac{1}{2}$ft inverted vertical engine for Sir Ralph Howard, Patent Fuel Works, Swansea.

56in high-pressure beam pumping engine for Osman Barret, Foxes Bridge Colliery, Forest of Dean.

Two 36in beam engines for Castle Pit, Merthyr Tydfil.

14in x $1\frac{1}{2}$ft high-pressure vertical engine for the Llwydcoed Ironworks of the Aberdare Iron Company.

12in engine for a copper mill for Henry Bath & Son, Swansea and Chile.

1863	24in x 4ft semi-portable horizontal engine for Port Phillip & Colonial Gold Mining Co., Australia.
	Two 27in x 5ft horizontal engines for Henry Crawshay, Cinderford.
	24in x 4ft horizontal engine for the Eaglesbush Tinplate Company.
	41in mill engine and a 24in x 3ft high-pressure A frame beam engine for Vivian & Sons, Hafod Copper Works, Swansea.
	Two 27in x 5ft winding engines for Foxes Bridge Colliery, Forest of Dean.
	6in x 9in engine for Vivian & Sons, Morfa Colliery.
	14in x $1\frac{1}{2}$ft inverted vertical engine for the Crown Preserved Coal Co Blackweir, Nr Cardiff.
	24in x 4ft engine for the Melincryddan Tinplate Works, Neath.
	10in x 1ft 8in horizontal pumping engine for Henry Bath & Son, Swansea & Chile.
	Engine for Clunes Mining Co., Victoria, Australia.
	24in vertical engine for Knight, Bevan & Sturge, Portland Cement Works, Northfleet.
	80in x 10ft Bull engine for Mr H.D. Hoskold, Forest of Dean.
	24in x 7ft rotative beam blowing engine with a 60in blowing cylinder and a 13ft flywheel for the Brynna Ironworks, Pencoed.
	20in horizontal winding engine for Mr Tissington.
	20in x 3ft horizontal engine for winding and pumping for the Bargoed Coal Co., Merthyr Tydfil.
1865	Two 20in x 2ft inverted vertical engines for the Plymouth Iron Co., Merthyr Tydfil.
	32in x 6ft 10in beam blowing engine for Henry Crawshay, Cinderford.
	26in x $2\frac{1}{2}$ft inverted vertical engine for blooming mills for Robert Crawshay, Cyfarthfa Ironworks.
	20in x 2ft inverted vertical engine for the Shelton Bar Iron Co., Staffordshire.
	Two 22in x 3ft horizontal engines for the Plymouth Ironworks.
	Two 27in winding engines for the Neath Abbey Coal Company.
	12in x 2ft 8in horizontal engine for Henry Bath & Son, Swansea and Chile.
	Two 25in winding engines for the Rhymney Iron Company.
1866	Two 18in horizontal engines for the Aberdulais Tinplate Works.
	16in x 3ft horizontal engine for Townshend, Wood & Co., Swansea.
	36in x 4ft engine and 20in x $3\frac{1}{2}$ft horizontal engine for the Rhymney Iron Company.
	40in beam engine for the Lydney Tinplate Company.
	22in winding engine for Henry Crawshay, Lightmoor Colliery.
	25in beam winding engine for Vivian & Sons, Morfa Colliery.
	12in x 2ft 8in horizontal engine for Henry Bath & Son, Swansea and Chile.
1867	Two 16in x 4ft horizontal engines for Vivian & Sons, Morfa Colliery, Taibach.
	10inx10in inverted vertical engine for rail punching machine for the Tredegar Iron Company.
	$38\frac{1}{2}$in mill engine for the Aberdulais Tinplate Works.
	20in x $3\frac{1}{2}$ft horizontal engine for the Rhymney Iron Company.

Two 27in horizontal winding engines for the Neath Abbey Coal Company, Stanley Pit.

12in x 1ft engine for the Shelton Bar Iron Company.

Two 27in x 5ft winding engines for Foxes Bridge Colliery, Forest of Dean.

26in x 2ft vertical engine for the Beaufort Tinplate Works, Morriston, Swansea.

26in x 2ft vertical engine for the Beaufort Tinplate Works, Morriston, Swansea.

34in mill engine for Alloway, Lydbrook.

1868   15in x 2ft 6in engine for Henry Bath & Son, Swansea and Chile.

21in x 10ft 3½in beam winding engine for Henry Crawshay, Causeway Mine Pit, Forest of Dean.

30in pumping engine and a 60in x 9ft beam pumping engine for Osman Barrett, Fair Play Pit, Forest of Dean.

80in x 10½ft beam pumping engine for the Dowlais Ironworks.

Two 28in engines for the Dunraven Colliery.

21in winding engine for Henry Crawshay, St Annal's Mine Pit, Forest of Dean.

15in x 2½ft horizontal engine for Henry Bath & Son, Swansea and Chile (for export).

21in x 5ft beam winding engine for Henry Crawshay, Buckshaft Mine Pit, Forest of Dean.

16in x 3ft winding engine for Osman Barrett, Fair Play Pit, Mitcheldean, Forest of Dean.

1869   24in x 2ft 9in condensing horizontal engine for Knight, Bevan & Sturge, Portland Cement Works, Northfleet, Kent.

Two 18in horizontal winding engines for the Neath Abbey Coal Company, Cwm Clydach Colliery.

24in x 4ft condensing horizontal engine for the Port Philip & Colonial Gold Mining Co., Australia.

24in x 2½ft horizontal engine for Robert Crawshay, Cyfarthfa.

26in x 2ft vertical engine for the Beaufort Tinplate Works, Morriston.

Haulage engine for Castle Pit, Merthyr Tydfil.

1870   30in condensing beam engine for T. Wood & Co., Briton Ferry Ironworks.

24in x 5ft horizontal winding engine for the Aberdare Iron Company.

6in x 9in inverted vertical engine for Barrett & Crawshay, Foxes Bridge Colliery, Forest of Dean.

12in haulage engine for the Neath Abbey Coal Company, Cwm Clydach Colliery.

16in x 1½ft inverted vertical winding engine for the Shakemantle Iron Mine, Forest of Dean.

15in engine for Osman Barrett, Easter Mine, Forest of Dean.

1871   Two 27in condensing horizontal engines and a 24in beam engine for Knight, Bevan & Sturge, Portland Cement Works, Northfleet, Kent.

20in x 2ft inverted vertical engine for the Aberdare Iron Co., Treforest Works.

12in x 3ft haulage engine for Cwm Clydach Colliery, Neath Abbey Coal Company.

Two 38in blowing engines for Cwmavon.

12in engine for Mr Sneezum.

12in x 1½ft horizontal pumping engine for the bottom of deep pit, Morfa Colliery,
10in x 1ft 3in vertical engine for driving rail punching machine for the
Plymouth Ironworks.
Two 22in horizontal winding engines for the Neath Abbey Coal Company.
Two 24in x 5ft horizontal winding engines for Henry Crawshay & Sons, Lightmoor
Colliery, Forest of Dean.
Two 14in x 3ft horizontal haulage engines for the Dowlais Ironworks.

1872	42in blowing engine for the Cefn Ironworks, Pyle, Glamorgan.
	34in x 3½ft horizontal mill engine for G.H. Banks, Llangennech Tinplate Works.
	10in portable horizontal engine for winding and pumping for the Neath Abbey Coal Company, Greenway Colliery.
	Two 27in vertical engines for Knight, Bevan & Sturge, Portland Cement Works, Northfleet Kent.
	Two 25in winding engines and an 18in winding engine for the Court Herbert Colliery.
	10in engine for driving a punching machine for the Briton Ferry Ironworks.
	24in x 3ft horizontal haulage engine for the Plymouth Iron Company.
	Two 13in horizontal winding engines for John Glasbrook, Morriston.
1873	24in x 1ft 6in condensing horizontal engine for Knight, Bevan & Sturge, Portland Cement Works, Northfleet, Kent.
	30in x 6ft beam engine for Foxes Bridge Colliery, Forest of Dean.
	Two 12in x 1ft 2in horizontal haulage engines for John Glasbrook, Morriston.
	15½in winding engine for Lightmoor Colliery, Forest of Dean.
	Two 22in x 3ft horizontal air compressing engines for the Plymouth Iron Company.
	Two 16in winding engines for Mr. Grenfell, Baglan Colliery.
1874	12in x 9in engine for the Shelton Bar Iron Company, Staffs.
	Two 12in x 1ft 2in horizontal haulage engines for John Glasbrook, Morriston.
1875	12in engine for Cripelo.
	24in x 4½ft engine for the Llangennech Tinplate Works.
	22in rotative beam engine and two 12in x 1ft 8in horizontal winding engines for Henry Crawshay, Cinderford, Forest of Dean.
	Two 22in x 4ft horizontal winding engines for the Alltwen Colliery Company.
	36in x 5ft beam mill engine for D. Edwards & Co., Duffryn Tinplate Works.
	Two 22in horizontal haulage engines for Dynevor & Dyffryn United Company, Brynddewy Colliery.
	Two 22in engines for Cefn Gorlau Colliery, Gowerton, Swansea..
	26in x 4ft horizontal mill engine for the Morriston Tinplate Works.
1876	70in x 12ft beam pumping engine for Henry Crawshay, Cinderford, Forest of Dean.

20in x 4ft horizontal engine for John Glasbrook, Morriston.

Two 25in horizontal haulage engines for the Gwladys Pit, Dulais Resolven Collieries.

1877   Two 30in x 3ft 6in horizontal mill engines for Mr H.I. Martin, Swansea.

12in haulage engine for the Main Colliery, Neath Abbey.

30in engine for Spain.

Two 25in x 4ft horizontal winding engines for Lewis T. Lewis, Dylais Merthyr Colliery.

41$\frac{1}{2}$in mill engine for Vivian & Sons.

40in rotative beam engine for William Roberts & Company, Liverpool.

1878   28in engine for David Glasbrook, Midland Tinplate Works, Swansea.

40in x 5ft beam mill engine for the Duffryn Tin Plate Company, Swansea.

Two 10in x 1ft 4in horizontal engines for Mr Roger Howells.

37in x 5ft mill engine for Glasbrook & Lewis.

22in x 3ft horizontal air compressing engine and a pair of 12in x 1ft 2in haulage engines for Edwin Crawshay, Forest of Dean.

1879   8in x 1$\frac{1}{2}$ft horizontal engine for Hutching's Patent Pickling Machine.

1879   Conversion of a 12in x 1ft 8in locomotive to a stationary engine for the Aberdulais Tinplate Works, Neath.

1880   30in x 4ft horizontal mill engine and 10in x 10in inverted vertical engine for the Gurnos Tinplate Works.

Two 16in winding engines for Mr. Grenfell, Baglan Colliery.

42in vertical condensing engine for the Pontardulais Tinplate Company.

43in x 3$\frac{1}{2}$ft vertical engine for William Griffiths & Co., Pontardulais.

25in x 4ft horizontal mill engine and 30in horizontal for the Clyne Tinplate Company, Resolven, Neath.

34in x 4ft tin mill engine for Edward Davies & Sons, Margam.

20in x 3$\frac{1}{2}$ft horizontal engine for cold roll mill and 6in x 9in inverted vertical engine for bar

shears for the Gurnos Tinplate Company.

14in x 1$\frac{1}{2}$ft inverted vertical engine for the Llynvi Vale Ironworks.

c1880   34in horizontal mill engine for the Midland Tinplate Company.

1881   32in horizontal air compressing engine for John Glasbrook, Cwm Pit Colliery.

7$\frac{1}{2}$in engine for D. Glasbrook.

1882   24in engine for general sale.

8in x 1$\frac{1}{2}$ft horizontal engine for working the 'Direct Motion' pickling machine as designed and arranged by the Neath Abbey Iron Company.

1882   70in x 12ft rotative beam pumping engine for Shakemantle Pit, Forest of Dean.

Pre 1840   12in x 3ft underground pumping engine for the Neath Abbey Coal Company.

Pre 1842   16in engine for Pwllfaron Colliery.

No date   New Trevithick engine for Mr Morris.
40in engine for Alloway, Lydbrook, Forest of Dean.
60in engine for the Ebbw Vale Ironworks.
14in x 2ft inverted vertical engine for driving saw mills for Lightmoor Colliery, Forest of Dean..
25in engine for the Llangennech Coal Company.
32in x 6ft beam engine for winding and pumping for Mr William Thomas, Lletyshenkin Colliery.
Two 24in x $3\frac{1}{2}$ft inverted vertical engines for the Old Castle Tinplate Company.
40in beam blowing engine for the Ruabon Ironworks.
Two 24in x 5ft rotative beam pumping engines for the Stourbridge Waterworks.
10in x 9in engine for sawing machine for the Tondu Ironworks.
20in x 2ft horizontal engine for Worcester Colliery.
19in beam engine for La Gurche, Antwerp.
16in beam engine for the Cyfarthfa Ironworks.
15in engine for Mr G. Insole, Maesmawr Colliery.
15in horizontal engine for the Forest of Dean Iron Company.

Appendix Three

The Marine Engineering Work of the Neath Abbey Iron Company.

[I] Ships engined by the company

1822   *Glamorgan*, a paddle steamer built by W. Evans of Rotherhithe. This vessel was fitted with two 27in simple side lever engines rated at 20hp each, the engines were later rebuilt to 29in.

1823   *Bristol*, a paddle steamer built at Bristol and fitted with two 31in simple side lever engines.

1824   *Lord Beresford*, a paddle steamer built by William Scott & Sons, Bristol. This ship was fitted with two simple side lever engines rated at 30hp each. In 1831 the ship was re-engined to give a total of 80hp.

1825   *Saint Pierre*, a paddle steamer used as a ferry built by Pride & Williams, Newport.

1827   *Worcester*, a paddle steamer used as a ferry built by William Scott & Sons.

1831   *Nautilus*, a paddle steamer built by the assignees of William Scott, Bristol. This vessel was fitted with two 32in simple side lever engines giving a total of 70hp.

1835   *Mountaineer*, a paddle steamer built by Patterson & Mercer of Bristol. This ship was fitted with two 45in x $4\frac{1}{2}$ft simple side lever engines.

1840   *Dragonfly*, a paddle tug built by N. Allen of Neath. This tug was fitted with a single 32in grasshopper side lever engine.

1849   *Firefly*, a screw steamer built for Chile by the Swansea Iron Shipbuilding Company. This ship was fitted with a pair of 13in x 1ft 7in V-twin engines.

1868   *Wave*, a small screw steamer built by Richard Allen, Pembroke Dock. It was fitted with a $7\frac{1}{2}$in x 7in inverted vertical engine.

[II] Ships built by the Neath Abbey Iron Company.

1842   *Prince of Wales*, length 120ft, 17.1ft breadth and 10ft depth. A paddle steamer of 182 tons gross, 106 tons nett; fitted with two 32in simple side lever engines. This ship was built for Joseph T. Price and was lengthened in 1854. The *Prince of Wales* was registered in 1876 as having two $31\frac{1}{2}$in x 3ft 1in simple side lever engines working at a pressure of 13psi. She was broken up in 1880-81.

1843   *Pioneer*, length 70ft, 16ft breadth and 9.4ft depth. A paddle tug of 19 tons nett; fitted with a single 32in grasshopper side lever engine. The *Pioneer* was built for Nathaniel Tregelles. Wrecked off Port Talbot.

1845   *Henry Southan*, length 103.6ft, 17.5ft breadth and 8.6ft depth. A screw steamer of 117 tons gross and 78 tons nett; fitted with two 28in engines. This ship was built for Henry Southan, Jnr of Gloucester but later sold and in 1855 lengthened. The *Henry Southan* was registered in 1876 as having two $29\frac{1}{2}$in x 1ft 8in inverted engines working at a pressure of 23psi. Hulked in 1881.

1846   *Neath Abbey*, length 97ft, 16.4ft breadth and 9ft depth. A screw steamer of 98 tons gross and 67 tons nett; fitted with a 13in inverted vertical engine. Wrecked off Nash Point in 1894.

1847   *Talbot*, length 134ft, 17ft breadth and 9.5ft depth. A screw steamer of 160 tons gross and 100 tons nett; fitted with two 18in engines, built for the Port Tabot Steam Vessel Company and in 1870 sold to France.

1848   *Charlotte*, length 83ft, 18.7ft breadth and 7.7ft depth. A screw steamer of 88 tons gross and 50 tons nett; fitted with a single 20hp engine. Converted to sail in 1866 and in 1882 dismantled and converted into a lighter for inland navigation.

1848   *La Serena*, length 141ft, 22ft breadth and 16ft depth. A barque of 373 tons built for a Swansea partnership which included Robert Eaton and Henry Bath.

1849   *John*, length 90.4ft, 18.4ft breadth and 7.1ft depth. A screw ketch of 109 tons gross and 93 tons nett; fitted with a 12hp engine. In 1874 this ship was owned by J.B. Brain of Cardiff.

1850   *Princess Royal*, length 114.5ft, 16.9ft breadth and 10ft depth. A screw steamer of 149 tons gross and 97 tons nett; fitted with a 24in x 1ft 9in inverted vertical engine. Broken up in 1875.

1851   *Spray*, length 48ft, 11.9ft breath and ft depth. A smack of 20 tons owned by Edwin Price and later sold to Falmouth.

1853   *Lapwing*, length 64.9ft, 9.4ft breadth and 5.4ft depth. A screw steamer of 20 tons gross and 13 tons nett; fitted with a 10in engine. *Lapwing* was ordered by the Francillon family of Gloucester to be used on the Gloucester Canal.

1853   *Ellen Bates*, length 211ft, 33.1ft breadth and 21.2 depth. A sailing ship of 1,098 tons built for Edward Bates of Liverpool. Her name was changed to *Scottish Tar* by 1882. She was wrecked on Engaro Island, south-west of Sumatra on 9 October1885.

1854   *Alliance* and *Resolution*. Two tugs to be used on the Severn between Gloucestershire and Shropshire. These tugs had 30in simple side lever engines.

A schooner yacht for Francis Crawshay.

1855   *Gannet*, length 55.6ft, 16.5ft breadth and 9.1ft depth. A ketch of 54 tons. In 1874 this vessel was owned by Garrich & Co. of Lerwick, Scotland.

Dart, length 42.2ft, 10.8ft breadth and 6.8ft depth. A schooner of 16 tons built for H.H. Price and sold in 1863 to Alexander Cansh of Birkenhead and registered at Liverpool.

1856   *Fearnought*. A three masted sailing ship of 1,175 tons built for Edward Bates of Liverpool. Wrecked on Long Island, Hong Kong on 20 July 1861.

Fleur de Marie. A small screw yacht with a 10in x 1ft inverted vertical engine built for H.H. Vivian.

1858   *Bahia*. A screw tug with a 10in inverted vertical engine built for Mr John Watson of London.

Norna, length 63.8ft, 14.5ft breadth and 8.2ft depth. A schooner of 31 tons built for H.H. Price, sold to Liverpool in 1865.

1862   *Charley*, length 87.8ft, 17.6ft breadth and 10.5ft depth. A paddle tug of 110 tons gross and 31 tons nett; fitted with a pair of 28in x 4ft grasshopper side lever engines. Built for a partnership which included H.H. Price and Theodore Fox. Sold to London in 1874 and later re-named *Defiance*.

1866   *Wotton*, length 64.7ft, 12.2ft breadth and 6ft depth. A screw steamer of 28 tons gross and 13 tons nett; fitted with a pair of 10in x 9in V-twin engines. Broken up in 1930.

1868   *Dora*, length 47ft, 12.3ft breadth and 7.9ft depth. A smack of 20 tons sold to Chester in 1877.

1877   *Flying Scud*, length 83.4ft, 17.1ft breadth and 8.4ft depth. A paddle tug of 74 tons gross and 16 tons nett; fitted with a second hand $32\frac{1}{2}$in x 4ft 2in side lever engine. Sold to Dundee in 1892 after serving at the port of Swansea.

[III] Separate marine engines built by the Neath Abbey Iron Company

1841 Two 36in simple side lever engines for a Neath-Porthcawl steamer.

1843 Engines for Lunell & Co., Bristol.

1848 Two 45 hp simple side lever engines for H.W. Harman & Pitcher, London.
35in oscillating engine for the Swansea Iron Shipbuilding Company.

1852 10in x 9in inverted vertical engine for Mr J.B. Martin, Bideford.

1883 Inverted vertical compound engine, HP 20in, LP 35in, stroke 2ft.

No date inverted vertical compound engine, HP 20in, LP 35in, stroke 2ft and steam pressure 80psi.

[IV] Dredgers built by the Neath Abbey Iron Company

1848 Wexford Harbour, a dredger with a 22in vertical engine.
Whitehaven Harbour, a dredger, 90ft in length, breadth 22ft and $8\frac{1}{2}$ft depth; fitted with a 24in x $2\frac{1}{2}$ft simple side lever engine.

1860 A dredger, 85ft in length and 22ft breadth; fitted with a simple side lever engine.

[V] Dredging engines built by the Neath Abbey Iron Company

1817 A 19in table engine for Hughes and Price.

1856 A 20in x 2ft vertical engine for Mr R.H. Michell, Cardiff.

[VI] Canal craft built by the Neath Abbey Iron Company.

1873 Steam barge.

1879 Canal launch fitted with a $4\frac{1}{2}$in x 5in engine for Mr Anlwyn or Alywin.

Appendix Four

Locomotives built by the Neath Abbey Iron Company

1830 *Speedwell*. An 0-4-0 locomotive with $10\frac{1}{2}$in x 24in cylinders built for Thomas Prothero for use on a 4ft 2in plateway. This locomotive had vertical cylinders with bell crank drive.

1831 *Hercules*. An 0-6-0 locomotive with $10\frac{1}{2}$in x 24in cylinders driving through bell cranks. Built for Thomas Prothero
An 0-6-0 locomotive with $10\frac{1}{2}$in x 24in inverted vertical cylinders driving through bell cranks. Built for Harford Bros. & Co., Ebbw Vale Ironworks.
A locomotive for Dare and Thomas.

1832 *Royal William*. An 0-6-0 locomotive with $10\frac{1}{2}$in inverted vertical cylinders driving through bell cranks. This locomotive was built for the 3ft 6in plateway of the Gloucester & Cheltenham Railway.
Industry. An 0-6-0 locomotive with horizontal $10\frac{1}{2}$in cylinders mounted on top of the boiler with a rocking beam drive. Built for Harfords, Davies & Co., of the Ebbw Vale Ironworks.
Perseverance. An 0-6-0 rack locomotive with inclined $10\frac{1}{2}$in x 20in cylinders. Built for the Dowlais Iron Company for use on the 4ft 2in Penydarren Plateway.
Yn Barod Etto. An 0-4-0 locomotive with inclined $8\frac{1}{2}$in x 20in cylinders. Built for the Dowlais Iron Company at a cost of £420 for use on the Penydarren Tramroad and the standard gauge rails inside the Dowlais Ironworks.

1834 *Camel*. An 0-6-0 locomotive with $10\frac{1}{2}$in x 24in inverted vertical cylinders driving through bell cranks. Built for the standard gauge Bodmin & Wadebridge Railway at a cost of £728.
Mountaineer. An 0-6-0 locomotive with $8\frac{1}{2}$in x 20in inclined cylinders. This locomotive cost £450 and was built for the Dowlais Iron Company.

1836 *Elephant*. An 0-6-0 locomotive with $12\frac{1}{2}$in x 24in vertical cylinders driving through bell cranks. This locomotive cost £800 and was supplied to the Bodmin & Wadebridge Railway.
Dowlais. An 0-6-0 locomotive with inclined $8\frac{1}{2}$in x 18in cylinders. A rack locomotive built for the Dowlais Iron Company at a cost of £604 19s 1d.

1837 A locomotive was used by H.H. Price to aid his construction of Sidmouth Harbour.

1838 *Charles Jordan*. An 0-6-0 locomotive with inclined $8\frac{1}{2}$in x 20in cylinders built for the Dowlais Iron Company.
John Watt. An 0-4-0 locomotive fitted with combined edge/plate wheels. This locomotive had $8\frac{1}{2}$in cylinders and was built for the Dowlais Iron Company.
An 0-4-4-0 locomotive with inclined $8\frac{1}{2}$in cylinders. Built for the Rhymney Iron Company

and used on a 4ft 2in plateway.

1839   A 10½in locomotive for the Rhymney Iron Company.

1840   A small locomotive with an adhesion device.

1844   *Lion*. A locomotive for Burrows and Teague.

1845   A locomotive for the Cwmavon works with 10½in cylinders.

1846   *Goliath*.

1846   Locomotives for William Crawshay, Hirwaun Ironworks.

1847   A locomotive is listed in the inventory of 1847 as being for sale.

1848   *Neath Abbey*. An 0-4-2 locomotive with 15in x 24in cylinders. Built to the standard gauge and sold to the Taff Vale Railway for £1,600.

1849   Four locomotives supplied to the Monmouthshire Canal & Railway Company. These were numbered 2 to 5 and were 0-6-0s with 15in x 24in cylinders. These locomotives were first used on a standard gauge plateway. No. 4 was sold to the Rhymney Railway in July 1856. No. 2 was renumbered No. 4 and was converted to railway working in 1857 and lasted until May 1875 when it was purchased by the Coalbrook Vale Colliery Co. No. 3 was sold to Messrs Budd & Holt as 'worn out' in May 1874. No. 5 was purchased by the Ebbw Vale Steel, Iron & Coal Co. Ltd in August 1874.

1854   An 0-6-0 saddle tank with 14in x 20in horizontal cylinders for J.&C. Bailey, Nantyglo Ironworks.

1855   An 0-6-0 saddle tank with 12in x 20in slightly inclined cylinders. Built for the Cinderford Iron Company's broad gauge Lightmoor Colliery line.
Caesar. An 0-6-0 saddle tank locomotive with 12in x 20in cylinders. Built to a gauge of 4ft 4in for the Morfa Colliery of Vivian & Sons.

1859   *Tubal Cain*. An 0-6-0 saddle tank with 12in x 20in horizontal cylinders. Built to a gauge of 4ft 4in for Vivian & Sons' Morfa Colliery.

1861   A locomotive with 10in x 18in cylinders built for Sims. Wylliams, Nevill & Co., Llanelli.

1862   *Abbot*. An 0-4-0 saddle tank with 8in cylinders. Built to a gauge of 2ft 8in and shown at the International Exhibition of 1862. Probably later sold to France.

c1862   A number of saddle tank locomotives with 8in x 15in cylinders employed on the 3ft gauge Neath Abbey Ironworks' line.

pre 1864 No. 2. A saddle tank with 8in x 16in cylinders employed on the Abernant Ironworks 2ft 9in line at Aberdare.

1864   Two saddle tank locomotives ordered by the Abernant Ironworks, Aberdare.
A number of small locomotives being built for South America, probably Chile.
A locomotive with 8in x 16in cylinders built for the Neath Abbey Coal Company.
Two 0-4-0 saddle tank locomotives with horizontal 8in x 16in cylinders. These were destined for the 2ft 8in line of the Plymouth Iron Company, Merthyr Tydfil.

1867   A 2-4-0 side tank locomotive with 8in x 16in inclined cylinders built for the Rhymney Iron Company's 3ft plateway.

1870   *Abercrave.* An 0-6-0 side tank locomotive with $8\frac{1}{2}$in x 16in cylinders, 2ft 8in gauge, for the Neath Abbey Coal Company. This locomotive was priced at £550.
An 0-4-0 saddle tank with $8\frac{1}{2}$in x 16in slightly inclined cylinders built to a gauge of 3ft 2in for Pascoe, Grenfell & Sons, Swansea.
Locomotive for 2ft 8in gauge for Neath Merthyr Coal Co., Clyne.
Tank locomotive with $8\frac{1}{2}$in x 15in cylinders for the Duffryn Graigola Coal Co., Neath

1871   An 0-4-0 saddle tank locomotive with $8\frac{1}{2}$in x 16in cylinders. This locomotive was built for Robert Crawshay of the Cyfarthfa Ironworks for duty on a 3ft plateway.

1874   An 8in x 16in cylinder locomotive, 2ft $8\frac{1}{2}$in gauge for Knight, Bevan & Sturge, Northfleet, Kent.

1875   A locomotive with 8in cylinders for Cefn Gorlau Colliery, Swansea.

1880   *Comet.* A locomotive for Knight, Bevan & Sturge, Northfleet, Kent.

1882   Locomotive for 2ft 8in gauge for Neath Merthyr Coal Co., Clyne.
There is also the possibility of a second-hand Neath Abbey locomotive named *Ironsides* having been purchased by the West Cornwall Railway in 1852.

An 0-4-0 saddle tank locomotive called *Sophie* which was built at Neath Abbey saw service at the Birch Rock Colliery, Pontardulais and was offered for sale in May 1906.

In September 1907 the Cheadle Works and Shipyard was dismantled and auctioned and the items included a 2ft 8in gauge locomotive.

Appendix Five

Gas plant built by the Neath Abbey Iron Company

Date	Customer
1820	W. George Junior, Ponypool
1820-30	Vivian & Sons, Hafod Works, Swansea
1821-23	Carmarthen Gas Company
1821-41	Swansea Gas Company
1822	Dover Gas Company
1829-31	Chepstow Gas Company
1830-31	Youghal Gas Company, County Cork, Ireland
1830	London
	Ross on Wye Gas Company
1831	James Wynn, Falmouth
1831-41	Williams, Foster & Co., Morfa Copper Works, Swansea
1832-41	Bridport Gas Company
1832-51	Neath Gas Company
1833-49	Barnstaple Gas Company
1833	Dorchester Gas Company
	Daniell, Nevill & Co., Llanelly
	Yeovil Gas Company
1834	Wellington Gas Company
1835	Witham Gas Company, Somerset
1835-40	Mr Caleb Cox, Bridgend, Glamorgan.
1836	Brecon Gas Company
	Haverfordwest Gas Company
	Saffron Walden Essex
1837-38	Exeter Commercial Gas Company
1837	Bodmin Gas Company
1839	Ashburton Gas Company
	Taibach Copper Works
	Truro Gas Company
1841	Bridgewater Gas Company
	Sidcot School, Somerset
	Tralee Gas Works, County Kerry, Ireland
1842	James Dewdney, Bradninch, Devon
1843	Brown & May, Colchester
	Fox Brothers, Tonedale, Wellington
1844-45	F.A. & J.A. de Elorza, Spain

1846	Vale of Neath Brewery
1847	Merthyr Gas Company
	Galway Gas Company, Ireland
1848-50	Aberdare Gas Company
1849-53	Cwmavon Gas Company
1851	Usk Gas Company
1856 or 1859	Torbay Gas Company
1862	P.S. Grenfell & Sons, Middle Bank Copper Works, Swansea
Undated	Llanelly Gas Company
	Fox Brothers, Uffculme, Devon

Appendix Six

Patents granted to the partners of the Neath Abbey Iron Company

Date   Patentees with description of patent

1812   Robert Were Fox with Joel Lean: improvements to the steam engine.

1823   Henry H. Price: apparatus for giving increased effect to paddles used in steam vessels.

1835   Joseph T. Price: railways and means of transporting carriages from one level to another.

1838   Joseph T. Price: constructing and adapting marine boilers for marine, stationary and locomotive engines; adapting and applying boilers to steam vessels.

1853   Henry H. Price: raising and forcing water and other fluids

Bibliography

Manuscript Sources

West Glamorgan Record Office, Swansea
Neath Abbey Ironworks Collection (D/DNAI), two deposits of the engineering drawings of the company.
Taylor Papers (D/D Xim), including extracts from the old notebook of H.F. Taylor.
Census return for the village of Neath Abbey, 1851.
Dynevor Collection (D/D D), including Neath Abbey Estate Papers.
Dyffryn Estate Papers.
Dyffryn Main Colliery Accounts (D/d Xgb).
Tennant Estate Papers (D/D T).
Main Colliery Collection (D/D MC).
Neath Library Manuscripts (D/D NLM)
Briton Ferry Estate Papers.
Glamorgan Record Office, Cardiff
Letter books of the Dowlais Iron Company.
Neath Antiquarian Society
Neath Abbey Coal Collection, 1855-1873.
Price Family Papers, Oxford
Talbot Family Papers, London
Ellison Family Papers, Swansea.
Birmingham Reference Library
Boulton & Watt Collection.
Matthew Boulton Papers.
Public Record Office Kew
Stockton & Darlington Railway Papers.
Minutes of the Surveyor General of the Ordnance (WO)
John Rylands University Library, Manchester
Committee Book of the Macclesfield Copper Company, 1774-1833 (EH 4 M4F)
Staffordshire Record Office, Stafford
Minute Book of the Cheadle Brass Wire Company (microfilm).
Cornish Record Office, Truro
Dissolution of Fox-Price partnership in the Neath Abbey Coal Company, 1856 (x394/59).
Lease of a field in Cadoxton, 1865 (x394/60).
Two balance sheets of the Neath Abbey Coal Company, one specifying the share of Alfred Fox, 1874 (x394/61-2)
Letters between D.R. Phillips and W.L. Fox regarding Neath Abbey, 1918-19 (x394/63)
Packet of notes on Neath Abbey Coal Company (x394/64).
Packet of papers relating to the history of Neath Abbey compiled by D.R. Phillips, c1928 (x394/65).
National Library of Wales, Aberystwyth
Aberpergwm Estate Collection

Library of the Society of Friends House, Euston Road, London.

Manuscript Dictionary of Quaker Biography

A Trip to Brynddewy Coal Mine, a poem by Elijah Waring, 10th Month 1813 (J.T. MSS 601).

University of London Library, Senate House, Mallet Street, London

Rastrick Papers, letters between Neath Abbey and Rastrick regarding drift engines supplied to the Dowlais Iron Company.

H.M. Customs and Excise Departmental Archives, Swansea and London Custom Houses

Swansea Shipping Registers, 1839-1886.

Science Museum Library, South Kensington, London

Rhys Jenkins Collection, collected material on the Neath Abbey Ironworks (Box 50, folder 6).

Newcastle Central Library

Tomlinson Collection, letter between J.T. Price and E. Pease, 22 December 1818.

Falmouth Public Library, Reference Department

Newspaper cuttings book made up by Mrs Wilson Lloyd Fox.

Bristol Record Office

Various leases

Primary Printed Sources

The Cambrian (1817-1886).

Children's Employment Commisssion, Vol 17 (1842).

Coste and Perdonnet, Sur la Fabrication de la Fonte et du Fer en Angleterre, *Annales Des Mines*, Tome V, Deuxieme Serie (1829).

The Engineer (1856-1886).

Fordyce, W., *A History of Coal, Coke, Coalfields and Iron Manufacture in Northern England* (1860).

Fox, *Charlotte, Recollections of our Old Home*, no date and printed for private circulation.

Francis, Grant Col., *The Smelting of Copper in the Swansea District of South Wales from the Time of Elizabeth to the Present Day* (1881).

Grantham, J., *Iron as a Material for Ship-Building* (1842).

Insole, H.R., and Bunning, C.Z., The Forest of Dean Colafield, *Journal of the British Society of Mining Students*, Vol VI, No 5 (1881).

Jeans, J.S., *History of the Stockton and Darlington Railway* (1875).

Lewis' Topographical Dictionary of Wales (1833).

Lloyd's Register of Shipping (1840-1886).

Mineral Statistics, 1855-1886.

Mining Journal (1840-1886).

Official Descriptive and Illustrated Catalogue of the Great Exhibition (1851).

Post Office Directory of Monmouthshire and the Principal Towns and Places in South Wales (1871).

Price, Anna, *Extracts form the Papers of Edwin Price* (1819).

Price, H.H., *Report relative to a Grand Western Communication from London into South Wales. with a comparitive view of the merits of the London and Windsor Railway schemes* (1834).

Price, H.H., *Report respecting the completion of the Grand Surrey Canal to the Thames at Vauxhall and the laying of a railway on the bank thereto to connect the Southampton, Croydon, Greenwich and proposed Brighton, Tunbridge Wells, Gravesend and Dover Railways, together with branches* (1835).

Price, H.H., *Report on the Harbour of Falmouth* (1835).

Price, H.H., *Report on the Establishment of a Ship Canal and Docks at the Port of Bridgewater* (1835).

Prosser, Richard B., *Birmingham Inventors and Inventions* (1881).

Reports of the Commissioners of Enquiry into the State of Education in Wales (1848).

Scamell & Co.'s City of Bristol and South Wales Directory (1852).

Scrivenor, H., *History of the Iron Trade* (1854).

The South Wales Coal Annual 1913-1925,

Trevithick, Francis, *Life of Richard Trevithick* (1872).

Warner, Richard, *Second Walk through Wales in August and September 1798*, (1813).

Woodcroft, Bennet, *Alphabetical Index of Patentees of Inventions from March 2nd, 1617 to October 1st, 1852* (1854).

Woodcroft, Bennet, *Alphabetical Index of Patentees and Applications for Patents of Inventions from 1st October, 1852 to 31st December, 1853* (1854).

Secondary Sources

Addis, J.P., *The Crawshay Dynasty: a study in industrial organisation and development, 1765-1867* (Cardiff, 1957).

Ashton, T.S., *Iron and Steel in the Industrial Revolution* (Manchester, 1924).

Barton, D.B., *A History of Copper Mining in Cornwall and Devon* (Truro, 1968).

Barton, D.B. *The Cornish Beam Engine* (Truro, 1969).

Barton, D.B., *Essays in Cornish Mining History*, Vol 2 (Truro, 1970).

Bick, D.E., *The Gloucester and Cheltenham Railway* (Lingfield, 1968).

Birch, A., *The Economic History of the British Iron and Steel History, 1784-1879* (1967).

Brett, R.L. (Ed), *Barclay Fox's Journal* (1979).

Buchanan, R.A. and Watkins, George, *The Industrial Archaeology of the Stationary Steam Engine* (1976).

Carr, J.C. and Taplin, W., *History of the British Steel Industry* (Oxford, 1962).

Chaloner, W.H., Charles Roe of Macclesfield (1715-1781): An Eighteenth Century Industrialist, Parts 1 & 2, *Transactions of the Lancashire and Cheshire Antiquarian Society* Vol LXII (1950-1951) & Vol LXIII (1952-1953).

Corlett, Ewan, *The Iron Ship* (Bradford on Avon, 1975).

Cox, Nancy, Imagination and Innovation of an Industrial Pioneer, the First Abraham Darby, *Industrial Archaeology Review*, Vol XII, No 2 (1990).

Craig, John, *The Mint. A History of the London Mint from AD 287 to 1948* (Cambridge, 1953).

Day, R. and Gale, W.K.V., Wiltshire Iron: 1855-1949, *Journal of the Historical Metallurgy Society*, Vol. 15, No 1 (1981).

Davies, T.G., *Howel Gwyn of Dyffryn and Neath* (Neath, 1992).

Deane Phylis, *The First Industrial Revolution* (Cambridge, 1969).

Dickinson, H.W. and Jenkins, Rhys, *James Watt and the Steam Engine* (Oxford, 1927).

Dictionary of National Biography.

Donald, M.B., *Elizabethan Copper* (1955).

Evans, Michael C.S., The Llandyfan Forges, *The Carmarthenshire Antiquary*, Vol. IX (1973).

Eyles, J.M., William Smith, Richard Trevithick and Samuel Homfray - Their Correspondence on Steam Engines, 1804-1806, *Transactions of the Newcomen Society*, Vol. XLIII (1970-71).

Farey, John, *A Treatise on the Steam Engine (1827)*, Vol. 2 (Newton Abbot, 1971).

Farr, G., *West Country Passenger Steamers* (Prescot, 1967).

Forester, Dean, Mr Keeling Buys a Locomotive, *Industrial Railway Record*, Vol. 1.

Fox, Hubert, Quaker Homespun. *The Life of Thomas Fox of Wellington, Serge Maker and Banker* (1958).

Fox, Joseph Hoyland, *The Woollen Manufacture at Wellington*, Somerset (1914).

Fox, Sarah E., (Ed), *Edwin Octavius Tregelles, Civil Engineer and Minister of the Gospel*, (1892).

Gale, W.K.V., *The British Iron and Steel Industry* (Newton Abbot, 1967).

Gale, W.K.V., Iron in the Cornish Industrial Revolution, *Journal of the Trevithick Society*, No 3 (1975).

Galloway, Robert, *Annals of Coal Mining and the Coal Trade* (1904).

Gibbs, D.E. and Roberts, R.O., The Copper Industry of Neath and Swansea: Record of a Suit in the Court of Exchequer, 1723, *South Wales and Monmouthshire Record Society Publications*, No 4 (1957).

Griffiths, John, *The Third Man. The Life and Times of William Murdoch, 1754-1838* (1992).

Guest, Revel and John, Angela V., *Lady Charlotte* (1989).

Hancock, H.B. and Wilkinson, N.B., The Journals of Joshua Gilpin 1795-1801, *Transactions of the Newcomen Society*, Vol. 32 (1959-60).

Harris, J.R. *The Copper King. A Biography of Thomas Williams of Llanidan* (Liverpool, 1964).

Harris, T.R., *Dolcoath, Queen of Cornish Mines* (Truro, 1974).

Harris, T.R., *Arthur Woolf, the Cornish Engineer* (Truro, 1966).

Harvey, Charles and Press, Jon, *Sir George White of Bristol 1854-1916* (Bristol, 1989).

Hocking, Charles, *Dictionary of Disasters at Sea During the Age of Steam* (1990).

Hoffman, W., *British Industry 1700-1950* (1955).

Hooper, W. Tregonning, Perran Foundry and its Story, *106th Annual Report of the Royal Cornwall Polytechnic Society*, New series, Vol. IX, Part (iii), (1939).

Ince, Laurence, The Neath Abbey Ironworks, *Industrial Archaeology*, Vol. 11, No 4 and Vol. 12, No 1, 1977.

Ince, Laurence, *The Neath Abbey Iron Company* (Eindhoven, 1984).

Ince, Laurence, *Richard Trevithick's Patent Steam Engine, Steam Power*, Vol. 1 (1984).

Ince, Laurence, *The Knight Family and the British Iron Industry*, 1692-1902 (Birmingham, 1991).

Ince, Laurence, The South Wales Iron Industry 1750-1885 (Birmingham, 1993).

Jenkins, Elis (Ed), *Neath and District, A Symposium* (Cowbridge, 1974).

John, A.H., Iron and Coal on a Glamorgan Estate, 1700-1740, *Economic History Review*, XIII (1943).

John, A.H., *The Economic Development of South Wales, 1750-1850* (Cardiff, 1950).

Jones, E.J., Scotch Cattle and Early Trade Unionism in Wales, *Economic History*, Vol. I (1928)

Law, R.J., *The Steam Engine* (1965).

Lewis, M.J.T., Steam on the Penydarren, *Industrial Railway Record*, No 59 (1975).

Lillie, William, *The History of Middlesbrough* (Middlesbrough, 1968).

Lloyd, John, *Old South Wales Ironworks* (1906).

Lowe, James, *British Steam Locomotive Builders* (Cambridge, 1975).

MacDermot, E.T., *History of the Great Western Railway*, (1927-31).

Marshall, C.F. Dendy, *A History of the Railway Locomotive Down to the End of the Year 1831* (1953).

Michel, Stephen, Cornish Foundries - What They Have Achieved, *Annual Report of the Royal Cornwall Polytechnic Society*, Part II (1932).

Michinton, W.E. (Ed), *Industrial South Wales* (1969).

Morton, John F., *Thomas Bolton & Sons Ltd.* (Ashbourne, 1983).

Morton, John F., *The Rise of the Modern Copper and Brass Industry in Britain, 1690-1750*. University of Birmingham PhD Thesis (1985).

Moss, M.S. and Hume, J.R., *Workshop of the British Empire* (1977).

Neff, J.U., The Progress of Technology and the Growth of Large Scale Industry In Great Britain 1540-1640, reprinted in, *Essays in Economic History*, Vol. I (1954).

Palmer, Marilyn and Neaverson, Peter, The Steam Engines at Glyn Pits Colliery, Pontypool: an Archaeological Investigation, *Industrial Archaeology Review,* Vol. XIII, No 1. (1990).

Pease, Alfred E. (Ed), *The Diaries of Edward Pease* (1907).

Pennington, R.R., The Cornish Metal Company, 1785-1792, *Journal of The Trevithick Society*, No 5 (1977).

Phillips, D. Rhys, *History of the Vale of Neath* (Swansea, 1925).

Pollard, S., *The Genesis of Modern Management. A Study of the Industrial Revolution in Great Britain* (1968).

Raistrick, Arthur, *Quakers in Science and Industry* (1968).

Raistrick Arthur, *Dynasty of Iron Founders* (Newton Abbot, 1970).

Riden, Philip, *John Bedford and the Ironworks at Cefn Cribwr* (Cardiff, 1992).

Roberts, C.W., *A Legacy from Victorian Enterprise* (Gloucester, 1983).

Roberts, R.O. The Smelting of Non-Ferrous Metals since 1750, Glamorgan County History, Vol. V, *Industrial Glamorgan from 1700-1970*, (Cardiff, 1980).

Rogers, K.H., *The Newcomen Engine in the West of England* (Bradford-on-Avon, 1976).

Rolt, L.T.C., *Thomas Telford* (1958).

Rolt, L.T.C., *Isambard Kingdom Brunel* (1972).

Saul, S.B., *The Myth of the Great Depression* (1969).

Southall, Hannah, The Price Family of Neath, *Friends Quarterly Examiner*, Vol. 28 (1894).

Treadwell, J.M., William Wood and the Company of Ironmasters of Great Britain, *Business History*, 16 (1974).

Vale, Edmund, *The Harveys of Hayle* (Truro, 1966).

Warren, J.G.H., *A Century of Locomotive Building by Robert Stephenson & Co. 1823-1923* (1923).

Watkins, George, *The Stationary Steam Engine* (Newton Abbot, 1968).

White, George, *Tramlines to the Stars, George White of Bristol* (Bristol, 1995).

Various Other Printed Material Contributing to the Biographies of the Fox Family of Falmouth and the Price Family of Neath Abbey.

Benson, R. Seymour, *Descendants of Isaac and Rachel Wilson*, Vol. II, (1912 & 1920), revised by M.E. and J.S. Benson (1962).

Boyce, Anne Ogden, *Records Of a Quaker Family, The Richardsons of Cleveland* (1889).

Fox, Samuel M., *Two Homes by a Grandson* (Plymouth, 1925).

Gay, S.E., *Old Falmouth* (1900-3).

Harris, Wilson, *Caroline Fox* (1944).

Quaker Records - An Index to the Annual Monitor (1813-1892).

References

1. T.R. Owen, Geology and Scenery in E. Jenkins (ed), *Neath and District. A Symposium* (Neath, 1974), pp 1-21.

2. D. Rhys Phillips, *The History of the Vale of Neath* (Swansea, 1925), pp. 414-417.

3. A.H. John, Iron and Coal on a Glamorgan Estate, 1700-1740, *Economic History Review*, XIII (1943) pp. 93-103.

4. D. Rhys Phillips, *History of the Vale of Neath*, p. 248.

5. Ellison Collection, Joshua Richardson's Notebook, 1847-73

6. D. Rhys Phillips, *History of the Vale of Neath*, p. 251.

7. K.H. Rogers, *The Newcomen Engine in the West of England*, (Bradford-on-Avon), p. 48

8. West Glamorgan Record Office, Swansea, Dynevor Estate Collection, D/D D 1205, Lease of collieries, 29 January 1791.

9. M.B. Donald, *Elizabethan Copper*, (1955), p. 343.

10. D. Rhys Phillips, *The History of the Vale of Neath*, p. 48.

11. John Craig, *The Mint. A History of the London Mint from AD 287 to 1948*, (Cambridge, 1953), pp. 179-180.

12. John F. Morton, The Rise of the Modern Copper and Brass Industry in Britain, 1690-1750, University of Birmingham PhD thesis, (1985), pp. 214-218.

13. D. E. Gibbs and R.O. Roberts, The Copper Industry of Neath and Swansea: Record of a Suit in the Court of Exchequer, 1723, *South Wales and Monmouth Record Society Publications*, No 4 (1957), pp. 129-131.

14. John F. Morton, The Rise of the Modern Copper and Brass Industry in Britain, 1690-1750, p. 325.

15. Col Grant Francis, *The Smelting of Copper in the Swansea District of South Wales from the Time of Elizabeth to the Present Day*, (1881), pp. 170-172.

16. John F. Morton, p. 327.

17. John F. Morton, p. 328.

18. John F. Morton, p. 328.

19. John F. Morton, p. 343.

20. J.M. Treadwell, William Wood and the Company of Ironmasters of Great Britain, *Business History*, 16 (1974), pp. 97-112.

21. West Glamorgan Record Office, Swansea, Dynevor Collection, D/D D 1197, Lease for twelve years between the Lords of the Abbey and the Mines Royal Company, 24 July 1771. This lease refers to the company's earlier lease of 24 March 1757.

22. J.R. Harris, *The Copper King. A Biography of Thomas Williams of Llanidan*, (Liverpool, 1964), pp. 18-55.

23. R.R. Pennington, The Cornish Metal Company, 1785-1792, *Journal of the Trevithick Society* No 5 1877, pp.76-88.

24. WGRO, DC, Neath Abbey Estate Papers, D/DDE/113-116, Rent Rolls of the Neath Abbey Estate 1786-1790.

25. Philip Riden, *John Bedford and the Ironworks at Cefn Cribwr*, (Cardiff, 1992), pp. 15-17 and communication with Peter King.

26. Col Grant Francis, pp. 74-79.

27. WGRO, DC, D 1206, Lease 1 June 1798.

28. Birmingham Reference Library, Mathew Boulton Papers, Box 318, No 35, An account of the names and situations of all the furnaces or houses employed in the respective collections for smelting iron, lead, copper and tin and also for making or procuring brass with as accurate an account as can be obtained of the quantity of each species of metal procured from the ores at each such furnace or smelting house within the last year, c1797.

29. *Mineral Statistics*, 1855-1861.

30. WGRO, D C, D/D D 1198, lease of 29 May 1792. D/D D 1199, lease of 30 May 1793

31. W.H. Chaloner, Charles Roe of Macclesfield (1715-1781): An Eighteenth Century Industrialist, Part *1*, *Transactions of the Lancashire and Cheshire Antiquarian Society*, Vol. LXII, (1950-1951), pp. 133-156.

32. W.H. Chaloner, Charles Roe of Macclesfield (1715-1781): An Eighteenth Century Industrialist, Part 2, *Transactions of the Lancashire and Cheshire Antiquarian Society*, Vol. LXIII (1952-1953), pp. 52-86.

33. W.H. Chaloner, Charles Roe, Part 2, p. 68.

34. John Rylands University Library, Manchester, EH4 M4F, Committee Book of the Macclesfield Copper Company, 1774-1833. All further references to the progress of this company originate from this source.

35. D. Rhys Phillips, *The History of the Vale of Neath*, p. 281.

36. D. Rhys Phillips, *The History of the Vale of Neath*, p. 282.

37. Staffordshire Record Office, Stafford, Minute Book of the Cheadle Brass Wire Company (microfilm), meeting 19 August 1803.

38. John F. Morton, *Thomas Bolton & Sons Ltd*, (Ashbourne, 1983), pp.13-19.

39. SRO, MBCBWC, meeting, 11 December 1810.

40. SRO, MBCBWC, meeting 6 November 1821.

41. WGRO, Swansea, DC, D/D D 1235/1/2, lease 25 March 1806.

42. *Mineral Statistics*, 1866.

43. *Mineral Statistics*, 1867.

44. WGRO, Swansea, DC, D/D D 1201, lease 20 November 1867.

45. R. Day and W.K.V. Gale, Wiltshire Iron: 1855-1949, *Journal of the Historical Metallurgy Society*, Vol. 15, No 1, 1981, pp. 18-38.

46. *Mining Journal*, 21 January 1871.

47. R.O. Roberts, The Smelting of Non-Ferrous Metals since 1750, *Glamorgan County History, Volume V, Industrial Glamorgan from 1700-1970*, 89.

48. D.Rhys Phillips, *The History of the Vale of Neath*, pp. 48-49.

49. Bristol Record Office, 4658/6b, lease of 9 June 1757 reciting earlier lease of 21 June 1727.

50. Nancy Cox, Imagination and Innovation of an Industrial Pioneer: the First Abraham Darby, *Industrial Archaeology Review*, Volume XII, No 2, 1990, p. 132.

51. Bristol Record Office, 4658/6b.

52. Michael C.S. Evans, The Llandyfan Forges, *The Carmarthenshire Antiquary*, Vol. IX, 1973, p. 139

53. Michael C.S. Evans, The Llandyfan Forges, p. 143.

54. Public Record Office, Kew, Minutes of the Surveyor General of the Ordnance, WO47 51, f.98.

55. PRO, MSGO, WO47 51, f.150 & f.192.

56. PRO, MSGO, WO47 51, f.542.

57. PRO, MSGO, WO47 53, f.267.

58. PRO, MSGO, WO47 53, f.582.

59. PRO, MSGO, WO47 54, f.39.

60. PRO, MSGO, WO47 54, f.152.

61. PRO, MSGO, WO47 55, f. 532.

62. PRO, MSGO, WO47 57, f.87

63. Laurence Ince, *The Neath Abbey Iron Company* (Eindhoven, 1984).

64. D. Rhys Phillips, *The History of the Vale of Neath*, p. 287.

65. WGRO, DC , D/D D 1198, lease 29 May 1792.

66. Arthur Raistrick, *Quakers in Science and Industry* (1968), pp. 330-331.

67. Birmingham Reference Library, Boulton &Watt Collection, G., C., G.R. & T. Fox to Boulton & Watt

concerning intercession with Pednandrea Adventurers, 22 May 1794.

68. BRL, B&W, George Fox to Boulton & Watt concerning investment in North Downs, 29 January 1784. this is one of many such letters between the Fox family and Boulton & Watt concerning investment in Cornish mines.

69. BRL, B&W, George Fox to Boulton & Watt, 21 September 1782.

70. BRL, B&W, G., C., R., G. & T. Fox to Boulton & Watt, 29 November 1797.

71. BRL, B&W, Boulton & Watt to Edward Fox,23 September 1792.

72. W. Tregonning Hooper, Perran Foundry and its Story, *106th Annual report of the Royal Cornwall Polytechnic Society*, New Series, Vol. IX, Part (iii), 1939, pp. 60-87.

73. Edmund Vale, *The Harveys of Hayle* (Truro, 1966), p. 51.

74. Arthur Raistrick, *Quakers in Science and Industry*, p. 331. Hubert Fox, *Quaker Homespun. The Life of Thomas Fox of Wellington, Serge Maker and Banker*, (1958). Joseph Hoyland Fox, *The Woollen Manufacture at Wellington*, Somerset, (1914).

75. Charlotte Fox, *Recollections of our Old Home*, no page numbers and printed for private circulation.

76. H.W. Dickinson & Rhys Jenkins, *James Watt and the Steam Engine* (Oxford, 1927), pp. 289-290.

77. BRL, B&W, unsigned letter from Falmouth to Boulton & Watt, 16 July 1792.

78. BRL, B&W, Boulton & Watt to the Foxes, 17 September 1792.

79. BRL, B&W, Boulton & Watt, Robert Were Fox to Boulton & Watt, 17 September 1792.

80. BRL, B&W, George C. Fox & Sons to Boulton & Watt, 30 May 1793.

81. BRL, B&W, Agreement between James Watt of Soho and Matthew Boulton and Robert Were Fox of Falmouth in the County of Cornwall, 1 November 1792.

82. John Griffiths, *The Third Man. The Life and Times of William Murdoch, 1754-1838*, (1992), p. 244.

83. National Library of Wales, Aberystwyth, Aberpergwm Collection, 2195, lease for ironstone mining, 21 September 1792.

84. H.B. Hancock, N.B. Wilkinson, The Journals of Joshua Gilpin 1795-1801, *Transactions of the Newcomen Society*, 32 (1959-60), pp. 15-28.

85. D. Rhys Phillips, *The History of the Vale of Neath*, pp. 289-290.

86. Laurence Ince, *The Knight Family and the British Iron Industry, 1692-1902*, (Birmingham, 1991), p. 119.

87. D. Rhys Phillips, *The History of the Vale of Neath*, p. 290.

88. D.B. Barton, *The Cornish Beam Engine* (Truro, 1969), p. 154.

89. BRL, B&W, Edward Fox to Boulton & Watt, 6 September 1794.

90. Birmingham Reference Library, Matthew Boulton Papers, Box 318, 23, Gilpin's Memorandum Book.

91. BRL, MBP, Box 318, 44, Statement of the expenses of Making Iron at Neath Abbey, June 30th 1799 to July 1st 1800.

92. BRL, MBP, Box 318, 40, Diary of James Watt Jnr. on his visit to South Wales, 1800.

93. *Svedenstierna's Tour of Great Britain 1802-03* (Newton Abbot, 1973), pp. 47-48.

94. Francis Trevithick, *Life of Richard Trevithick*, Vol. 2 (1872), pp. 153-154. J.M. Eyles, William Smith, Richard Trevithick and Samuel Homfray - Their Correspondence on Steam Engines, 1804-1806, *Transactions of the Newcomen Society*, Vol. XLIII, (1870-71),p. 154. Laurence Ince, Richard Trevithick's Patent Steam Engine, *Stationary Power*, Vol. 1, (1984),pp. 67-75.

95. WGRO, Neath Abbey Ironworks Collection, M/206.

96. G. Farr, *West Country Passenger Steamers*, (Prescot, 1967).

97. *The Cambrian*, 6 December 1817.

98. D. Rhys Phillips, *The History of the Vale of Neath*, p. 291.

99. WGRO, NAI, W/3/2, Inventory of Works, 31 May 1847.

100. D. Rhys Phillips, *The History of the Vale of Neath*, p. 293.

101. D. Rhys Phillips, *The History of the Vale of Neath*, p. 294.

102. Science Museum, London, Rhys Jenkins Collection, Box 50, folder 6, 55, unidentified newspaper cutting dated 4 May 1929.

103. WGRO, Census return for the village of Neath Abbey, 30 March 1851.

104. WGRO, Taylor Foundry Papers, Extracts from old notebook of H.F. Taylor.

105. Laurence Ince, *The South Wales Iron Industry 1750-1885* (Birmingham, 1993), pp. 161-167.

106. D. Rhys Phillips, *The History of the Vale of Neath*, p. 293.

107. D.B. Barton, *The Cornish Beam Engine*, p. 281.

108. D.B. Barton, *The Cornish Beam Engine*, p. 156.

109. *The Engineer*, 1 January 1864, 3.

110. *The Post Office Directory of Monmouthshire and the Principal Towns and Places in South Wales* (1871), 326.

111. *The Engineer* 3 April 1874, 3.

112. D. Rhys Phillips, *The History of the Vale of Neath*, p. 294.

113. *Lloyds Register of Shipping* 1880, entry for Flying Scud.

114. WGRO, DC, D/D D 1204, lease commencing Ladyday 1876.

115. C.W. Roberts, *A Legacy from Victorian Enterprise* (Gloucester 1983), p.217.

116. R.A. Buchanan and George Watkins, *The Industrial Archaeology of the Stationary Steam Engine* (1976), p. 77.

117. M.S. Moss and J.R. Hulme, *Workshop of the British Empire* (1977), pp. 114-115.

118. M.S. Moss and J.R. Hulme, *Workshop of the British Empire*, p. 73.

119. R.J. Law, *The Steam Engine* (1965), pp. 8-10.

120. D.B. Barton, *The Cornish Beam Engine*, p. 185.

121. John Farey, *A Treatise on the Steam Engine* (1827), Vol. 2 (Newton Abbot, 1971), p. 7.

122. Arthur Raistrick, *Dynasty of Iron Founders* (Newton Abbot, 1970), p. 163.

123. Laurence Ince, Richard Trevithick's Patent Steam Engine, *Steam Power*, Vol1, (1984), pp. 67-75.

124. D.B. Barton, *Essays in Cornish Mining History* (Truro,1970), p. 15.

125. WGRO, NAI, L 34(ii), Trevithick's Engine from Penydarren.

126. Science Museum, London, Rhys Jenkins Collection, Box 50, folder 6, sheet 32.

127. Francis Trevithick, *Life of Richard Trevithick*, Vol. 2, (1872), 153-154.

128. John Farey, A Treatise on the Steam Engine (1827), Vol. 2, p. 13.

129. T.R. Harris, *Dolcoath: Queen of Cornish Mines* (Truro, 1974), p. 31.

130. Edmund Vale, *The Harveys of Hayle*, p. 103.

131. D.B. Barton, *The Cornish Beam Engine*, pp. 37-38.

132. WGRO, NAI, M/206, Sundry views for a 16in engine for Mr Williams, Scorrier House, 2 August 1809.

133. R.J. Law, *The Steam Engine*, p. 22.

134. For Woolf's compound pumping engines in Cornwall see, John Farey, *A Treatise on the Steam Engine* (1827), Vol. 2, pp. 94-98 & 101-117. T.R. Harris, *Arthur Woolf, The Cornish Engineer* (Truro, 1966), pp. 55-58.

135. D.B. Barton, *The Cornish Beam Engine*, p. 33.

136. D.B. Barton, *The Cornish Beam Engine*, p. 41.

137. T.R. Harris, *Arthur Woolf, The Cornish Engineer*, pp. 84-88.

138. D.B. Barton, *The Cornish Beam Engine*, pp. 43-44.

139. D.B. Barton, *The Cornish Beam Engine*, p. 154.

140. Edmund Vale, *The Harveys of Hayle*, pp. 143-146.

141. D. Rhys Phillips, *The History of the Vale of Neath*, p. 757.

142. Edmund Vale, *The Harveys of Hayle*, pp. 222.

143. W. Tregonning Hooper, Perran Foundry and its Story, 106th *Annual report of the Royal Cornwall Polytechnic Society*, New Series, Vol. IX, Part (iii), 1939, pp. 73-77.

144. WGRO, NAI, M/151/1-151/4, Drawings for engine for James Ozanne, Guernsey, 1833-1835 & M/158/1-158/2, Drawings for engine for N. Perchard, Jersey, 1830.

145. H.R. Insole and C.Z. Bunning, The Forest of Dean Coalfield, *Journal of the British Society of Mining Students*, Vol. VI, No 5 (1881), pp. 84-85.

146. R.A. Buchanan and George Watkins, *The Industrial Archaeology of the Stationary Steam Engine*, p. 170.

147. Marilyn Palmer and Peter Neaverson, The Steam Engines at Glyn Pits Colliery, Pontypool: an Archaeological Investigation, *Industrial Archaeology Review*, Vol. XIII, No 1, (1990), pp. 7-34.

148. 52½beam blowing engines were built for the Blaenavon Ironworks, Plymouth Ironworks, Penydarren Ironworks, Cyfarthfa Ironworks, Hirwaun Ironworks, British Iron Co., Pontypool, Leigh and George, Pontypool, Golynos Ironworks, Cambrian Iron and Spelter Co., Rhymney Ironworks, Clydach Ironworks and Ystalyfera Ironworks.

149. Coste and Perdonnet, Sur la Fabrication de la Fonte et du Fer en Angleterre, *Annales des Mines*, Tome V, Deuxieme Serie, (1829), pp. 477-481.

150. D.B. Barton, *The Cornish Beam Engine*, p. 265. In 1839 the Neath Abbey Ironworks supplied a blowing engine to the Victoria ironworks, Ebbw Vale with a 122in blowing cylinder. Harvey & Co. of Hayle had quoted for building this engine at £3,700.

151. For descriptions of table engines see, George Watkins, *The Stationary Steam Engine* (Newton Abbot, 1968), p. 14 and R.J. Law, *The Steam Engine*, p. 16-17.

152. George Watkins, *The Stationary Steam Engine*, p. 10.

153. WGRO, NAI, S/59/87, Drawing of marine engine, 10in cylinder, 9in stroke for Mr J.B. Martin, Bideford, 14 May 1852. This drawing of an inverted vertical marine engine bears the note, 'engine thus for the Aberdare Iron Co., 27 August 1852.

154. *The Engineer*, Vol. 53, 16 June 1882, p. 443.

155. D.Rhys Phillips, *The History of the Vale of Neath*, p. 294.

156. G. Farr, *West Country Passenger Steamers*, pp. 4-5. The Neath Abbey Ironworks Collection contains a number of engineering drawings related to *Britannia* and indicates that the ship remained at Neath Abbey for over 2 months.

157. WGRO, NAI, S/1/1, report of the *Arrow*, built by Evans, Rotherhithe, 18 January 1822 at Dover. S/58/2(I), Descriptions of steam packets. S/58/2(ii), Sketches and descriptions of main beams, sweep rods, cylinder cover, air pumps and blow valve, air bucket and slide box for blow hole.

158. For the development of the iron ship see, Ewan Corlett, *The Iron Ship* (Bradford-on-Avon, 1975), pp. 24-27.

159. J. Grantham, *Iron as a Material for Ship-Building* (1842), p. 5.

160. Grahame Farr, *West Country Passenger Steamers*, p. 171.

161. WGRO, NAI, S/11/1-S/11/57. These drawings not only include details of the Henry Southan but also of the *Clara*. The *Clara* had been built at Liverpool by John Grantham in 1842 and was a screw steamer of 42 tons. She was purchased by Henry Southan in 1845 and underwent a refit at Neath Abbey. The Neath Abbey engineers must have learnt a good deal from studying her construction and mode of propulsion.

162. WGRO, NAI, S/58/67, Method of Connecting the Beams, Frames and Gunwhale of Iron Steamers, 17 March 1842.

163. WGRO, NAI, S/53/1-S/58/99, Dredger drawings.

164. Information concerning Edward Bates and the two sailing ships built for him by Neath Abbey was kindly supplied by M.K. Stammers, Keeper of Maritime History, Merseyside County Museums.

165. *The Cardiff and Merthyr Guardian*, 9 August 1856.

166. *The Cambrian*, 25 August 1876.

167. Newcastle Public Library, Tomlinson Collection, Letter from J.T. Price to Edward Pease, 22 December 1818.

168. J.S. Jeans, *History of the Stockton and Darlington Railway* (1875), pp.51-52.

169. Public Record Office, British Transport Historical Records, Records of the Stockton and Darlington Railway Company, Rail 667/910, 912 & 926.

170. The Tredegar locomotive is dealt with in, J.G.H. Warren, *A Century of Locomotive Building by Robert Stephenson & Co. 18232-1923* (1923), pp. 154-155. Information concerning the Penydarren engine is contained in , M.J.T. Lewis, Steam on the Penydarren, *Industrial Railway Record*, No 59, (April 1975), pp. 15-18.

171. James W. Lowe, *British Steam Locomotive Builders* (Cambridge, 1975), p. 575.

172. WGRO, NAI, L/22/1-L/23/14, Drawings related to the Royal William.

173. D.E. Bick, *The Gloucester and Cheltenham Railway* (Lingfield,1968), pp. 46-47.

174. M.J.T. Lewis, *Industrial Railway Record*, No 59, (April 1975).

175. Four of these locomotives were supplied to the Monmouthshire Canal and Railway Co. in 1849, WGRO, NAI, L/33/1.

176. WGRO, NAI, L/2/1-2/3, Drawings relating to a locomotive for J. and C. Bailey, 1853.

177. D.K. Clark, On the Locomotive Engines in the International Exhibition of 1862, *The Engineer*, 1 January 1864, p.3.

178. For a description of some Neath Abbey locomotives working at Welsh ironworks, see, Dean Forester, Mr Keeling Buys a Locomotive, *Industrial Railway Record*, Vol. 1, pp. 58-64.

179. D.Rhys Phillips, *History of the Vale of Neath*, pp. 439-440. Price Family Papers, The Price Family, begun by Alice M. Price, October 1888. An account of Peter Price's Life, written by Henry Habberley Price, undated.

180. BRL, B&W, Watt to Boulton, 4 August 1781.

181. Price Family Papers, Peter Price's Certificate of Attendance at the Freemasonry Lodge, Philadelphia, 20 May 5774 (the Freemason's date of 5774 is equivalent to AD 1774).

182. L.T.C. Rolt, *Thomas Telford* (1958), p.135.

183. William Lillie, *The History of Middlesbrough* (Middlesbrough, 1968) p. 54,

184. Henry H. Price, *Report on the Establishment of a Ship canal and Docks at the Port of Bridgewater* (1835), p. 7.

185. National Library of Wales, Aberystwyth, Nevil, Druce and Co Papers, book L.V., No 25, Henry H. Price, Plan of the Harbour of Swansea and of the River Tawe from the Piers to the Forest Weir with the Proposed improvements.

186. M. Messenger, Harbours that didn't happen, *The Western Morning News*, 1 August 1973.

187. WGRO, NAI, M/136, Plan of Dock gates for Montrose Wet Dock.

188. Library of the Society of Friends, Euston Road, London, Dictionary of Quaker Biography.

189. Sir Alfred E Pease (Ed), *The Diaries of Edward Pease* (1907), p. 390.

190. Glamorgan Record Office, Cardiff, Dowlais Iron Company Letters, Joseph Tregelles Price to Josiah John Guest, 10 April 1824.

191. GLO, DIC, Joseph Tregelles Price to Josiah John Guest, 1 July 1826.

192. Sarah E. Fox (Ed.), *Edwin Octavius Tregelles, Civil Engineer and Minister of the Gospel* (1892), entry for September 1820.

193. D. Rhys Phillips, *The History of the Vale of Neath*, p. 440.

194. *Report of the Commissioners of Enquiry into the State of Education in Wales* (1848), p. 159.

195. *Children's Employment Commission* (1842), p. 564.

196. D. Rhys Phillips, *The History of the Vale of Neath*, p. 441.

197. E.J. Jones, Scotch Cattle and Early Trade Unionism in Wales, *Economic History*, Vol. 1, (1928), pp. 385-393.

198. Sarah E. Fox (Ed.), *Edwin Octavius Tregelles*, entry for 7 June 1831.

199. Sarah E. Fox (Ed.), *Edwin Octavius Tregelles*, entry for 23 October 1831.

200. *Annual Monitor* (1856), pp. 156-166.

201. *The Cambrian*, 29 December 1854.

202. Hannah Southall, The Price Family of Neath, *Friends Quarterly Examiner*, Vol. 28 (1894), p. 191.

203. Goronwy J. Jones, *Wales and the Quest for Peace* (Cardiff, 1969).

204. Talbot Family Collection, C.H. Waring, Recollections of My Life. C.H. Waring, Notes and Memoranda on the Waring Family.

205. Revel Guest and Angela V. John, *Lady Charlotte* (1989), pp. 99-100.

206. Talbot Family Collection, C.H. Waring, Recollections of My Life. C.H. Waring, Notes and Memoranda on the Waring Family.

207. Ellison Collection, Letter, C.S. Price, Cape of Good Hope to J.T. Price, 20 May 1854.   Letter of Good Character for C.S. Price from Concordia Mines, Cape of Good Hope, 17 April 1854.

208. Charles Hocking, *Dictionary of Disasters at Sea During the Age of Steam* (1990), p. 145.

209. Ellison Collection, Memorial to Hannah Isabella (Annabella) Price, died 2 June 1898, privately printed.

210. Ellison Collection, Certificate of Registration for the Companies Act, Edwin Price & Co., Ltd, 1 February 1906.

211. R.L. Brett (Ed.), *Barclay Fox's Journal* (1979), pp. 185-191.

212. WGRO, Dyffryn Gwyn Estate Papers, Box 10, Lease of 12 August 1806.

213. D. Rhys Phillips, *The History of the Vale of Neath*, p. 249.

214. For this accident and other minor ones see, Robert Galloway, *Annals of Coal Mining and the Coal Trade* (1904), Volume 2, pp. 104-124.

215. WGRO, Neath Library Manuscripts No 3, Report Book of Joshua Richardson, notes on the Report on the Collieries belonging to the Neath Abbey Coal Company at Briton Ferry by William P. Struvé, 3 February 1849.

216. WGRO, NLM, Report Book of Joshua Richardson, J.T. Price's Remarks and Observations on W.P. Struves's report, 7 February 1849.

217. WGRO, NLM, Report Book of Joshua Richardson, Report by Joshua Richardson on Briton Ferry regarding the South Wales Railway, 5 March 1850.

218. WGRO, Briton Ferry Estate Papers, Nos 822 & 823, Surrender of leases, 8 February 1853.

219. T.G. Davies, *Howel Gwyn of Dyffryn and Neath* (Neath, 1992).

220. D. Rhys Phillips, *The History of the Vale of Neath*, pp, 251.

221. WGRO, DC, D/D DE/125, Rental and Royalties for the Year ending Ladyday 1857.

222. WGRO, DC, D/D DE/126, Rental and Royalty account for the Year ending Ladyday 1866.

223. Neath Antiquarian Society, Neath Abbey Coal Company Collection.

224. NAS, NACC, Report 18 January 1868.

225. NAS, NACC, Reports for 1868.

226. NAS, NACC, Report 1 February 1868.

227. NAS, NACC, Report 21 March 1868.

228. NAS. NACC, Report 8 February 1868.

229. NAS, NACC, Report 29 February 1868.

230. NAS. NACC, Report 7 May 1868.

231. NAS, NACC, Report 20 June 1868.

232. NAS, NACC, Report 11 June 1868

233. NAS, NACC, Report 8 August 1869

234. NAS. NACC, Report 24 October 1868.

235. NAS, NACC, Report 14 November 1868.

236. NAS. NACC, Report 10 October 1868.

237. NAS, NACC, Report 19 December 1868.

238. NAS, NACC, Report 13 November 1868.

239. WGRO, DC, D/D D 1207, Lease of 1 February 1870.

240. WGRO, DC, D/D D 1208 Mortgage for £5,500 between The New Dynevor Coal Company and Wm. Edw. Jones of Brighton, 24 June 1872 and D/D D 1214, Mortgage for £4,000 between The New Dynevor Coal Company and Maria Alston of Wembdon, Somerset.

241. NAS, NACC, Report 22 January 1870.

242. NAS, NACC, Report 5 March 1870.

243. NAS, NACC, Report 6 August 1870.

244. NAS, NACC, Report 14 May 1870.

245. NAS, NACC, Report 2 July 1870.

246. NAS, NACC, Report 17 September 1870.

247. NAS, NACC, Report 13 August 1870.

248. NAS, NACC, Report 25 March 1871.

249. NAS, NACC, Report 6 May 1871.

250. NAS, NACC, Report 10 June 1871.

251. NAS, NACC, Report 12 August 1871.

252. NAS, NACC, Report 19 July 1871

253. NAS, NACC, Report 30 December 1871.

254. NAS, NACC, Report 25 January 1873.

255. NAS, NACC, Report 26 April 1873.

256. NAS, NACC, Report 17 May 1873.

257. NAS, NACC, Report 9 June 1873.

258. Cornwall Record Office, Truro, X394/61-2, Last balance sheets of the Neath Abbey Coal Company, 1874.

259. D.Rhys Phillips, *The History of the Vale of Neath*, p. 250.

260. WGRO, D/d Xgb 12, Draft Profit and Loss Accounts, the Dyffryn Main Colliery Company, October 22 1874.

261. *Mineral Statistics*, 1874-1889.

262. WGRO, DC, D/D D 1215, Memoranda of Agreement for Rent Arrears with the Dynevor, Dyffryn and Neath Abbey United Colliery Company Ltd., 1 January 1880.

263. WGRO, Tennant Estate Papers, D/D T 697, Prospectus of the Main Colliery Company, 21 June 1889.

264. The outline history of the Main Colliery Company has been constructed using parts of this collection, namely, West Glamorgan Record Office, Swansea, Main Colliery Collection, D/D MC 1, Minutes of General Meetings, D/D MC 2/1 Directors' Minute Books 1889-1928, D/D MC 6, Annual Reports and Statements of Accounts, 1890-1925, D/D MC 117, R. Vaughan Price's Summaries of Annual Accounts, Costs and Output, 1889-1918.

265. WGRO, MC, The Main Colliery Company Limited, Report on the Collieries by Mr Henry T. Wales, November 9th , 1895.

266. *The South Wales Coal Annual*, 1913-1925.

267. WGRO, D/D MC 12(2ii) Edmund Hann, Private Report, 28 September 1914.

268. WGRO, D/D GW 4, The Dyffryn Mineral Estate, report by Robert T. Rees, 22 January 1915.

269. George White, *Tramlines to the Stars*, George White of Bristol (Bristol, 1995). Charles Harvey and Jon Press, *Sir George White of Bristol 1854-1916* (Bristol, 1989).

270. Charles Hocking, *Dictionary of Disasters at Sea During the Age of Steam* (1990), p. 443.

271. WGRO, D/D MC 155/5, Newspaper Cutting Book, the last few years of the Main Colliery Company and the problems that beset it are vividly recounted in this collection of various cuttings.

272. WGRO, D/D GW 4, Lease dated 10 May 1932.

Index